The 2018 and 2019 Indonesian Elections

The 2018/2019 Indonesian elections were among the most divisive elections in Indonesian history, where identity politics and ethno-religious sentiments were prevalent not just during the 2019 presidential election, but also during the 2018 regional executive elections as well. Contributors to this edited volume analysed the dynamics between identity politics, national and local politics and produce findings and insights that will inform prospective readers regarding the future of identity politics and how it may affect Indonesian politics for the intermediate future.

This book is an up-to-date study addressing contemporary Indonesian politics that should be read by Indonesian Studies and more broadly Southeast Asian Studies specialists. It is also a useful reference for those studying Electoral Politics, Religion and Politics, and Comparative Politics.

Leonard C. Sebastian is Associate Professor and Coordinator of the Indonesia Programme at the S. Rajaratnam School of International Studies (RSIS), Nanyang Technological University (NTU), Singapore. He is also Professor (Adjunct), Institute for Governance and Policy Analysis, University of Canberra.

Alexander R. Arifianto is a Research Fellow with the Indonesia Programme, Institute for Defence and Strategic Studies, S. Rajaratnam School of International Studies (RSIS) – Nanyang Technological University, Singapore.

Routledge Contemporary Southeast Asia Series

The aim of this series is to publish original, high-quality work by both new and established scholars on all aspects of Southeast Asia.

Tourism and Development in Southeast Asia
Edited by Claudia Dolezal, Alexander Trupp and Bui T. Huong

Ethnographies of Development and Globalization in the Philippines
Emergent Socialities and the Governing of Precarity
Edited by Koki Seki

The Political Economy of Growth in Vietnam
Between States and Markets
Guanie Lim

ASEAN and Power in International Relations
ASEAN, the EU, and the Contestation of Human Rights
Jamie D. Stacey

The Army and Ideology in Indonesia
From Dwifungsi to Bela Negara
Muhamad Haripin, Adhi Priamarizki and Keoni Indrabayu Marzuki

The 2018 and 2019 Indonesian Elections
Identity Politics and Regional Perspectives
Edited by Leonard C. Sebastian and Alexander R. Arifianto

Embodied Performativity in Southeast Asia
Multidisciplinary Corporealities
Edited by Stephanie Burridge

For more information about this series, please visit: www.routledge.com/Routledge-Contemporary-Southeast-Asia-Series/book-series/RCSEA

The 2018 and 2019 Indonesian Elections

Identity Politics and Regional Perspectives

Edited by Leonard C. Sebastian and Alexander R. Arifianto

Routledge
Taylor & Francis Group

LONDON AND NEW YORK

First published 2021
by Routledge
2 Park Square, Milton Park, Abingdon, Oxon OX14 4RN

and by Routledge
52 Vanderbilt Avenue, New York, NY 10017

Routledge is an imprint of the Taylor & Francis Group, an informa business

British Library Cataloguing-in-Publication Data
A catalogue record for this book is available from the British Library

Library of Congress Cataloging-in-Publication Data
A catalog record has been requested for this book

ISBN: 978-0-367-46780-7 (hbk)
ISBN: 978-0-367-63230-4 (pbk)
ISBN: 978-1-003-03100-0 (ebk)

DOI: 10.4324/9781003031000

Typeset in Times New Roman
by Wearset Ltd, Boldon, Tyne and Wear

Contents

Figures

Tables

Contributors

Editors

Leonard C. Sebastian is Associate Professor and Coordinator of the Indonesia Programme, Institute for Defence and Strategic Studies, S. Rajaratnam School of International Studies (RSIS), Nanyang Technological University, Singapore and Professor (Adjunct), Institute for Governance and Policy Analysis, University of Canberra, Australia.

Alexander R. Arifianto is a Research Fellow with the Indonesia Programme, Institute for Defence and Strategic Studies, S. Rajaratnam School of International Studies (RSIS) – Nanyang Technological University, Singapore.

Contributing authors

Chaula R. Anindya is a Research Analyst with the Indonesia Programme of the S. Rajaratnam School of International Studies (RSIS), Nanyang Technological University, Singapore.

Jonathan Chen is an Associate Research Fellow with the Indonesia Programme, S. Rajaratnam School of International Studies (RSIS), Nanyang Technological University, Singapore.

Dedi Dinarto is a Research Associate with the Indonesia Programme of the S. Rajaratnam School of International Studies (RSIS), Nanyang Technological University, Singapore.

James Guild is a PhD Candidate in Political Economy at the S. Rajaratnam School of International Studies (RSIS), Nanyang Technological University, Singapore.

Syafiq Hasyim is a Lecturer at Faculty of Social Sciences and Director of Library, International Islamic University Indonesia, Jakarta, Indonesia.

Chris Lundry is a Profesor-investigador and the Academic Coordinator for the Center for Asian and African Studies at El Colegio de México in Mexico City.

Keoni Marzuki is an Associate Research Fellow with the Indonesia Programme, S. Rajaratnam School of International Studies (RSIS), Nanyang Technological University, Singapore.

Andar Nubowo is a Ph.D. student in the Department of Philosophy, École Normale Supérieure de Lyon, France and a Lecturer at Muhammadiyah University of Surakarta, Indonesia.

Adhi Primarizki is a Visiting Research Fellow with the Indonesia Programme, S. Rajaratnam School of International Studies (RSIS), Nanyang Technological University, Singapore.

Tiola is a Senior Analyst with the Indonesia Programme, S. Rajaratnam School of International Studies (RSIS), Nanyang Technological University, Singapore.

Adri Wanto was an Associate Research Fellow at the Indonesia Programme, S. Rajaratnam School of International Studies, Nanyang Technological University, Singapore. He is currently a lecturer at Raja Ali Haji University in Tanjung Pinang, Riau Island Province.

Acknowledgements

This book project has involved numerous individuals and institutions that have contributed immensely during its fieldwork stage, chapter writing, production, and finalisation stage, so it may now come into fruition. Many chapters of the book were originally conceptualised as part of a research project initiated by the Indonesia Programme, S. Rajaratnam School of International Studies (RSIS), Nanyang Technological University (NTU), Singapore, focusing on the regional political trends in Indonesia before and after the 2019 Indonesian general election.

We would like to thank the Indonesia Programme's current and former staff members who were part of this research project, including Chaula R. Anindya, Alexander R. Arifianto, Dedi Dinarto, Syafiq Hasyim, Jonathan Chen, Keoni Marzuki, Andar Nubowo, Adhi Primarizki, Tiola, and Adri Wanto. In addition, we also would like to thank two external contributors – James Guild and Chris Lundry – who had kindly contributed their chapters – respectively on the Indonesian political economy and on the regional elections in Sumba, East Nusa Tenggara, as part of this book project as well.

We also thank our editorial assistants – Syed Huzaifah Mohamed Alkaff, Jefferson Ng Jin Chuan, James Guild, and Jonathan Chen, who had spent significant time to edit and finalise each book chapter for this book project. Our thanks to Chris Lundry as well for his willingness to review and provide feedback to several draft chapters. Lastly, we thank our contributors for patiently enduring several rounds of revision and resubmission process. We hope that the long hours spent on researching, writing, and revising these chapters are now paying off.

We thank the S. Rajaratnam School of International Studies (RSIS) for providing generous support for this research project. The views and opinions expressed in this book are solely those of its editors and contributors. It does not in any way represent those of RSIS.

We thank RSIS for its support for the project. In particular, we acknowledge the support of Professor Ralf Emmers, Dean of the School, and Ambassador Ong Keng Yong, RSIS Executive Deputy Chairman. Ambassador Ong's support for the Indonesia Programme's ongoing projects is greatly appreciated.

Lastly, we thank our Routledge counterparts, namely Simon Bates (senior editor) and Tan Sheng Bin (acquisition specialist) for supporting this book project from the beginning and guiding us through the submission process. We also thank two anonymous reviewers whom have provided substantive and helpful feedback for the initial draft of this book. Much of the feedback has been incorporated into the final draft.

We, the contributors, bear responsibility for the views, interpretations, and any errors in the book.

Abbreviations

Bawaslu	*Badan Pengawas Pemilihan Umum* (General Election Supervisory Agency)
Berkarya	*Partai Berkarya* (Working Party)
DI/TII	*Darul Islam/Tentara Islam Indonesia* (Darul Islam/Indonesian Islamic Army)
DPR	*Dewan Perwakilan Rakyat* (Indonesian House of Representatives)
DPRD I	*Dewan Perwakilan Rakyat Daerah Tingkat I* (Provincial Legislative Council)
DPRD II	*Dewan Perwakilan Rakyat Daerah Tingkat II* (District or City Legislative Council)
FPI	*Front Pembela Islam* (Islamic Defenders Front)
Gerindra	*Partai Gerakan Indonesia Raya* (The Great Indonesia Movement Party)
GDP	Gross Domestic Product
Golkar	*Partai Golongan Karya* (Party of Functional Groups)
HTI	Hizb ut-Tahrir Indonesia
KPU	*Komisi Pemilihan Umum* (Indonesian Election Commission)
MUI	*Majelis Ulama Indonesia* (Council of Indonesian Ulama)
NasDem	*Partai Nasional Demokrat* (National Democratic Party)
NGO	Non-Governmental Organisations
NTT	*Nusa Tenggara Timur* (East Nusa Tenggara)
NU	Nahdlatul Ulama
PAN	*Partai Amanah Nasional* (National Mandate Party)
PBB	*Partai Bulan Bintang* (Crescent and Star Party)

PD	*Partai Demokrat*
	(Democratic Party)
PDI-P	*Partai Demokrasi Indonesia – Perjuangan*
	(Indonesian Democratic Party of Struggle)
Perda	*Peraturan Daerah*
	(Regional Government Regulations)
Perludem	*Perkumpulan Untuk Pemilu dan Demokrasi*
	(Association for Election and Democracy)
Perppu	*Peraturan Pemerintah Pengganti Undang-Undang*
	(Government Regulation in lieu of Law)
Pilkada Serentak	*Pemilihan Kepala Daerah Serentak*
	(Simultaneous Regional Government Executive Election)
PKB	*Partai Kebangkitan Bangsa*
	(National Awakening Party)
PKS	*Partai Keadilan Sejahtera*
	(Prosperous Justice Party)
POM	*Persatuan Orang Muda Melayu*
	(Malay Youth Association)
PPP	*Partai Persatuan Pembangunan*
	(United Development Party)
PR	Proportional Representation
PRRI	*Pemerintah Revolusioner Republik Indonesia*
	(Revolutionary Government of the Republic of Indonesia)
RIS	*Republik Indonesia Serikat*
	(Federated Republic of Indonesia)
TNI	*Tentara Nasional Indonesia* (Indonesian Armed Forces)

1 Introduction

The 2018 and 2019 Indonesian elections – identity politics and regional perspectives

*Leonard C. Sebastian
and Alexander R. Arifianto*

Introduction

The recently concluded 2019 Indonesian general election had been one of the most divisive elections in Indonesian history. The dramatic increase in identity-based politics to mobilise voters and its deliberate employment by politicians to jostle for political advantage occurred on a scale that has not been seen since the era of 'stream' (*aliran*) politics that divided Indonesia during the 1950s.

The study compiled in this edited volume finds that during the 2019 presidential election, identity politics was widely used during the campaign season by both the supporters of incumbent president Joko Widodo (commonly known as Jokowi) and his opponent Prabowo Subianto. Jokowi was supported by a coalition of secular–nationalist and moderate Islam parties – specifically the Indonesian Democratic Party of Struggle (PDI-P) and the National Awakening Party (PKB), the party affiliated with Nahdlatul Ulama (NU). The alliance between PDI-P and NU, Indonesia's largest Muslim organisation, represented Indonesia's pluralist coalition. Meanwhile, Prabowo Subianto was backed primarily by conservative Islamist groups – many whom had participated in the 2016 and 2017 Defending Islam rallies (*Aksi Bela Islam*) in Jakarta against former governor Basuki Tjahaja Purnama (commonly known as 'Ahok'). The rallies were the precursor of identity-based politics that took place both during the 2018 simultaneous regional elections (*pilkada*) – which elected local executives of 17 provinces and 154 districts and cities throughout Indonesia – but especially during the 2019 general election itself.

The widespread usages of identity politics during the 2018 simultaneous regional executive elections and the 2019 Indonesian general election is a troubling sign of Indonesian politics for the years to come – as Islamism has become increasingly prominent in Indonesian politics. Political Islam plays on the growing desire among many pious Muslims to have Islamic values be reflected in Indonesia's political and legal institutions – both at the national and local levels. This can be seen in the influence of senior religious clerics such as Ma'ruf Amin – who became president Jokowi's vice-presidential nominee. Similarly, a large number of national and regional politicians sought endorsements from Islamist clerics ranging from Rizieq Shihab – leader of the Islamic Defenders

Front (FPI) and chief organiser of the Defending Islam Movement, Tengku Zulkarnain, the controversial Salafi preacher who is also an official of the Council of Indonesian Ulema (MUI), and popular online preachers with millions of online followers such as Abdul Somad, Abdullah Gymnastiar (Aa Gym), and Hanan Attaki. They underscore that visible demonstrations of religious piety have become extremely important as a large number of the Indonesian population has become more religious and are using their religiosity to inform their viewpoints, especially in political matters.

Local history often plays a role in determining the saliency of identity politics in different Indonesian regions. Buehler (2016) found in his research that provinces that participated in the 1950s/1960s Darul Islam (DI) rebellion – seeking the establishment of an Indonesian state based upon Islamic principles – tend to adopt local Islamic regulations (*perda shari'a*) than provinces with no prior experience with the DI. Due to this historical legacy, religiously inspired identity politics are more salient in former DI provinces like West Java, West Sumatra, and South Sulawesi. These provinces have strong theologically conservative Islamic groups dominating regional politics, which affected the political discourses within these regions, motivating candidates and activists alike to resort to identity-based 'black campaigns' against their opponents. The importance of conservative Islamist groups in regional politics also meant that gubernatorial candidates for West Java and South Sulawesi needed to play the role of a pious Muslim and court support from clerics who ran Islamic groups and boarding schools during the course of the electoral campaign.

In addition, provinces with a long history of intra-ethnic rivalry and competition also saw a high incidence of identity politics. This can be seen in West Kalimantan – where the long-standing rivalries between Malays, Dayaks, and Chinese ethnic groups morphed into inter-religious rivalries between the Muslim Malay, the Christian Dayak, and Chinese ethnic groups. The rivalries between the different groups was evident in the 2018 gubernatorial election, featuring candidates that only represented their respective ethno-religious groups – respectively Malay–Muslim Sutarmidji and Dayak Christian Karolin Margaret Natasa. Nonetheless, Islamisation does not necessarily translate directly into increased usages of identity politics within a given province or region. Mitigating factors – such as the strong presence of moderate Islamic organisations like NU and Muhammadiyah, will shape how Islam and identity politics are being expressed within a given region.

Identity politics plays a smaller role in provinces where there was no history of past Islamist rebellion and where theologically moderate Islamic groups like NU dominates local politics. Meanwhile, this was reflected in elections in East and Central Java provinces. In fact, elections in these provinces were dominated by issues relating to candidate personality and patron–client relationships between candidates and their party supporters, rather than identity-based politics. Nevertheless, some form of identity politics can still be seen in the gubernatorial campaign in both provinces – as seen in the last-minute maneuvering by Gerindra and Prosperous Justice Party (PKS) parties against Saifullah Yusuf and Puti Guntur

Soekarno from the PKB–PDI-P coalition that resulted in their electoral defeat against their challenger Khofifah Indar Parawansa – Emil Dardak. A similar manoeuvre can also be seen in Central Java in the re-election candidacy of incumbent governor Ganjar Pranowo from PDI-P and his opponent Sudirman Said backed by Gerindra Party.

The role of identity politics differs in its scale and intensity across Indonesia's many electoral battlegrounds. While it is significant for the presidential election and many gubernatorial election races, its role is significantly attenuated in regional races for regents (*bupati*) and mayoral elections, as well as Indonesian House of Representatives (DPR) and regional legislative (DPRD) elections. Instead of identity politics, these races tend to be mired by historical grievances between different ethno-religious groups. Candidate ties to local networks often based on patron–client relations with notable local politicians and power brokers instead of loyalties to political parties. Indeed, the scholarship on Indonesian regional politics over the past decade has shown that political parties at the regional level continue to weaken and become divided along numerous factions formed based on their leader's patron–client ties. Candidates for local executives and legislatures are often selected based on political patronage and connections rather than based on achievements or party loyalty (e.g. Aspinall & Sukmajati 2016, Aspinall & Berescott 2019, Muhtadi 2019).

The question underlies this edited volume – are the 2018 regional elections and 2019 general elections in Indonesia a watershed moment in Indonesian politics characterised by divisive identity politics or a continuation of electoral politics characterised by political pragmatism and patron–client relationship? Or are they somewhere in between? In this edited volume, we would like to probe the saliency of identity politics during the 2018 regional executive and 2019 national and regional legislative elections. We define 'identity politics' as: any political act that utilises rhetoric, images, metaphors, and symbols that are meant to portray members of ethnic and/or religious groups (both as individuals or as a collective) in a negative or derogatory manner. In this edited volume, we want to understand the factors behind the prevalence of identity politics in critical battleground regions throughout Indonesia during the 2018/2019 Indonesian elections. We also want to find how do they relate to local historical legacies, socio-political, and demographic variables within these regions that either promotes the high usages of identity politics or alternatively – the lack of them – during the 2018/2019 elections in these regions.

The 2019 Indonesian general election was also the largest single-day election in the world – with more than 20,000 elected positions contested among 245,000 candidates, and 7 million poll workers administering the election, it was also one of the most complex election systems ever administered in the world. Independent monitoring Non-Governmental Organisations (NGOs) like Perludem have expressed concerns regarding the complexities and possible irregularities that might arises under the current system. Our edited volume argues that the current design of the Indonesian electoral system is also playing a significant role in increasing party fragmentation and personalisation of election campaigns during the 2018/2019 Indonesian elections.

Indonesian electoral system under challenge

The use of identity politics during the 2018 regional election and the 2019 general election has made the Indonesian electoral system – which is already marred with problems such as the increasing personalisation of candidates and widespread money politics – to become even more fragile. Election observers believed that the elections were plagued by several issues, including: 1) increased prevalence of identity politics and polarisation during both the gubernatorial and presidential election campaigns; 2) the massive complexity of the election administration which had to manage five different elections simultaneously; and 3) the use of an open proportional representation (PR) system, which contributed to the widespread use of money politics by candidates in national and local legislative races. In addition, there are other issues related to the conduct of the election, including: the lack of substantial voter education at the grassroots level and the increased attacks against election management institutions such as the Indonesian Election Commission (KPU) and the Election Supervisory Agency (*Bawaslu*) that threatens to erode their reputation as fair and impartial Indonesian election managers in future elections to come.

The main legal framework for the 2019 election was Law No 7/2017 on General Elections, which was a comprehensive law that combines three previously separate election laws covering the legislative elections, presidential election, and election management. The law retains the electoral threshold provisions for both the presidential and legislative elections as prescribed by previous laws. The presidential threshold stipulates that a presidential candidate shall be nominated by a party that manages to reach 25 per cent of popular votes casted in the presidential election or control 20 per cent of the House of Representatives (DPR) seats. As Indonesia's party system is fraught with consistent fragmentation – none of the parties that sat in the DPR elected in 2014 was able to meet the bar set by this threshold – necessitating the need to develop coalitions between multiple parties so they may be able to nominate a presidential candidate. This created incentives for all parties to form 'grand coalitions' based on their need for political spoils and patronage (i.e. the 'cartel party' and 'promiscuous power-sharing' arrangement stated by Slater (2004) and Slater and Simmons (2012)). Some of the parties aligning with president Jokowi – for instance *Partai Golongan Karya* (Party of Functional Groups, Golkar) and the United Development Party (PPP) – were driven by these motives when they agreed to join his party coalition, after they had backed Prabowo during the 2014 presidential contest (Mietzner 2016).

However, the post-212 political climate also created incentives for several parties to band together on an identity-based platform, to back Prabowo Subianto's presidential candidacy. It was especially so among the ranks of Prabowo Subianto's supporters – who came from the ranks of conservative Islamist parties such as Prosperous Justice Party (PKS) affiliated with the *Tarbiyah* movement influenced by Ikhwanul Muslimin (Muslim Brotherhood) theology and the National Mandate Party (PAN), which is aligned with Muhammadiyah, Indonesia's second-largest

Islamic organisation – where many of its activists are committed to the idea of promoting a more orthodox interpretation of Islam. PKS has benefitted the most from its close alliance with Prabowo and became the second-largest Islamic party in Indonesia (based on its total DPR vote share) after touting the retired general as 'the most Islamic presidential candidate'.[1] The high presidential threshold – which made it difficult for parties to nominate presidential candidates of their own – was blamed by a number of electoral reform experts as factors contributing to the identity-based polarisation between Jokowi and Prabowo camps during the campaign season.[2]

Law No 7/2017 calls for a national election for five different national and regional offices to be held simultaneously in 2019. Namely they were held for the following offices: the presidency, House of Representatives (DPR), Regional Representatives Council (DPD), Provincial Legislative Council (DPRD I), and District or City Legislative Council (DPRD II). Featuring 245,000 candidates that contested approximately 20,000 public offices, the election took place in 800,000 polling stations and was supervised by nearly 7 million poll workers (Bland 2019). Organising what some observers have called the biggest single-day elections in the world was certainly a major challenge for the poll workers – who had to administer, supervise, and hand-count the ballots for five different elections in each polling booth – all in a single day.

The high number of poll workers who died within weeks after the election was held – estimated to be 424 people (Grayman 2019) testified not just to the exhaustion of poll workers who had to perform the above tasks at the polling booth, and often also had to deal with threats and intimidation campaigns staged by certain candidates and/or their party sponsors, which openly questioned the electoral integrity of the election process. The number of threats and intimidation at the polling booth has increased significantly compared to previous elections, signifying a growing scepticism among some candidates and parties regarding the fairness of the election process. While some of it can be attributed to the increased usages of identity politics during the 2019 election, it can also be attributed to the growing dissatisfaction towards Indonesian democratic system and institutions, something that shall be elaborated later in this section.

Despite the large number of poll workers deployed to administer the election, little effort was expanded by KPU, the government, and by candidates themselves to educate prospective voters on the use of five different ballot papers, each a different colour, being utilised simultaneously on election day and the accompanying election procedures. Voters were not informed regarding the large ballot papers they needed to fill for DPR and DPRD elections – due to the large number of candidates running for these elections within a single constituency. And most did not know the names of the majority of candidates that appeared on the ballot papers. The lack of adequate voter education resulted in the large number of spoiled ballots in the legislative elections. The number of spoiled ballots were estimated to be 17 million (approximately 11.1 per cent of all votes casted) for the DPR election and 19 million for the DPD election.[3] Arguably, the lack of adequate information regarding election procedures and candidates, also resulted in the large incidents of money politics in the national and legislative elections – as shall be elaborated below.

The 2019 Indonesian election was also held under an open and decentralised manner where voters were able to vote for individual candidates but not necessarily their political parties, by punching at the name of the candidates at the polling booth. This takes place under the open-list proportional representation (PR) system Indonesia has been using since the 2009 election. First established after a successful Constitutional Court challenge by minor political parties, the open PR system was initially hailed as an innovation that would have resulted in a greater choice for Indonesian voters and a reduced role for political parties, as individual candidates – not parties – were supposed to be the focus of the election and party control over candidates are supposed to be minimised.

However, by 2019 the open-list PR system has promoted further party fragmentation and heavy personalisation of electoral campaigns both at the national and local levels, as candidate's personal characters, attributes, and networks have become the primary determinants of electoral success, while party's role during the campaigns – except in constituencies contested by senior party figures – have become almost nonexistent except during the nomination process. As individual candidates bear the primary responsibilities for writing up their campaign materials, managing their campaign activities, and most importantly, raising funds to support their own campaigns, the use of money politics is increasingly becoming more widespread in both national and local election campaigns. It is driven by both the need for candidates to obtain as many votes as possible within their respective constituencies, the dilution of campaign messages and issues with candidates from 16 political parties competing against each other within a single constituency, and the lack of voter education campaigns conducted by national and local governments, the Indonesian Election Commission (KPU), and individual candidates themselves.

Arguably, the most serious threat arising from the 2019 Indonesian election was the eroding trust towards electoral management agencies, namely KPU and Bawaslu. Unlike in previous elections where much of the negative campaigning and attacks were targeted towards candidates, this year much of the attacks came from Prabowo, who frequently accused these agencies of favouring Jokowi while claiming that they were complicit in unsubstantiated plot to rig the election results. Prabowo's frequent accusations were followed up by politicians and religious leaders aligned to him. They frequently made false allegations on social media alleging the Jokowi campaign and the KPU have engaged in massive electoral fraud.

For instance, Democratic Party politician Andi Arief, alleged there were up to 10 million 'fictional voters' that were already casted for Jokowi that were stored in sealed containers parked in Tanjung Priok port in Jakarta (BBC News Indonesia, 3 January 2019). In addition, conservative Islamic preacher Haikal Hassan alleged there were 13 million 'mentally ill' voters who were able to vote without proper checking by KPU (Kumparan.com, 25 April 2019). These allegations were rebutted by KPU, which stated that there were only tens of thousands votes that were casted fraudulently or by mentally ill patients – making the total number of spoiled votes to be much less significant than what Arief had claimed[4] (interview, Pramono Ubaid Tanthowi, 25 June 2019). Nevertheless, 'fake' allegations such as these have helped to lower public confidence against KPU, especially among Prabowo supporters. In a survey conducted by Saiful Mujani Research Consultancy (SMRC), nearly one-quarter of Prabowo supporters indicated they had little or no confidence in KPU's professionalism, compared to just 3.6 per cent of Jokowi's supporters (Tirto.id, 11 March 2019). The misinformation campaign directed by Prabowo supporters against the institution – culminating in the 22 May 2020 demonstration in front of KPU's office that led to the deaths of ten people and injured hundreds more – had resulted in further deterioration of KPU's reputation among Prabowo supporters which could have incrementally eroded public trust towards Indonesian electoral management institutions by the time of the next general election scheduled in 2024.

Features of the book

The 2018 and 2019 Indonesian Elections: Identity Politics and Regional Perspectives highlights the need to study different Indonesian regions in order to capture the similarities and the differences driving electoral results in six battleground regions. This will provide important data to inform scholars, policymakers, and the general public on a range of issues including candidate strategies, the statutory framework regulating the election system, and how identity politics influenced results in each region.

The chapters included as part of this edited volume are based on field research conducted by the contributing authors in eight Indonesian regions: West Java, Central Java, East Java, North Sumatra, West Sumatra, South Sulawesi, West Kalimantan, and East Nusa Tenggara. We selected these regions for our in-depth election study because they represent key battleground states where supporters of both presidential candidates fought very fierce campaigns. The demographic and political dynamics of each region led to a wide variety of results that clearly show the impact of identity politics during the campaigns, and how they interact with other features of local politics, candidate–party relationship, and other localised contexts.

The regions we are covering in this volume vary widely in the degree of support towards presidential candidates and political parties, as well as the intensity of identity politics that played out during the campaigns. In this book, we focus our study on national and regional election dynamics by highlighting four main themes that we believe are crucial to understanding the 2018 regional elections as well as how they influenced the 2019 general election and their likely impact in the future. The four main themes are:

1 **Historical background of electoral politics in each covered regions:**
   Each chapter of our edited volume begins with a short historical overview of electoral politics within each of the provinces covered in the book. In

their chapters the authors include the following in each sub-topic: 1) history of electoral contestation between different political parties and socio-political groups (ethnic, religious, social class, etc.) within the province, 2) demographic and geographical features within a region that might have shaped its political culture and electoral politics, and 3) the role of political Islam within the province, including Islamic movements which had history of being politically active within the province and whether or not the province was affected by the DI/TII Islamic rebellion during the 1950s and 1960s.

2   **The relationship between regional executive candidates and political parties**: Our edited volume studies coalition-building, relationships between different key personalities, and the process of power-brokering between political parties and candidates in gubernatorial elections. We discuss how prospective candidates were chosen during the recruitment process and which factors (party loyalty, ethno-religious identity, financial/patron–client considerations, etc.) were important in shaping candidate selection within a given region. We also examine patterns of coalition-building between parties at the provincial level and probe whether coalition-building for regional executive candidates was based on ideological/identity-based considerations or on pragmatic and transactional considerations.

3   **Identity politics at the regional level:** The contributors of the edited volume detailed how Islamic groups and activists utilised identity politics to influence the outcomes of the presidential and regional elections. The analysis will look at how identity politics were employed during the presidential campaign to mobilise voters, and how identity politics and polarisation helped to shape voter turnout. Lastly, we will examine the impact of identity politics during the 2018 regional executive elections and the 2019 presidential and legislative elections.

4   **Implications of the election results on the future of Indonesian politics:** Each chapter in this edited volume will link the election results within a given province to the projected dynamics of national Indonesian politics over the medium term (5 to 10 years). This situates the significance of regional electoral dynamics within a broader framework of how national Indonesian politics have evolved since the 1998 *Reformasi* and the implications this has on the future direction of democracy and identity politics in the world's third-largest democracy. As we do not advance any particular theoretical framework or ideological viewpoint in this volume, our conclusions are solely based on empirically grounded assessments of what Indonesian politics actually look like in the aftermath of the 2018/2019 Indonesian elections, instead of what it should look like according to theoretical or normative models.

By focusing on the four themes mentioned above, we highlight how these topics and issues are being played out in key battleground regions throughout Indonesia, which socio-political issues have more salience in certain provinces as opposed to others, and explain how variations in election results are often linked to underlying national and regional dynamics.

Within the past several years, the majority of scholars studying Indonesian politics are divided into two distinct camps: the first group, the oligarchy school, which argues that despite democratic reforms of the past two decades, Indonesian politics are still controlled by a small number of very wealthy and powerful elites, who dominate electoral politics and policymaking in Indonesia from the top to bottom level of governance (Robison and Hadiz 2004, Hadiz 2010 & 2016). While the oligarchy school emphasises that powerful elites with large concentrations of material wealth will have an outsized impact on electoral and policy outcomes in Indonesia, analytically and methodically it is challenging to view oligarchs as a monolithic group. There is also growing resistance from new groups and actors from civil society that employ non-material power resources to challenge oligarchic dominance. While the oligarchy school argues that new actors can be co-opted by oligarchs, Indonesia's democratic environment also provides opportunities for the mobilisation of interest groups with independent agendas to shape policy and electoral outcomes.

The second dominant school of thought is the liberal pluralist school, which sees Indonesia as a democratic polity where politics and policies are shaped by competition among organised groups representing different interests in society (e.g. Mietzner 2012, Ford & Pepinsky 2014). A common theme promoted by this school after the 2018/2019 Indonesian elections (e.g. Mietzner 2018, Power 2018, and Warburton and Aspinall 2019) is that Indonesia is experiencing a period of democratic stagnation and regression, as civil liberties are gradually eroded by undemocratic uses of government power, ranging from the imprison-ment of several politicians and activists affiliated with Prabowo Subianto to security officials' harassment against pro-Prabowo groups like #2019GantiPresiden (#2019ChangePresident).

However, the liberal pluralist school presents an image of Indonesian politics in 'black or white' terms and seems to ignore long-standing historical and socio-cultural features of Indonesian politics that predates post-1998 *Reformasi* era. We argue in this volume that these historical, socio-political, and demographical features are important for us to understand the features of election results and specifically the factors that had shaped it (e.g. identity politics), especially at regional level. While we are not advancing a new theoretical framework to offer an alternative views from both oligarchy and liberal pluralist approaches to Indonesian politics, we believe that long-term historical, demographical, and other socio-cultural factors, helped to explain the election outcomes both at the regional and national level, particularly why are identity politics more salient in some of the provinces studied in this edited volume, and why is it less signi-ficant in other provinces during both the 2018 regional and 2019 general elections.

Lastly, *The 2018 and 2019 Indonesian Elections: Identity Politics and Regional Perspectives* seeks to assess Indonesia's democratic health and if elect-oral dynamics and candidates' pathway to power at the regional level contribute to the ongoing discussion on issues relating to pluralism and oligarchy. We find evidence of growing political polarisation from identity politics that have shaped the nature of democratic contestation, with consequences for both pluralism and minorities in Indonesia. At the same time, we highlight the great diversity of political actors involved in regional politics and therefore contribute to discussions on the contours of oligarchy in Indonesia. The volume will offer a wealth of insights for readers who are studying political populism, identity politics, and comparative politics of emerging democracies.

Chapter outline

While the main findings from the empirical chapters will be further detailed in the concluding chapter of this book, we would like to highlight some of the key conclusions of our study below.

First, identity politics was the feature of the presidential election campaign in many of the provinces we studied, where the use of identity-based 'black campaign' could be seen in provinces which are considered as hotbeds for growing Islamic conservatism (such as West Java and South Sulawesi) and also in provinces known to be more religiously moderate and eclectic such as East Java. The involvement of Alumni 212 alumni who volunteered for the Prabowo campaign and activists of hardline groups who were also heavily involved in his campaign, were quite significant in contributing to this outcome. Alumni 212 activists can be found volunteering for the Prabowo campaign in Padang, West Sumatra, Pontianak, West Kalimantan, and Madura Island, East Java. Even in moderate urban cities like Surabaya, they were active mobilising voters in low–middle income areas that could potentially become swing districts where Jokowi and Prabowo campaigns actively competed for votes. Hence, identity politics were crucial elements that shaped the presidential campaign's discourses. It also helped to solidify support for Prabowo among conservative Muslim voters across Indonesia, and also contributed to his electoral victory in provinces such as West Java, West Sumatra, and South Sulawesi.

Second, while identity politics plays an important role in some provinces like North Sumatra and West Kalimantan – where inter-ethnic rivalry has shaped local political competition for decades – generally it has not been a major factor in most provinces. In strongly Islamic provinces like West Java and South Sulawesi – virtually all politicians running for gubernatorial or regional executives in these provinces used their Islamic credentials to boost their standing among prospective voters, making it difficult for any one of them to 'out-Islamise' the other candidates by utilising identity-based campaigns. In more moderate provinces like East Java, the predominance of NU – a moderate Islamic organisation helped to promote a largely conducive campaign where candidates were discussing local-level political issues rather than engaging in identity politics.

Local political contexts also shaped the intensity of identity politics in the different localities that we study. Regions with a long history of ethnic-based contestation like West Kalimantan – which witnesses a fierce contestation between gubernatorial candidates from ethnic Javanese/Malay and ethnic Dayak background – tend to have more intense identity-based politics both at the regional and national-level campaigns. However, local contexts often helped to tame the frequency of identity politics within a given region. For instance, in South Sulawesi voters were reacting against the local established elites like the Kalla family by voting against the candidates supported by the elites. For instance, they voted against Munafri Arifuddin – candidate for the Makassar mayor who was a member of the Kalla family and was backed by all major political parties. Hence, South Sulawesi voters seem to care more about electing representatives that are more responsive to their concerns rather than engaging in identity politics.

Finally. while identity politics can also be quite strong in regions where there was plenty of Alumni 212 activists who utilised identity-based politics on Prabowo's behalf during the campaign season, in others where the Jokowi coalition parties were perceived to be strong there are fewer identity-based campaigns. In such regions, some legislative candidates from Prabowo-supporting parties toned down their level of support and often spoke in praise of Jokowi. This can be seen in regions of East Java where there is an overwhelming support for Jokowi, such Mataraman or even part of Surabaya with an overwhelming PDI-P constituency. The reversed happened in regions where Jokowi is not popular among the local voters, like Madura Islands (East Java) or Pontianak (West Kalimantan), where FPI and other hardline groups predominated the political discourse during the election.

Our contributors consist of scholars and researchers – both those affiliated with the Indonesia Programme, S. Rajaratnam School of International Studies (RSIS), Nanyang Technological University, Singapore, and external contributors we invited to contribute their chapters into our edited volume. All contributors are specialists in the region we requested them to focus their chapter on and all have an extensive network with regional politicians, local government officials, religious leaders, and other civil society activists based in the respective regions they work on. The outline of each chapter on this edited volume can be found below:

Chapter 2 analyses Jokowi's developmentalist economic policy – particularly with regard to infrastructure – and how it impacted the 2018/2019 Indonesian elections. In this chapter, James Guild explores whether good economic policy still matter to electoral outcomes or would identity politics trump everything else. During the presidential campaign, Jokowi ran on a broadly popular policy platform, one that emphasised major infrastructure projects, and he won comfortably in 2019 which suggests that Indonesian voters are still willing to reward popular policies at the polls. Nevertheless, a closer look at the island of Java, which has received the bulk of infrastructure investment and big-ticket projects, shows that while Jokowi was less vulnerable to identity politics than former Jakarta governor Basuki Tjahaja Purnama, his support in the provinces of West, East, and Central Java was still contingent to some degree on ethnic and religious divisions.

Chapter 3 analyses the national and regional elections in West Java, the most populous province in Indonesia. Authors Keoni Marzuki and Chaula R. Anindya argue that identity politics played a role during the province's gubernatorial race in June 2018, but because all four candidates portrayed themselves as 'pious' Islamic candidates, the impact was somewhat lessened. Former Bandung mayor Ridwan Kamil – a Jokowi supporter – managed to win. Ridwan Kamil's election did not, however, translate into victory for Jokowi the following year as Prabowo carried the province with 60 per cent of the votes. Kamil did endure a last-minute surge of attacks from supporters of retired General Sudradjat – who was backed by the Gerindra/PKS coalition contributing to the latter's strong performance on election day. Nevertheless, he managed to win the election as he recruited Tasikmalaya regent Uu Ruzhanul Ulum – whose family run one of the largest Islamic boarding schools in West Java, giving the pair very strong Islamic credentials. They also found Jokowi's image in the province to be severely tarnished after a series of accusations that he is not a pious Muslim circulated widely on social media, damaging the president's electoral prospects in a province dominated by conservative Islamist voters.

Chapter 4 discusses national and regional elections in East Java. As the second-largest Indonesian province in terms of population, East Java was pivotal in Jokowi's electoral strategy against Prabowo. In this chapter, Alexander R. Arifianto finds that like elsewhere in Indonesia after the 2016/2017 Defending Islam rallies, Islamism and identity politics were important features in East Java. However, they did not entirely dominate political discourses during the gubernatorial election. The chapter further details how this dynamic was not limited to urban cities like Surabaya and Malang, but was also present in several rural regions like Madura Island, where support for the Defending Islam rallies and Islamic Defenders Front (FPI) was significant. Nevertheless, Jokowi managed to win overwhelmingly in East Java thanks to the support of NU, which has a large number of followers in the province. Jokowi's supporters aligned with his PDI-P party, which managed to develop an effective alliance with NU and deliver East Java voters in a landslide for the president. In contrast, the 2018 gubernatorial election in East Java was rather lacking overt identity politics, since both of the candidates running – respectively Saifullah Yusuf and Khofifah Indar Parawansa – came from the rank of the province's political elites and both also affiliated with elite Nahdlatul Ulama families. Much of the campaign focuses on their personalities and local issues rather than on substantive issues or identity politics.

Chapter 5 highlights election results in Central Java, the province where Jokowi enjoyed the highest margin of victory in Java – approximately 77 per cent of votes – and proved to be a significant base of support that helped him win re-election. In his analysis, Syafiq Hasyim finds that despite the changing religious orientation of Central Javanese residents from syncretic (*abangan*) to more pious Muslims, most still prefer to support presidential and legislative candidates from nationalist parties like Jokowi's Indonesian Democratic Party of Struggle (PDI-P). Most Central Java Muslims are also followers of Nahdlatul Ulama – the largest Muslim organisation in Indonesia – which embraces and promotes a moderate interpretation of Islam and supported Jokowi during the presidential election. While the number of conservative Islamist voters have increased significantly in in urban areas like Yogyakarta and Solo, the number of moderate Muslims voting for Jokowi in Central Java still far exceeded their numbers, resulting in Jokowi's 77 per cent electoral support achieved during the presidential election – the largest margin in Java island.

Chapter 6 covers national and regional elections in North Sumatra. The fourth most populous province in Indonesia (with approximately 13 million residents), North Sumatra is politically divided along distinct ethno-religious lines between native Malays and Javanese Muslims who largely supported Prabowo Subianto, and Batak and Chinese Indonesian Christians who primarily backed Jokowi. In their analysis, Tiola and Adhi Primarizki find that polarisation between the two camps started during the 2018 North Sumatran governor's election between Djarot Saiful Hidayat – who was supported by Batak Christians and moderate Muslims – and retired Lieutenant General Edy Rahmayadi, who was thought to have strong Islamic credentials and was supported by conservative Muslims living in the province. Voters in Muslim-majority regencies and cities are more likely to support Edy, while those in Christian-majority regions are more likely to support Djarot. This polarisation continued to shape the political landscape through the presidential election.

Chapter 7 covers national and regional elections in West Sumatra. In the presidential election, the province produced the largest margin of victory for Prabowo Subianto, with 87 per cent of the vote going to his ticket. In their analysis, Adri Wanto and Leonard C. Sebastian explain that Prabowo's victory over Jokowi in the province can be tied to two main factors: 1) the history of activism in the province dating back to the *Pemerintah Revolusioner Republik Indonesia* (Revolutionary Government of the Republic of Indonesia, PRRI) rebellion during the 1950s and 2) a history of distrust against parties linked to the Sukarno legacy and in this context, the PDI-P, which has never won more than five provincial legislative seats in an election since 1998. These historical legacies, along with the fact that Prabowo managed to secure endorsements from many notable religious and traditional (*adat*) leaders, contributed to his landslide victory there.

Chapter 8 analyses national and regional elections in South Sulawesi. With 6 million people, South Sulawesi is the largest province on Sulawesi island and also the largest province in Eastern Indonesia. In 2014 voters in the province voted strongly for Jokowi, but in 2019 they reversed this by overwhelmingly voting for Prabowo Subianto. In this chapter Dedi Dinarto and Andar Nubowo explain this reversal by noting that in 2019 Jokowi's ticket did not include a 'native son' while in 2014 his running mate was Jusuf Kalla who was born in South Sulawesi and helped shore up votes in the province. Long dominated by established political elite families like the Kallas and the Limpos, South Sulawesi politics are increasingly becoming more competitive, as new entrants – particularly those with strong Islamic credentials and affiliated with large Islamic groups such as Wahdah Islamiyah – gained more political influence over the past decade or so. In the absence of a prominent elite politician native to South Sulawesi who was Jokowi's running mate in his 2014 election bid, the province flipped to his opponent in the most recent cycle. In addition, voters evinced a general distrust towards much of the provincial political elite. This, along with growing Islamic conservatism, contributed to Prabowo's victory in South Sulawesi.

Chapter 9 discusses national and regional elections in West Kalimantan. Despite having a relatively small population of 4.4 million people, West Kalimantan is an important case for studying how identity politics can polarise voters from different ethnic and religious backgrounds during the provincial governor race in June 2018 as well as the presidential race in April 2019. Based on his research in the province, Jonathan Chen analyses the ethno-religious dynamics between candidates of the 2018 gubernatorial election in West Kalimantan between Sutarmidji (a Javanese Muslim) and Karolin Margaret Natasa (a Dayak Christian who is the daughter of incumbent governor Cornelis). He concludes that ethnic politics and tensions played an important role in West Kalimantan province between the three largest ethnic groups and their hyphenated identities: Malay–Muslims, Dayak–Christian, and the Chinese who are either Christian or Buddhist. However, the conflict between the three groups worsened due to mobilisation by hardline groups such as FPI in ethnic Malay-dominated districts like Pontianak. The divisive campaigns resulted in the victory of Sutarmidji against Karolin in the gubernatorial election and an overwhelming victory for Prabowo Subianto within the Malay-dominated Pontianak metropolitan region. Nevertheless, the majority of the electorate favoured Jokowi in the province since the latter managed to get support from both ethnic Dayaks and Chinese, which constitute a substantial percentage of the province's population.

Chapter 10 discusses national and regional election dynamics in East Nusa Tenggara (NTT), particularly in Sumba. With a population of 5.2 million, NTT is an Indonesian province where the majority population are non-Muslims (55.4 per cent Roman Catholics, 34.2 per cent Protestant). In his analysis, Chris Lundry finds that traditional nobility (*bangsawan*) played an important role in shaping the electoral behaviour of the NTT electorate. His chapter describes how residents of NTT and other Christian or Hindu-dominant provinces were motivated to support Jokowi shaped by impressions formed during the presidential debates based on his perceived stance for and Prabowo's stance against pluralism. It was in the regional gubernatorial and legislative elections that the influence of *bangsawan* had more of an effect on the results. Although there was certainly some effort by traditional leaders to get people to vote for Jokowi, Lundry argues that the question of pluralism was the major factor in most of voters' mind when they overwhelmingly voted for Jokowi in the 2019 presidential election. 88.5 per cent of NTT voters supported Jokowi – giving him the second-largest margin of victory in Indonesia.

Chapter 11 is the concluding chapter, which summarises the main findings of the empirical chapters and relates these findings to the four main themes of the book that were outlined in the introductory chapter. It also outlines the main empirical contribution and policy implications of the analyses contained in the book.

Notes

1 Interview with Titi Anggraini, Executive Director, Association for Elections and Democracy (Perludem) (Jakarta, 22 August 2019).
2 Interview with Titi Anggraini (Jakarta, 28 June 2019).
3 Interview with Titi Anggraini (Jakarta, 28 June 2019).
4 Interview with Pramono Ubaid Tanthowi, Commissioner, Indonesian Election Commission (KPU) (Jakarta, 25 June 2019).

Bibliography

Aspinall, E. and W. Berenschot. 2019. *Democracy for Sale: Elections, Clientelism, and the State in Indonesia*. Ithaca, NY: Cornell University Press.

Aspinall, E. and M. Sukmajati (eds.). 2016. *Money Politics, Patronage, and Clientelism at the Grassroots*. Singapore: National University of Singapore Press.

BBC News Indonesia. 2019, 3 January. 'Andi Arief, Tujuh Kontainer berisi Surat Suara dan Hoaks Lain Terkait Pilpres' ['Andi Arief, Seven Containers Filled with Ballots and Other Hoaxes Related to the Presidential Election']. Retrieved from www.bbc.com/indonesia/indonesia-46744492.

Bland, B. 2019, 3 April. 'The Mind-Boggling Challenge of Indonesia's Election Logistics', *The Interpreter*. Retrieved from www.lowyinstitute.org/the-interpreter/mind-boggling-challenge-indonesian-election-logistics.

Buehler, M. 2016. *The Politics of Shari'a Law: Islamist Activists and the State in Democratizing Indonesia*. New York: Cambridge University Press.

Ford, M. and T.B. Pepinsky (eds.). 2014. *Beyond Oligarchy: Wealth, Power, and Contemporary Indonesian Politics*. Ithaca, NY: Cornell University Southeast Asia Program.

Grayman, J. 2019, 7 May. 'Death by Overwork: The Complicated Cases of the Indonesian Election', *Indonesia at Melbourne*. Retrieved from https://indonesiaatmelbourne.unimelb.edu.au/death-by-overwork-the-complicated-case-of-the-indonesian-election/.

Hadiz, V. 2010. *Localising Power in Post-Authoritarian Indonesia: A Southeast Asian Perspective*. Stanford, CA: Stanford University Press.

Hadiz, V. 2016. *Islamic Populism in Indonesia and the Middle East*. New York: Cambridge University Press.

Kumparan.com. 2019, 25 April. 'Saat KPU Terusik Cuitan Haikal Hassan soal Hoaks 13 Juta Orang Gila' ['When KPU Was Disrupted by Haikal Hassan's Hoax Regarding 13 million 'Insane Voters']. Retrieved from https://kumparan.com/kumparannews/saat-kpu-terusik-cuitan-haikal-hassan-soal-hoaks-13-juta-orang-gila-1qxGveRrzaW.

Mietzner, M. 2012. 'Indonesia's Democratic Stagnation: Anti-Reformist Elite and Resilient Civil Society', *Democratization*, Vol. 19 (2): 209–229.

Mietzner, M. 2016. 'Coercing Loyalty: Coalitional Presidentialism and Party Politics in Indonesia', *Contemporary Southeast Asia*, Vol. 38 (2): 209–232.

Mietzner, M. 2018. 'Fighting Illiberalism with Illiberalism: Islamist Populism and Democratic Deconsolidation in Indonesia', *Pacific Affairs*, Vol. 91 (2): 261–282.

Muhtadi, B. 2019. *Vote Buying in Indonesia: The Mechanics of Electoral Bribery*. New York: Palgrave Macmillan.

Power, T.P. 2018. 'Jokowi's Authoritarian Turn and Indonesia's Democratic Decline', *Bulletin of Indonesian Economic Studies*, Vol. 54 (3): 307–338.

Robison, R. and V. Hadiz. 2004. *Reorganising Power in Indonesia: The Politics of Oligarchy in an Age of Markets*. New York: Routledge.

Slater, D. 2004. 'Indonesia's Accountability Trap: Party Cartels and Presidential Power after Democratic Transition', *Indonesia*, Vol. 78: 61–92.

Slater, D. and E. Simmons. 2013. 'Coping by Colluding: Political Uncertainty and Promiscuous Powersharing in Indonesia and Bolivia', *Comparative Political Studies*, Vol. 46 (11): 1366–1393.

Tirto.id. 2019, 11 March. 'Kepercayaan ke KPU Rendah: Tanda Upaya Delegitimasi Berhasil?' [Confidence for KPU is Low: Sign That Delegitimization Effort is Successful?]. Retrieved from https://tirto.id/kepercayaan-ke-kpu-rendah-tanda-upaya-delegitimasi-berhasil-djaW.

Warburton, E. and E. Aspinall. 2019. 'Explaining Indonesia's Democratic Regression: Structure, Agency, and Popular Opinion', *Contemporary Southeast Asia*, Vol. 41 (2): 255–285.

2 Indonesia's 2019 presidential election

Does policy still matter?

James Guild

Introduction

Despite broadly popular policies focused on improving Jakarta's infrastructure and economy, the incumbent governor of Jakarta, Basuki Tjahaja Purnama, commonly known as Ahok, was defeated in the 2017 Jakarta gubernatorial election as his opponents leveraged divisive identity politics to oust him. With the presidential election just 2 years off, these events begged the question: did good policy still matter to electoral outcomes, or would identity politics trump all?

Indonesian president Joko 'Jokowi' Widodo also ran on a broadly popular policy platform, one that emphasised major infrastructure projects, an improved investment climate and steady Gross Domestic Product (GDP) growth. He won comfortably in 2019, which suggested that Indonesian voters are still willing to reward popular policies at the polls. However, a closer look at the island of Java, which has received the bulk of infrastructure investment and big-ticket projects, showed that while Jokowi was less vulnerable to identity politics than Ahok, his support in the provinces of West, East, and Central Java was still contingent on demographics, as well as the strength and composition of provincial political coalitions.

The evidence in support of this is that all three provinces have seen stable macroeconomic performance, as well as large-scale investment activity and infrastructure development. Yet West Java still broke heavily against Jokowi in the 2019 election, likely due to the existence of unfavourable political dynamics at the provincial level as well as social and religious demographics. Meanwhile, Jokowi increased his vote share in the Javanese-majority provinces of East and Central Java, suggesting good economic policy can translate into electoral support, but only if the existing demographics and political structures are favourable to begin with.

This chapter will discuss Jokowi's performance in 2014 and 2019 in the aforementioned provinces. These cases have been selected because East, Central, and West Java are the most populous provinces in Indonesia and the distribution of votes in Java is crucial to securing a viable path to the presidency. Moreover, the voting behaviour and demographic make-up in these provinces very clearly demonstrates the interplay between economic performance, demographics, and local political coalitions. It underscores the hypothesis that economic policymaking cannot overcome embedded structural factors.

East, West, and Central Java are large provinces that are economically, culturally, and politically important. The demographic make-up of the provinces provides a good opportunity to examine the hypothesis that majority-Javanese provinces were likely to vote Jokowi, while Javanese-minority areas voted against him – even when all cases showed evidence of strong macroeconomic fundamentals, and were on the receiving end of substantial cash transfers from the central government and saw major infrastructure project development. In other words, if policy could overcome demographics and political coalitions, it would be reasonable to expect that West Java's stable macroeconomic performance and the development of big infrastructure projects would have netted Jokowi more support. That his support was virtually unchanged in the province from 2014 to 2019 suggests policy can only do so much in the face of embedded structural obstacles such as unfavourable demographics or political coalitions.

The chapter begins with some background on the major issues, then discusses in turn the impact of economic policies, provincial political coalitions, and demographics on Jokowi's performance in each province. The purpose of this analysis is not to rigorously test a particular hypothesis or to make a claim of causality or to exhaustively explore every facet of provincial identity politics. The purpose, in line with the overall tone and approach of this edited volume, is to create a descriptive account of how these variables interacted during the election at a more removed conceptual level with a particular emphasis on the limits of economic policy. Therefore, the discussion of identity politics and political coalitions is meant to be illustrative, rather than conclusive or exhaustive.

The concepts, themes, and interactions described in this chapter will be developed in greater detail in the following chapters but the main conclusion is that good economic policy is useful up to a point, and likely helped Jokowi consolidate his already strong support base in East and Central Java. Yet the results in West Java clearly indicate that even though economic indicators in the province were generally good and large-scale infrastructure projects proceeded at scale, this was not sufficient to overcome entrenched social, religious, and political cleavages.

Background

In April 2017 the popular incumbent governor of Jakarta was defeated by Anies Baswedan in the gubernatorial election. Several months later he was jailed on blasphemy charges widely believed to be fraudulent (Lamb 2017). In the run-up to the election, a massive anti-Ahok demonstration was held in Central Jakarta on 2 December 2016, which became known as Action 212. This demonstration was organised primarily by hardline Islamist groups seeking to use Ahok's Chinese ethnicity and Christianity as a wedge issue to mobilise grassroots opposition against him. It worked as Anies defeated him by a comfortable margin after securing the support of ultra-conservative political parties such as the Prosperous Justice Party (PKS) and groups like Islamic Defenders Front (FPI) who exploited divisive identity politics to attack the incumbent (Ramadhani et al. 2017).

Analysis of Ahok's defeat in the immediate aftermath suggested several possible causes. One analyst concluded Ahok's brash manner and narrow focus on infrastructure development upset the city's business and political elites, and his forced resettlement of squatter compounds (*kampung*) to make room for housing developments caused a social backlash against him (Wilson 2017). A more detailed analysis relying on survey data showed that broadly speaking Jakarta's middle class actually had a favourable opinion of his policies; yet it was religion that was a more important determinant of voter behaviour. Even among Jakartans who approved of Ahok's performance as governor, voters identifying as Muslim were overwhelmingly more likely to have voted against him (Mietzner & Muhtadi 2017).

This naturally begged the question of how much policy still mattered in Indonesia's electoral politics. If identity politics were more important than popular policies in driving voter behaviour, then crafting a sound policy agenda would be less important than getting the endorsement of the right religious or ethnic groups and their leaders. The events of 2017 clearly influenced president Jokowi, himself a former governor of Jakarta who had made pro-growth policies focused on infrastructure development the cornerstone of his national economic narrative and governing agenda (Guild 2019b).

When Jokowi first took office in 2014 he was faced with a fairly trenchant opposition in the legislature, but after a rough first year he horse-traded sufficiently to organise a more stable political coalition backing his economic agenda which included deregulation, elimination of subsidies for the oil and gas industry, tax amnesty, and a narrow focus on infrastructure development (Emont 2016). With a broader coalition backing him, and a couple of cabinet reshuffles, he was able to roll out an expansionary fiscal policy that helped buoy GDP growth at 5 per cent annually, which is steady if not spectacular, while significantly growing the country's stock of fixed capital (Guild 2019c).

One of the most striking examples of Jokowi's impact on infrastructure development is in the toll road sector. During the administration of his predecessor Susilo Bambang Yudhoyono (2004–2014) around 229 kilometres of toll roads were built throughout Indonesia. From 2015 to 2018, that number increased to 718 kilometres (BPJT 2018). That is a threefold increase in less than half the time, much of it built in Java, and can be directly attributed to Jokowi's policies, particularly his ramping up of the use of the state's eminent domain law to accelerate land acquisition (Guild 2019a).

The energy sector shows similarly scaled up development. Jokowi pledged to expand installed capacity by 35,000 MW, a promise he ultimately fell short on. But he did substantially ramp up the scale and pace of energy project development. Looking only at mega-power projects, for those over 1,000 MW, his administration oversaw financial closing of seven projects valued at over $17 billion which are currently under construction, all but one of them in Java (see Table 2.1).

Table 2.1 Summary of mega-power projects under development as part of 35,000 MW Programme

Project	Location	Cost (USD billion)	Capacity (MW)	Status (2019)
Batang PLTU	Central Java	4.2	2,000	Construction
Cirebon II	West Java	2.1	1,000	Construction
Cilacap #4	Central Java	1.389	1,000	Construction
Tanjung Jati B	Central Java	4.194	2,000	Construction
PLTU Jawa 7	Banten	1.8	2,000	Construction
Jawa Satu	West Java	1.8	1,760	Construction
Indramayu II	West Java	4	2,000	Delayed
Sumsel-8	South Sumatra	1.680	1,240	Construction

Source: Author calculation based on media reports and World Bank documents.

These projects draw in billions of dollars in foreign direct investment to the provinces where they are located, provide jobs, technology, and skills transfer and have a multiplier effect on regional economies. Once completed, these 7 projects alone will add 11,000 MW of new generating capacity to the grids in Java and Sumatra.

In addition to these efforts targeted at particular sectors, Jokowi also ramped up cash transfers from the central to the provincial and district-level governments. For instance, in 2018 the government transferred a total of IDR 152.28 trillion to provincial governments, more than double the amount in 2015.[1] District governments received far larger transfers, with the biggest bump coming when Jokowi first took office. In 2014, district governments received 408.98 trillion in cash transfers; in 2016 that figure had increased to 513.37 trillion.[2] Jokowi also pioneered the Dana Desa or Village Fund which is specifically earmarked for development projects in rural villages, and disbursed IDR 59.8 trillion in 2017 alone (BPS 2018).[3] Measuring the precise impact of these transfers on GDP or fixed capital falls outside the scope of this chapter, but the headline numbers alone indicate the extent to which the Jokowi administration was willing to disburse funds to local governments for development purposes.

Monetary policy during Jokowi's first term has also been recognised as an important component of macroeconomic stability, keeping inflation and interest rates manageable even in the face of unfavourable global trade and financial headwinds. In part, this is because Jokowi nominated widely respected technocrats to serve in key positions, such as Sri Mulyani as Minister of Finance (Triggs et al. 2019). This strategy has been credited with keeping the Indonesian economy on an even keel over the last several years.

While not an exhaustive account of Jokowi's national economic policies, these examples are sufficient to broadly support the claim that his administration was narrowly focused on accelerating the pace and scale of infrastructure development and investment, embracing expansionary fiscal measures, and maintaining macroeconomic stability. It is also worth noting that the majority of the infrastructure projects described above occurred in Java, which underlines the importance of the island's most populous provinces when it comes to understanding the political economy of development.

Yet the experience with Ahok suggests that even broadly popular infrastructure development and expansionary fiscal policy might leave a politician vulnerable to attacks from hardline Islamist groups. This is likely what prompted Jokowi to nominate the conservative Muslim cleric and influential chairman of the Council of Indonesian Ulema (MUI) – the supreme religious authority in Indonesia charged with issuing *fatwas*) Ma'ruf Amin as his vice-presidential running mate in late 2018, as a pre-emptive step to inoculate his ticket against criticism from hardliners (Fealy 2018).

During the presidential campaign of 2018 and early 2019, Jokowi's opponent Prabowo Subianto, who he had previously defeated in 2014, predictably leaned into identity politics. He secured the support of a conservative coalition, including many of the same groups and parties that drove grassroots opposition of Ahok like PKS and FPI. Groups unofficially associated with the Prabowo campaign attacked Jokowi for not being sufficiently religious, especially on social media, while Prabowo stoked nativist rhetoric by accusing his opponent of selling Indonesia's national assets to foreigners, a questionable claim in heavily protectionist Indonesia (McRae & Tomsa 2019).

Despite these efforts, Jokowi won by a comfortable 10-point margin in April 2019 and the outcome of the election was never seriously in doubt according to pollsters (Tehusijarana et al., 2019). This suggests two things. One is that broadly speaking his popular policy agenda focused narrowly on economic growth and infrastructure development did in fact matter and helped propel him to victory. It also reveals that a Javanese Muslim, like Jokowi, is much less vulnerable to attacks rooted in identity politics.

But narrowing the focus from the national to the provincial level reveals a more complex picture. This analysis will focus on three of the most populous and most economically and politically important provinces in Indonesia – West, East, and Central Java. The voting shares for these provinces in 2014 and 2019 are summarised in Table 2.2.

The interesting thing about these vote totals is that voter behaviour in West Java remained virtually unchanged from 2014 to 2019, with Jokowi receiving

Table 2.2 Summary of vote totals in 2014 and 2019 presidential elections by province

Province	2014 Jokowi (%)	2014 Prabowo (%)	2019 Jokowi (%)	2019 Prabowo (%)
West Java	40.22	59.78	40.07	59.93
Central Java	66.65	33.35	77.29	22.71
East Java	53.17	46.83	65.79	34.21

Source: Indonesian Election Commission (KPU).

just over 40 per cent of the vote both times. In East and Central Java, by comparison, his support increased considerably from 2014 to 2019. This would suggest that through some combination of policies and political coalition-building, he was able to boost his support in those provinces by over 10 per cent. Yet West Java voters were impervious to similar tactics, and Jokowi was unable to move the needle at all during his first 5-year term.

This analysis feeds into ongoing scholarly debate on the history of democracy in Indonesia, and specifically the drivers of election results that appear to be changing. In the immediate post-1998 reform era, elections were held in 1999 and 2004. Work by William Liddle and Saiful Mujani (2007) on these elections found that leadership and party identification were the most important variables influencing the election results. Religious identity, political economy, and other demographic variables were found to not be significant.

By 2019, ideology had started to make a comeback as a significant factor. The return of political ideology and political Islam, hearkened back to the turbulent political landscape of the 1950s when politics were organised around ideological and partisan factions (Fossati 2019). As will be discussed in a later section, for instance, the strength of the Prosperous Justice Party in West Java appears to have been significant in Jokowi's defeat there. Tom Pepinsky (2019) in his analysis of voting behaviour in the 2019 election identified ethnicity as the most important variable; that is, Javanese-majority areas voted for Jokowi and Javanese-minority areas did not. This was true even when other variables were introduced into the model.

What the literature and the voting results from 2019 suggest is that political coalitions and demographics are becoming increasingly important. The question is whether or not sound economic policy and macroeconomic performance can make a difference even in the face of unfavourable structural conditions. The following sections will expand on some of the aforementioned drivers of voting behaviour and how they impacted Jokowi's chances in the 2019 election, looking at economic performance, provincial-level politics, coalition-building, and demographics as possible explanations for his performance in East, Central, and West Java. Again, the details of these demographic and political trends will be developed in more detail in later chapters, but this discussion will hopefully provide a concise overview of the big picture trends at work, and how they relate to economic performance.

Economic performance

The island of Java is the most populous island in the Indonesian archipelago, with the largest share of national GDP, which is what makes a detailed analysis of its three largest provinces a useful point of inquiry for this chapter.

Java – specifically West, East, and Central Java – has been the recipient of large amounts of infrastructure investment during Jokowi's first term. To just to give a brief snapshot of the scale and scope of these development efforts, billions of dollars had flowed into the power projects described above, of roughly US$10 billion in Central Java and US$3.9 billion in West Java (see Table 2.1). A new international airport valued at IDR 2.6 trillion or approximately US$185 million was recently opened in Kertajati, West Java (Dipa 2019). The Trans Java Toll Road, a multi-billion dollar highway, is nearing completion and will traverse all three provinces. This not only helps increase fixed capital formation, but it reduces transaction costs – it is now possible to travel by car from Solo to Surabaya in around 3 hours, about half the time it took before the road was completed.[4]

As discussed above, the rapid acceleration in toll road development is a particularly telling result of Jokowi's economic efforts. The Bogor–Ciawi–Sukabumi Toll Road in West Java helps illustrate this. This toll road has been in some form of planning and development since 1997, but has continually been held up by breakdowns in coordination and difficulties with land acquisition and financing (Dahono & Bagus 2018). The project changed hands multiple times, with no real progress being made until 2015 (Jokowi's first full year in office) when the state-owned builder PT. Waskita Toll Road took a majority stake and development was suddenly fast-tracked. The entire road will eventually span 54 kilometres and is valued at IDR 7.7 trillion or US$550 million.

As of this writing the first section had been completed, with the remaining three sections under construction. It is clear the project was stalled until Jokowi specifically set as a goal the acceleration of these kinds of projects, and then created a policy framework designed to overcome hurdles and expedite project development. This project alone will generate trillions of rupiah in investment activity in West Java, hundreds of jobs, and increased economic activity along the toll road corridor once it is complete. This is a clear example of a province, in this case West Java, directly benefitting from Jokowi's economic policies.

This cross-section of some of the major infrastructure projects under development in East, West, and Central Java gives an idea of Jokowi's infrastructure efforts there. But looking at aggregate data will help complete the picture. As mentioned above, Jokowi engineered an increase in direct cash transfers to provincial and district-level governments and Java received substantially increased revenue flows from these efforts. As shown in Figure 2.1, direct transfers from the central government to district governments in West, Central and East Java experienced a significant increase from 2015 to 2016. District governments in West Java alone received IDR 44.7 trillion (US$3.19 billion) in 2018, while East Java received the largest share at IDR 53 trillion (US$3.79 billion).

Coupled with the distribution of Dana Desa funds, this influx of cash from the central government to local appropriators helps boost economic activity, especially expenditures designed to maintain and expand the stock of fixed capital. During my fieldwork in Yogyakarta in 2017 and 2018 it was common to see small-scale local infrastructure projects such as the re-paving of roads or expansion of bridges being undertaken, which had previously been neglected. But direct cash transfers from the central government to the regions do not capture the full extent of government efforts to boost economic activity. This is because government spending does not account for the large amount of investment and development activities being

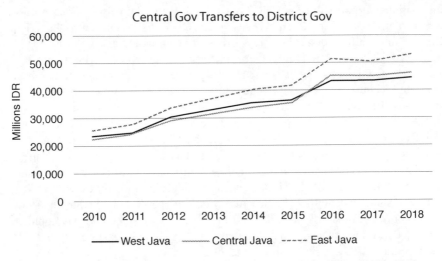

Figure 2.1 Central government transfers to district governments in Java 2010–2018.

carried out by State Owned Enterprises. A better way to more completely gauge the health of the economic environment is to also look at aggregate indicators such as foreign and domestic investment, exports, and GDP growth.

In order to create a more conducive investment and business environment, Jokowi passed 12 economic reform packages during the first half of his presidency. These were designed to eliminate red tape and regulatory hurdles and boost business activity through 'deregulation, tax incentives, elimination of redundancies, predictability, and harmonization' (Hayden 2016). The extent to which these reforms can be explicitly tied to subsequent economic performance is unclear, but that is not the point of this analysis nor does this analysis make a claim of causality. The point is to note that the Jokowi administration enacted a fairly significant number of regulatory and procedural reforms designed to boost investment activity including infrastructure development, increase exports, and stimulate GDP growth. Tables 2.3, 2.4 and 2.5 and Figure 2.2 describe some of the major macroeconomic indicators (GDP, exports, and investment) in each province during Jokowi's first term.

Table 2.3 Annual percentage growth in regional GDP at 2010 constant prices

	2012 (%)	2013 (%)	2014 (%)	2015 (%)	2016 (%)	2017 (%)	2018 (%)
West Java	6.5	6.33	5.09	5.04	5.67	5.29	5.64
East Java	6.64	6.08	5.86	5.44	5.57	5.46	5.5
Central Java	5.34	5.11	5.27	5.47	5.25	5.26	5.32

Source: Indonesian Statistical Agency (BPS).

Table 2.4 Foreign direct investment (in millions USD)

	2012	*2013*	*2014*	*2015*	*2016*	*2017*	*2018*
West Java	4,210	7,124	6,561	5,738	5,470	5,100	5,573
C. Java	241	464	463	850	1,030	2,400	2,372
East Java	2,298	3,396	1,802	2,593	1,941	1,400	1,333

Source: Investment Coordinating Board (BKPM).

Table 2.5 Domestic investment (in billions IDR)

	2012	*2013*	*2014*	*2015*	*2016*	*2017*	*2018*
West Java	11,383	9,006	18,726	26,272	24,070	38,400	42,278
C. Java	5,797	12,593	13,601	15,410	30,360	19,900	27,474
East Java	21,520	34,848	38,131	35,489	46,349	45,000	33,333

Source: Investment Coordinating Board (BKPM).

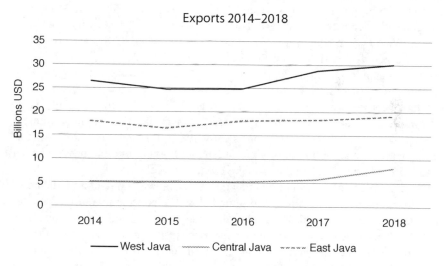

Figure 2.2 Non-oil and gas exports to Java island, 2014–2018.

The data on regional GDP shows that growth was on a declining trend until around 2014–2015 when it was stabilised in all three provinces at between 5 and 5.5 per cent annually thereafter. West Java in particular saw the steepest decline from 6.5 per cent to 5.04 per cent in 2015, before seeing a rebound as Jokowi's first term got underway. This is not spectacular growth, but it very closely mirrors the trend in national GDP which suggests these provinces, from an aggregate production point of view, are doing no better or worse than the rest of the country. It is also worth noting that GDP growth was on a downward slope until Jokowi took office when it stabilised at 5–6 per cent. Again, the point of this analysis is not to make any claims of causality, but it is not difficult to imagine a counterfactual where, in the absence of the infrastructure development and expansionary fiscal policies described above, the growth rate continued to decline rather than even out at 5 per cent.

The data on exports is more clear-cut. In all three provinces it has increased in the second half of Jokowi's term. West Java has been the largest exporter, sending nearly $30 billion of non-oil and gas goods abroad in 2018. It is of course possible, even likely, that this is a function of the depreciation in the rupiah over that time period, or some other exogenous factor. But from a political economy standpoint, exports from these particular provinces have increased under Jokowi's administration, after he passed numerous regulatory reforms and policy packages designed to achieve precisely that goal. Whether or not his policies actually caused the increase, he would not be much of a politician if he did not try to take credit for it.

The data on investment is a little harder to parse. Foreign direct investment has steadily increased year over year in Central Java, has remained fairly stable at around $5 billion a year in West Java, and after surging to $2.5 billion in 2015 has gradually declined in East Java. Domestic investment has steadily risen each year in West Java, reaching IDR 42 trillion ($3 billion) in 2018. East Java again saw a surge of over IDR 45 trillion ($3.2 billion) in 2016 and 2017 before declining again, and Central Java has seen significant volatility, peaking at IDR 30 trillion ($2.14 billion) in 2016. Investment activity in East and Central Java has thus been up and down, although partially this is due to especially large inflows in 2015 and 2016. But of interest to this analysis is that investment inflows in West Java have been consistently strong throughout Jokowi's presidency, with over $5 billion in foreign investment flowing into the province each year and steadily increasing domestic investment as well.

The final piece of data to be examined is a baseline social welfare indicator – the percentage of people considered to be below the poverty line, organised per province and compared against the national average from 2012 to 2018 (Figure 2.3). This data tells a clear story – the number of poor in Indonesia as a percentage of the population is on the decline and has been for several years. The trend lines in Central and East Java appear to be converging, although still higher than the national average, while in West Java the percentage of poor is well below the national average and has been getting even further under it since 2017. There is a limit to how much this data can explain, of course. It is probable that the well-off urban residents of Bogor, Depok and Bekasi are bringing the average down and we do not know how much of this trend is due to existing circumstances or to Jokowi's policies.

But it still forms an important part of a larger story. The evidence presented thus far demonstrates quite clearly that overall economic conditions in East, West, and Central Java are stable with many positive indicators. Cash transfers from the central government have increased, exports have increased, GDP has

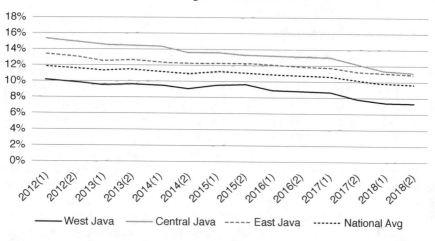

Figure 2.3 Percentage of poor population in the three largest Javanese provinces, 2012–2018.

remained stable, and the poverty rate is steadily declining. There are numerous transportation and energy infrastructure projects underway, many of which had previously remained stalled for years or even decades. Investment activity is mostly up, with billions of dollars and trillions of rupiah flowing into each province.

Even more interestingly, economic indicators in West Java are particularly good. Of the three provinces being looked at in this chapter West Java has the highest exports, has the lowest poverty rate and is the largest recipient of Foreign Direct Investment (FDI). Domestic investment has also been steadily increasing year over year. There are major toll road, airport, and energy projects in the province worth billions of dollars that are either under construction or already complete. In other words, the province has been the beneficiary of sound economic policy that has kept growth steady and seen a proliferation of new infrastructure projects, investment inflows, and improved social welfare indicators. And yet, voter support for Jokowi did not increase in any significant way from 2014 to 2019.

This suggests that economic policymaking alone cannot explain voting behaviour in the 2019 presidential election. If a vote for Jokowi could be linked solely to investment activity, GDP growth, infrastructure development, poverty rate, cash transfers or other economic indicators he would have performed much better in West Java. This would indicate that steady aggregate economic performance alone is insufficient to win elections when there are other mitigating circumstances, which recalls the experience of Ahok in Jakarta – it is fairly uncontroversial to assert that his policies were popular and effective. And yet, this ultimately was unable to prevent his defeat and jailing. The key determinant in that case may have been identity politics, and the following section will examine the role of politics and demographics in the 2019 election.

Politics and demographics

Why did stable economic performance in West Java not secure Jokowi more support in the province? Political coalition-building is one possible alternative explanation.

In 2019, the provincial legislature of West Java was dominated by Gerindra and the Prosperous Justice Party or PKS, a conservative Islamic party. With a combined 46 seats, these two parties commanded nearly 40 per cent of the legislature. PKS and Gerindra both backed Prabowo for president, and PKS in particular has long been opposed to Jokowi. This may help explain Jokowi's poor performance in the province, as PKS is a powerful political presence. In addition to holding a significant number of local legislative seats, the provincial governor from 2008 to 2018, Ahmad Heryawan, hailed from PKS. At the national level, West Java sent 13 legislators from PKS to sit in the DPR in 2019, an increase over the 11 members it fielded in 2014. Meanwhile, Jokowi's main political supporter, the Indonesian Democratic Party of Struggle (PDI-P), lost five seats from its West Java delegation.

By comparison, PKS has a minimal presence in East and Central Java. In 2019, East Java sent two PKS members to the national legislature, and Central Java sent five. In the East Java provincial legislature, PKS members held less than 4 per cent of the seats making them something of a non-entity. Meanwhile, the PDI-P consolidated its control over the Javanese heartlands, fielding 25 national legislators from Central Java and 20 from East Java, a sizable increase from 2014. The governorship of Central Java has also remained comfortably in PDI-P hands since 2008.

With the support of PDI-P in Central Java all but assured, Jokowi moved in 2019 to consolidate his political base in East Java by strengthening ties with the PKB party, a moderate Islamic-based organisation that has a strong presence in East Java. The new governor of East Java, Khofifah Indar Parawansa, hails from PKB and Jokowi appointed three PKB members: Agus Suparmanto, Ida Fauziyah, and Abdul Halim Iskandar, to respectively run the Ministry of Trade, Ministry of Manpower, and the Ministry of Villages, Under-developed Regions and Transmigration in his new cabinet. Having PKB as part of his coalition is a shrewd move, as the party sent a combined 32 lawmakers from East and Central Java to the DPR in 2019.

The composition of these provincial political coalitions appears likely to have been a factor in presidential voting behaviour in East, West, and Central Java. In 2019, Jokowi secured the support of all the major political parties with the exception of Gerindra, PKS, PAN, and the Democrat Party, which backed Prabowo. The subsequent legislature voting results, both national and provincial, are summarised in Tables 2.6 and 2.7.

The parties backing Prabowo secured 53.3 per cent of the provincial legislature seats in West Java, but only 32.5 per cent in East Java and 28.33 per cent

Table 2.6 DPR delegates according to province and membership in presidential coalitions

Province	Prabowo coalition seats	Percentage	Jokowi coalition seats	Percentage
West Java	48	52.75	43	47.25
Central Java	18	23.68	58	76.32
East Java	25	28.74	62	71.26

Source: Indonesian House of Representatives (DPR).

Table 2.7 DPRD I delegates according to province and membership in presidential coalitions

Province	Prabowo coalition seats	Percentage	Jokowi coalition seats	Percentage
West Java	64	53.33	56	46.67
Central Java	39	32.50	80	66.67
East Java	34	28.33	86	71.67

Source: Indonesian Election Commission (KPU).

in Central Java, meaning the members of local legislatures in East and Central Java were overwhelmingly drawn from parties that supported Jokowi. There is a similar pattern at the national level, with parties backing Prabowo in West Java sending 48 members to the national legislature, compared to 18 and 25 in Central and East Java. By comparison 76.3 per cent of Central Java's delegates in the national legislature were drawn from parties backing Jokowi, and 71.3 per cent in East Java.

Clearly, political party networks were an important factor in Jokowi's election prospects. He did poorly in West Java, where opposition parties like PKS and Gerindra have a strong presence, even despite numerous economic policies and indicators that might have been expected to improve his profile in the province. He did well in Central and East Java, where allies such as the PDI-P and PKB are prominent, and where friendly faces hold the governorships. These provinces also benefitted from his economic policymaking, such as the provision of infrastructure and stable economic growth, perhaps benefitting even less than West Java. Yet their support increased from 2014 to 2019. This is likely because people in East and Central Java liked Jokowi's economic record, and he had a solid political coalition there. But the role of demographics also cannot be ignored.

There is no doubt that 2019 was a polarising, divisive campaign. Political operators in Indonesia are increasingly homing in on identity politics in order to drive wedges between political coalitions, and Prabowo's antagonistic rhetoric during the campaign inflamed underlying tensions. He openly embraced the support of Islamist groups like the Islamic Defenders Front (FPI) and worked to paint Jokowi and his more moderate Muslim backers (such as the National

Table 2.8 2018 provincial demographics, according to ethnicity and religion

Province	Javanese (%)	Sundanese (%)	Other (%)	Islam (%)	Other (%)
West Java	10	79	11	97	3
Central Java	98	0	2	96	4
East Java	80	0	20	96	4

Source: Indonesian Statistical Agency (BPS).

Awakening Party (PKB) and Nahdlatul Ulama (NU)) as insufficiently conservative (Warburton 2019). As mentioned above, the conservative Islamic party PKS is very popular in West Java, reflecting the province's more conservative nature. It is also possible that ethnic cleavages helped tilt the vote in Prabowo's favour in West Java. Table 2.8 summarises the ethnic and religious demographics of West, Central, and East Java.

In all of these provinces, Islam is overwhelmingly the dominant religion. However, Islam in West Java tends to be more conservative, as evidenced by the prominent role in politics played by PKS. East and West Java are the heartland of NU, the moderate-leaning Islamic organisation that has long advocated for pluralism, and which staunchly supported Jokowi in 2019. West Java, by contrast, is where the militant Islamist group *Darul Islam* was born. It is also the Indonesian province that recorded the highest number of acts of religious intolerance in 2018 (McBeth 2019). This is why Prabowo prominently championed his association with Rizieq Shihab, the exiled leader of FPI, during campaign stops in West Java – to bolster his own Islamic credentials while painting Jokowi as insufficiently committed to Islamist principles.

Ethnicity is also likely to have been a factor, as the ethnically homogenous Javanese-majority province of Central Java voted strongly for Jokowi, as did the province of East Java where Javanese are likewise a majority. Meanwhile, in West Java the Sundanese ethnic group is by far the dominant group, composing some 79 per cent of the population. While I cannot say conclusively that ethnic identity was the major factor in determining the West Java results, work by Tom Pepinsky (2019) has shown that both religion and ethnicity were important in 2019. In particular, he showed that non-Muslims were more likely to vote for Jokowi, but also that Jokowi did better in Javanese-majority areas than in non-Javanese-majority areas. The bigger the Javanese population, the better Jokowi did in 2019. This conforms with the voting results in West Java, where Javanese compose only 10 per cent of the population.

To fully test this hypothesis would require a large-n statistical analysis, which falls outside the scope of this chapter. But it does seem likely that ethnic and religious identity played a significant role in Jokowi's large margins of victory in East and Central Java, as well as the scale of the defeat he suffered in West Java. West Java is not a Javanese-majority province, and it is more religiously conservative. These factors are known to disadvantage Jokowi, and indeed he failed to gain any ground at all in the province over his performance in 2014, even despite solid economic performance in the province during his first term.

Conclusion and future implications

This data suggests that Jokowi was less vulnerable than Ahok to the use of grassroots identity politics attacking his religious and nationalist credentials. At the national level, these attacks failed to have an impact as Jokowi coasted to a convincing victory on the back of popular growth-oriented economic policies. However, a look at the provincial-level data in a number of cases on Java shows that ethnicity, religion, and local political coalitions likely did play a role in shaping electoral outcomes, even in the face of popular policies targeted at infrastructure development.

East, West, and Central Java have all been the recipients of large-scale investment in power plants, toll roads and other infrastructure projects. West Java alone has seen over US $5 billion in foreign direct investment flow into the province every year of Jokowi's presidency, seen exports rise to almost $30 billion a year, received billions in direct transfers from the central government, and has seen poverty fall. Despite this, the province broke overwhelmingly towards Jokowi's opponent, Prabowo Subianto.

The big picture take away from this analysis is that yes policy does matter, but only up to a point. In Ahok's case, popular polices were ultimately not able to overcome the pull of identity politics and his status as a double minority worked against him in the Jakarta election. Jokowi, as a Javanese Muslim, was not as vulnerable to these types of identity-based attacks but they still had an effect. Structural conditions – ethnic and religious demographics, and political party coalitions – appear to have been significant factors in determining his electoral performance at the provincial level, and it appears that even sound economic policies were not able to overcome the inertia of these dynamics. In particular, the way in which economic performance, demographics, and politician coalitions interacted in West Java is very strong evidence in support of this conclusion.

To fully flesh out the relationship between ethnic and religious identity, economic policy and political coalitions would require a more comprehensive statistical analysis that aggregates these variables at the provincial and district level throughout Indonesia and models their relationship with voting behaviour in the 2019 election. That is beyond the scope of this chapter, which merely looks at three important provincial-level cases in Java in order to highlight and discuss some broad conceptual trends. Given the extent to which Jokowi has associated his presidency with economic development, investment, and pro-growth policies this would be a fruitful and important line of research to continue pursuing. However, the central finding of this study – which is that strong economic performance does not necessarily translate into electoral success when demographics and political coalitions are not conducive, is an important finding. It suggests that getting the policy right is only one part of the puzzle, and not even the most important part.

As the effectiveness of identity-based campaign strategies becomes clearer, the use of religion and ethnicity as wedge issues in political campaigning is likely to accelerate in the future, deepening existing social cleavages in Indonesian society and hardening the political and social polarisation already underway. Popular policies can help ameliorate these forces, especially if a candidate is a member of one of the dominant ethnic or religious groups, but they do not appear capable of escaping the gravitational pull of identity politics entirely.

Notes

1 $10.88 billion USD at an exchange rate of 14,000, which is the rate that will be used throughout for exchange conversions. Figures calculated by author from BPS government financial reports.
2 At an exchange rate of 14,000 that converts to USD $29.21 billion in 2014 and $36.67 billion in 2016. Figures calculated by author from BPS government financial reports.
3 $4.27 billion USD at an exchange rate of 14,000.
4 The author has personally verified this.

Bibliography

BPJT. (2018). *Progress Report*. This report is updated on a rolling basis. Retrieved from: http://bpjt.pu.go.id/konten/progress/beroperasi.

BPS. (2018). *Laporan Keuangan Pemerintah* 2017 [Annual Statement of Account of the Indonesian Government, 2017 Edition].

Dahono, Y., & W. Bagus. (2018, 3 December). 'This New Toll Road Drastically Cuts the Time It Takes You to Drive to Sukabumi'. *Jakarta Globe*. Retrieved from https://jakartaglobe.id/news/this-new-toll-road-drastically-cuts-the-time-it-takes-you-to-drive-to-sukabumi/.

Dipa, A. (2019, 28 March). 'Cargo Services to Help Boost Underused Kertajati Airport'. *Jakarta Post*. Retrieved from www.thejakartapost.com/news/2019/03/28/cargo-services-to-help-boost-underused-kertajati-airport.html.

Emont, J. (2016, 19 October). 'Visionary or Cautious Reformer? Indonesian President Joko Widodo's Two Years in Office'. *Time*. Retrieved from https://time.com/4416354/indonesia-joko-jokowi-widodo-terrorism-lgbt-economy/.

Fealy, G. (2018, 28 August). 'Ma'ruf Amin: Jokowi's Islamic Defender or Deadweight?' *New Mandala*. Retrieved from www.newmandala.org/maruf-amin-jokowis-islamic-defender-deadweight/.

Fossati, D. (2019). 'The Resurgence of Ideology in Indonesia: Political Islam, Aliran and Political Behaviour'. *Journal of Current Southeast Asian Affairs*, Vol. 38 (2), pp. 119–148.

Fossati, D., D. Simandjuntak & U. Fionna. (2016, 7 January). 'A Preliminary Assessment of Indonesia's Simultaneous Direct Elections (*Pilkada Serentak*) 2015'. *ISEAS Perspective*. Retrieved from www.iseas.edu.sg/images/pdf/ISEAS_Perspective_2016_1.pdf.

Guild, J. (2019a, November). 'Land Acquisition in Indonesia and Law No. 2 of 2012'. *Asian Development Bank Institute Working Paper No. 1036*. November 2019. Retrieved from www.adb.org/publications/land-acquisition-indonesia-and-law-no-2-2012.

Guild, J. (2019b, 22 March). 'In Defence of Jokowinomics'. *New Mandala*. Retrieved from www.newmandala.org/in-defence-of-jokowinomics/.

Guild, J. (2019c, 28 August). 'Is Indonesia's State-led Development Working?' *East Asia Forum*. Retrieved from www.eastasiaforum.org/2019/08/28/is-indonesias-state-led-development-working/.

Hayden, S. (2016, 26 May). 'With a Dozen Economic Reform Packages under His Belt, Indonesia's Jokowi Settles In'. *Center for Strategic and International Studies*. Retrieved from www.csis.org/analysis/dozen-economic-reform-packages-under-his-belt-indonesia%E2%80%99s-jokowi-settles.

Lamb, K. (2017, 9 May). 'Jakarta Governor Ahok Sentenced to Two Years in Prison for Blasphemy'. *The Guardian*. Retrieved from www.theguardian.com/world/2017/may/09/jakarta-governor-ahok-found-guilty-of-blasphemy-jailed-for-two-years.

Liddle, W., & S. Mujani. (2007). 'Leadership, Party, and Religion: Explaining Voting Behavior in Indonesia'. *Comparative Political Studies* Vol. 40 (7), pp. 832–857.

McBeth, J. (2019, 9 April). 'The Battle for West Java'. *Asia Times*. Retrieved from https://asiatimes.com/2019/04/the-battle-for-west-java/.

McRae, D., & D. Tomsa. (2019, 8 March). 'Another Fork in the Road for Democracy?' *Inside Indonesia*. Retrieved from www.insideindonesia.org/another-fork-in-the-road-for-democracy.

Mietzner, M., & B. Muhtadi. (2017, 5 May). 'Ahok's Satisfied Non-voters: An Anatomy'. *New Mandala*. Retrieved from www.newmandala.org/ahoks-satisfied-non-voters-anatomy/.

Pepinsky, T. (2019, 28 May). 'Religion, Ethnicity, and Indonesia's 2019 Presidential Election'. *New Mandala*. Retrieved from www.newmandala.org/religion-ethnicity-and-indonesias-2019-presidential-election/.

Ramadhani, N., S. Batu, & I. Budiari. (2017, 20 April). 'Anies Rides Islamist Wave'. *The Jakarta Post*. Retrieved from www.thejakartapost.com/news/2017/04/20/anies-rides-islamist-wave.html.

Tehusijarana, K., M.A. Sapiie, G. Ghaliya, & N. Ramadhani. (2019, 22 May). 'It's Over: Jokowi Wins'. *The Jakarta Post*. Retrieved from www.thejakartapost.com/news/2019/05/21/its-over-jokowi-wins.html.

Triggs, A., F. Kacaribu, & J. Wang. (2019). 'Risks, Resilience, and Reforms: Indonesia's Financial System in 2019'. *Bulletin of Indonesian Economic Studies* Vol. 55 (1), pp. 1–27.

Warburton, E. (2019, 16 April). 'Polarisation in Indonesia: What if Perception is Reality?' *New Mandala*. Retrieved from www.newmandala.org/how-polarised-is-indonesia/.

Wilson, I. (2017, 19 April). 'Jakarta: Inequality and the Poverty of Elite Pluralism'. *New Mandala*. Retrieved from www.newmandala.org/jakarta-inequality-poverty-elite-pluralism/.

3 The 2018 simultaneous regional elections and 2019 simultaneous national elections in West Java province

Keoni Marzuki and Chaula R. Anindya

Introduction

Indonesian politicians view the West Java province as one of Indonesia's most important electoral battlegrounds due to its sheer population size and voter base. It is the most populous province with about 49 million inhabitants and also the country's largest vote bank, with roughly 32 million voters that comprise about 20 per cent of the total national voter population. Given its demographic weight, West Java is one of the most important electoral battlegrounds in the country. Two elections were recently held in West Java province within a short time-frame: the 2018 simultaneous regional executive elections and the 2019 simultaneous national elections. The 2018 *pilkada serentak* in the province saw 16 different elections at the city/regency level and a gubernatorial election. The 2018 West Java gubernatorial election was framed as a preliminary to the 2019 presidential election that injected national-level dynamics into a routine regional election. Similarly, the 2019 simultaneous national elections were hotly contested with West Java as a key battleground province in the presidential election. president Joko 'Jokowi' Widodo, who was seeking his second and final presidential terms, faced his rival, Lieutenant General (Ret.) Prabowo Subianto who won decisively in West Java province in the 2014 national election cycle.

This chapter looks at both the 2018 and 2019 elections from the perspective of West Java. Analysing the trajectory of both elections, the demographics of the province, the candidates as well as their electoral strategy, illuminates important dimensions of how the path to electoral victory must conform to the priorities of the voters. Islam stands out as the most important single consideration in voter choice in both elections due to the large number of religiously conservative voters. As a barometer for growing religious conservatism in the rest of Indonesia, the West Java case study shows how the path to political victory must increasingly accommodate religious aspirations.

This chapter is organised as follows. The first section covers the history of electoral politics in West Java to better understand electoral dynamics during the 2018 West Java gubernatorial election and the 2019 national elections in West Java. The second section outlines the ticket-formation of the gubernatorial election and illustrates the complex dynamics surrounding them. It is followed by a discussion on the electoral dynamics surrounding the 2019 national elections in West Java and its result. Finally, the section ends with conclusions regarding coalition-building process at the regional level, the role of identity politics and trajectory of West Java politics and how it relates to the broader Indonesian politics.

A brief history of electoral politics in West Java

Islam is and has always been an intrinsic part of politics in West Java even during the time of the proclamation of the Indonesian state. In the late 1940s till 1960s, West Java was *Darul Islam/Tentara Islam Indonesia's* (DI/TII) – a rebel group bent on establishing a sovereign Islamic state – stronghold in Java (Formichi 2012). Led by the charismatic Sekarmadji Kartosuwiryo, the leader of the rebellion, DI/TII broke out due to at least two factors, namely the disillusionment over the fledgling republican government to surrender West Java back to the Dutch following the Renville Agreement (Hefner 2012, p. 63) and aspiration to establish Indonesia as a sharia-based Islamic state (Horikoshi 1975), which Islamic-based political parties at the time failed to accommodate through political channels. The group had surrendered as its leader was captured and executed by the Indonesian government and, though it was virtually disbanded, remnants and offshoots of the group exist to this day. The ripple of DI/TII's legacy can also be felt in West Java politics today.

Memories of the rebellion laid the foundation of political Islam activism and a conservative interpretation of Islam, particularly in the Priangan Mountains (in the Eastern part of the province) where DI/TII enjoyed the most significant support. Many of Kartosuwiryo's surviving followers went on to establish Islamic boarding schools (*pesantren*) in the province. For instance, Choer Affandi, one of Kartosuwiryo's disciples, who founded Miftahul Huda Islamic boarding school in Manonjaya, Tasikmalaya – one of West Java most prolific traditionalist *pesantren*. The incorporation of DI alumni into religious institutions and Islamic boarding schools in West Java influenced religious education and promoted conservative interpretations of Islam (Pamungkas 2018). Groups with a stronger puritan outlook such as the Islamic Union (Persis) and the Association for Cooperation between Islamic Boarding Schools (Buehler 2013) continue to play important roles in the socio-cultural life of West Javans. In contrast, the teachings of the two mainstream moderate Islamic organisations Nahdlatul Ulama and Muhammadiyah, whose strongholds are in Central and Eastern Java, have become less prominent over time in the development of Islam in West Java.

The footprints of Islam in West Java electoral politics can be traced to the 1955 general elections. Four parties, namely Indonesian National Party (PNI), The Council of Indonesian Muslim Associations Party (Masyumi), Nahdlatul Ulama (NU) and the Indonesian Communist Party (PKI), dominated the national parliament, as well as West Java. Despite the dominance of secular–nationalist parties in West Java, accumulating a combined total of 51.38 per cent of the total votes in the province, Masyumi garnered the most votes (Feith 1957, Buehler 2016, p. 117). Masyumi is an Islamic-based party that advocated the broader adoption of Islamic sharia law and the establishment of an Indonesian Islamic state (Tanuwidjaja 2010, p. 32). The party's major victory in West Java offers a glimpse of the mobilisational power of political Islam in the province. During the New Order, the United Development Party (PPP), an umbrella party of Islamic-based parties, enjoyed a strong following in West Java (Kadir 1999, p. 36). Though secular–nationalist parties would continue to come out as the winner in subsequent legislative elections in post-Suharto Indonesia (Ananta et al. 2005, Suryadinata 2002), Islamic-based political parties traditionally enjoy strong and consistent support in West Java. The rise of *Partai Keadilan Sejahtera* (Prosperous Justice Party/PKS) and the relatively consistent support for Islamic Development Party (PPP) in the post-Suharto era West Java province reflected the continuation of this pattern.

Past West Java regional elections provide an illustration as to how Islam plays a role in West Java politics. The 2008 West Java gubernatorial election, for example, shows that candidate backed by Islamic-based political parties were able to defeat better-resourced candidates with strong name recognition (especially the incumbent governor) and support from secular–nationalist parties that dominated the provincial legislature (Mietzner 2011, p. 135). Then-candidate Ahmad Heryawan and Dede Yusuf – backed by two Islamic-based parties of PKS and *Partai Amanat Nasional* (National Mandate Party/PAN) – won the election, partly due to their outsider status in West Java politics, the mobilisation of young Muslim voters, and the leverage on Yusuf's action-movie stardom (Junaidi 2008, p. 583, Mujani & Liddle 2009, p. 583, Hamayotsu 2011a). In the 2013 gubernatorial election, Heryawan once again won the election, having adroitly combined populist appeals (Aspinall 2013, p. 112) with an Islamist agenda (Arifianto 2016). Under governor Heryawan and PKS, the agenda of religiously conservative groups was promoted in return for their electoral support. (Kramer 2014).

Aside from Islam, concentration of nationalist voters in the Northern coast of the province is another important hue in West Java politics. In the past, the sub-region was home to nationalist and communist supporters who voted for PNI and PKI respectively (Lanti et al. 2019). The anti-communist purge in the 1960s, however, decimated the small pockets of communist supporters in West Java (Hindley 1964, p. 222) and eventually threw the PKI support base into disarray. Meanwhile, the majority of secular–nationalist voter base were subsumed under the *Golongan Karya* (Functional Groups/Golkar) during the Soeharto era, leaving only a small base of fervent nationalist voters that are loyal to the Indonesian Democratic Party (PDI) and later the Indonesian Democratic Party of Struggle (PDI-P), the successors to PNI. Finally, the industrialisation in West Java, particularly in the areas of Bekasi and Karawang, have raised the visibility and significance of labour unions as political players. Direct elections had encouraged labour unions to exert pressure on candidates to side with them in wage negotiations in return for

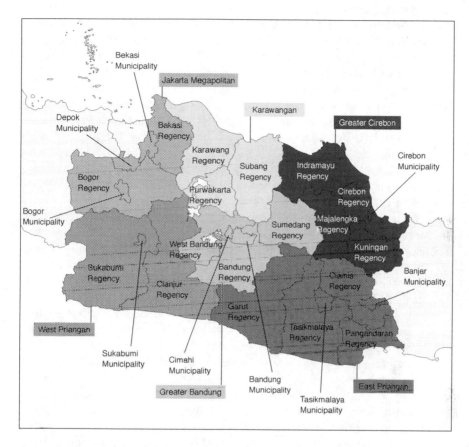

Figure 3.1 Map of West Java and its sub-regions.

mobilisation of votes. While the exact membership number of labour unions in West Java is difficult to determine, their large presence provides an incentive for local executives to court the unions in order to gain votes (Caraway & Ford 2020).

2018 West Java gubernatorial elections: parties, candidates, and the battle for the gubernatorial tickets

The 2018 gubernatorial elections featured four candidate pairs. Reflecting the electoral conditions of the West Java province, the governor and vice-governor pair had to enjoy broad appeal from both conservative Islamic voters as well as secular–nationalist voters. A quick examination of the province's demographics explains why this is so. The province is relatively homogenous because 97 per cent of the population are Muslim and 80 per cent of the inhabitants are Sundanese – with Javanese, Cirebonese, and Betawi people as the other main ethnic groups in the province. Nonetheless, voters have diverse political beliefs. Some regions, such as the East Priangan regions are bastions of religiously conservative voters (Nainggolan 2018). Urban centres, such as the Greater Bandung region, are more moderate and cosmopolitan, even though Depok, Bogor, and Bekasi (satellite cities of Jakarta), have become more religiously conservative over time due to strong PKS presence (Hamayotsu 2011b, p. 975). The North coast and Northwestern part of West Java had traditionally supported the secular–nationalist party PDI-P. Given the province's demographic profile, candidate pairs that can draw votes from religious and non-religious voters will have a distinct advantage.

As stipulated by Law No. 10/2016 on Regional Elections, gubernatorial candidate hopefuls can form a governor and vice-governor ticket provided that they can secure endorsement from a political party or a coalition of parties with at least 20 per cent of the seats at the Regional House of Representatives (DPRD I) or 25 per cent of the total votes in the previous legislative election. While it is theoretically possible to run as an independent candidate, candidate hopefuls must obtain support from about 2.1 million registered voters (in the case of West Java province) by collecting identification and signatures from voters. The logistical challenges involved to run as an independent candidate naturally favour political parties, who assume the role of gatekeepers that determine the eligibility of candidates who can run. The key point here is that prospective candidates cannot run without accommodating party interests.

Ridwan Kamil, the Berkeley-educated architect and former mayor of Bandung, was a case in point. He had built his reputation and popularity through innovative policies such as the Bandung smart city, improvement in public services, and revitalisation of public spaces (Arifianto 2016). However, he faced difficulties in securing firm support for his candidacy from the political parties because the parties endorsing him, namely National Democratic Party (NasDem), People's Consciousness Party (Hanura) Golkar, National Awakening Party (PKB), and PPP, threatened to rescind their endorsements if he did not select their preferred running mate. To alleviate the pressure, Kamil organised a convention to choose his running mate where he strategically picked Uu Ruzhanul Ulum of PPP, the two-term regent of Tasikmalaya. Ulum is the grandson of Affandi and his lineage granted him some controlling interest within Miftahul Huda and its vast regional network of alumni and affiliates. Ulum's affiliation to the education institution and its networks would be an important source of votes and his lineage would help strengthen Kamil's religious credentials. Golkar poorly received Kamil's decision to hold a convention as he chose Ulum over their presumptive candidate and retracted their endorsements (Sasongko 2017). The catalyst of Golkar's pulling out the plug on Kamil was the arrest of Setya Novanto, Golkar's chairperson, on corruption charges (Nursanti 2017).

The PDI-P had 20 seats in West Java provincial parliament. Consequentially, PDI-P did not need to form a coalition to endorse a gubernatorial candidate. PDI-P decided to form its own gubernatorial ticket by endorsing Tubagus Hasanudin, a member of the House of Representatives, and Anton Charliyan, a former West Java police chief, near the registration deadline. Several candidate hopefuls had approached PDI-P for their endorsements, but negotiations fell through as the candidate hopefuls repudiated PDI-P's demand of selecting PDI-P cadre as their running mate. Candidates were also reminded of the fate of ex-Jakarta governor Basuki Purnama who ran on a PDI-P ticket, which made them wary of forming an alliance with PDI-P (interview, Ita Winarsih, 18 September 2018). The PDI-P had no choice but to form their own ticket and to use this opportunity to gauge the party's electability for the 2019 simultaneous presidential and legislative elections in West Java (Fikri 2018).

Another coalition of parties, consisting of the Great Indonesia Movement Party (Gerindra), the National Mandate Party (PAN), and PKS, had initially formed a gubernatorial candidate ticket – endorsing then-incumbent West Java vice governor Deddy Mizwar and vice mayor of Bekasi, Ahmad Syaikhu, a cadre of PKS. Similar to Kamil, Mizwar had a strong name recognition not only because of his incumbency, but also because of his acting background and Islamic credentials built upon his relations with religiously conservative groups and his frequent role as a cleric. However, Gerindra abruptly retracted its endorsement, when Mizwar publicly embarrassed Prabowo Subianto – Gerindra's chief party patron. The affront led to the loss of his endorsement (Rikang et al. 2017). Following this incident, Mizwar's successfully approached the Democrat Party (PD) to endorse his candidacy. However, Mizwar's approach to PD without consulting his other coalition partners led to PKS and PAN rescinding their endorsements (Nadlir 2019). With a new faction in control, Golkar offered an alliance with Mizwar, this time proposing Dedi Mulyadi, then-regent of Purwakarta as his running mate. Golkar's initial course of action to endorse Kamil was not without controversy as the central leadership of the party overrode the aspiration of its regional leadership. As the party's regional chairman, Mulyadi was up in arms when the party central leadership proposed a running mate for Kamil without consulting the regional branch (Sarwanto 2017), subsequently burying his prospects to run, either as a gubernatorial or vice-governor candidate from Golkar. Mulyadi's rising profile and popularity as promoter of religious tolerance (Sutisna 2016, Soeriaatmadja 2017) and Sundanese culture (Dipa & Aruperes 2015) made him an important electoral asset.

Gerindra was quick to endorse retired major general Sudrajat as the party's gubernatorial candidate following their falling out with Mizwar. The majority of PKS sympathisers were dumbfounded when Gerindra pulled the rug out of Mizwar as the vice governor has ties to conservative Islamic groups (such as the Anti-Shia National Alliance), enjoyed good relations with PKS, and had a high public profile. Gerindra's choice seemed like a poor one. The Harvard-educated retired two-star general and Indonesia's former ambassador to China was a complete outsider in West Java politics, having spent most of his military career overseas as military attaché. Prabowo was quick to ease the tension in his coalition by persuading PKS and PAN to accept his party's proposition, as well as pairing Sudrajat with Syaikhu, a PKS cadre, to appease his coalition partners (Ihsanuddin 2017).

Table 3.1 2018 West Java gubernatorial candidates

No.	Gubernatorial candidate	Vice-gubernatorial candidate	Endorsing political parties	Total seats in regional House of Representatives
1	Ridwan Kamil	Uu Ruzhanul Ulum	NasDem, PKB, PPP, Hanura	24
2	Tubagus Hasanuddin	Anton Charliyan	PDIP	20
3	Sudrajat	Ahmad Syaikhu	Gerindra, PKS, PAN	27
4	Deddy Mizwar	Dedi Mulyadi	Demokrat, Golkar	29

Source: Author's calculation.

Identity politics in West Java gubernatorial election: campaign promises, visits to *pesantren*, and online slanders

The four candidates essentially promised similar campaign programmes to bring economic benefits to the province. Kamil–Ulum promised to provide government's assistance to develop a centre of entrepreneurship for villages in West Java, as well as to develop various tourist attractions. Meanwhile, Mizwar–Mulyadi campaigned to establish a perpetual zone for agriculture and improve the ease of doing business in the province. Sudrajat–Syaikhu, on the other hand, promised to create 1 million new jobs, improve the quality of education, as well as installing every village in West Java with Internet connectivity. Similarly, Hasanuddin–Charliyan promised to embrace digital technology as a mean of oversight for civil service performance and boost the efficiency of public services. But the race turned out to be less about a contest of ideas and policy programmes as religious issues quickly dominated the candidates' attention.

To begin with, the four candidate pairs had Islamic-themed campaign promises to compete for the Islamic vote, tending to focus on empowering or benefitting Islamic boarding schools. Kamil, for example, promised to endorse regional bylaws aiming to improve the welfare of religious teachers (*ustadz*) in the province, whereas Hasanuddin pledged to allocate one trillion rupiah (about US$70 million) for mosques and Islamic boarding schools that would fund for scholarships and building improvements (Marzuki 2018). Similarly, Sudrajat espoused to establish a madrasah-based polytechnic, where students will not only learn religious subjects, but also essential skills such as culinary skills and creative skills that prepares them to contribute directly to the economy (Permadi 2018).

The candidates also paid visits to several Islamic boarding schools (*pesantren)* across the province and gave their respects to the leaders of the *pesantren*. The candidates sought endorsement from these schools because their networks tend to make them important vote-getters. All of the candidates, for example, sought to obtain endorsement from Miftahul Huda, one of the most renowned *pesantren* in

West Java, with numerous affiliate branches and widespread alumni network called *Himpunan Alumni Miftahul Huda* (Hamida). In early 2018, Sudrajat and Mizwar separately visited Miftahul Huda to secure its endorsement. Kamil's choice of Ulum as his running mate was partly motivated by his familial ties to the *pesantren*. Even then, the school was divided by factions and Ulum had to put in considerable effort to persuade his family members to support his candidacy. Apart from Islamic boarding schools, the candidates also sought to obtain endorsements from the growing number of media and Internet-savvy preachers, who have more influence in urban West Java. As Internet penetration rate grew over time, the influence of the new media preachers has partially marginalised the role of traditional Islamic scholars in rural West Java. Sudrajat–Syaikhu were the only pair that had some considerable success in obtaining endorsements from these preachers, thanks to their PKS connection and campaign assistance from the outgoing West Java governor, Ahmad Heryawan. Several leading preachers, such as Hanan Attaki of *Pemuda Hijrah* (Temby 2018), 'Mamah' Dedeh Rosidah, and Abdullah 'Aa Gym' Gymnastiar lent support to the pair. Endorsements that flooded social media supported the narrative that voting for Sudrajat–Syaikhu was an religious obligation (Power 2018, p. 317).

Meanwhile, some candidates, particularly Kamil and Mulyadi, were the subjects of online religious slander, forcing them to prove their religious credentials. Kamil was portrayed as a secular Muslim, a supporter of the LGBT community in Bandung, a closeted adherent of the Shi'ite 'deviant' sect and a supporter of the religious minorities – the 'infidels' (Sutari 2018). Mulyadi was targeted due to his affinity for traditional Sundanese culture, which frequently earn him a reputation as a witch doctor (*dukun*). The FPI branch in Purwakarta even tried to frame him as an idol worshipper, which is considered to be a cardinal sin in Islamic theology. To address these rumours, both candidates went to great lengths to dispel them. Kamil displayed his minor haj trip to Mecca and touted his lineage as the grandson of Kyai Muhjiddin, a Nahdlatul Ulama religious scholar and part of a Hisbullah resistance group that fought against colonialism. He also appeared in a sermon with up-and-coming young preacher Adi Hidayat to dispel the LGBT rumour. Mulyadi sought to dispel such rumours by demonstrating his religiosity – visiting a number of Islamic boarding school in various sub-regions of West Java. He even changed his appearance, sporting the more common black *peci* to project an image of a pious Muslim. Kamil's and Mulyadi's experiences highlight the challenges of running for political office in a religiously conservative province like West Java – candidates are vulnerable to politically motivated character assassination, as well as ways to cope with slanderous activities.

One candidate in particular demonstrated a complementary strategy on top of pandering to the Islamic constituents. At the second round of gubernatorial candidates' debate held at Universitas Indonesia, Sudrajat–Syaikhu sparked a controversy by introducing the tagline '*2018 Asyik Menang, 2019 Ganti Presiden* (2018 Asyik Wins, 2019 Change the President)' – a modification of the existing '*2019 Ganti Presiden*' movement popularised by the anti-Jokowi movement (Bempah 2018). The significance of the statement was that if the duo won in West Java, they would support Prabowo Subianto in his 2019 presidential run and thereby lead to the replacement of president Jokowi. The daring stunt rode on Prabowo's popularity in West Java and subsequently acted as a rallying call that attracted his loyalists to the Sudrajat–Syaikhu pair. To add some context, Prabowo obtained 14.1 million votes – compared to Jokowi's 9.5 million votes – in West Java during the last presidential election. Sirojudin Abbas, Programme Director at the Saiful Mujani Research and Consulting estimated that 30 to 35 per cent of Kamil' and Mizwar's voters base were swing voters (Pramono et al. 2018). Getting Prabowo supporters in that pool to swing to them was a brilliant masterstroke.

According to a survey by *Kompas* in May 2018, the stunt seemed to pay dividends as the pair's electability showed an upward trend, albeit only slightly, after the debate was held. By April 2018, the frequent use of the tagline has allowed it to grow organically and made it as an unofficial rallying call. *Kompas* released an in-depth polling that focuses on the different sub-regions of West Java to look where each respective candidate was leading. The poll indicated that Kamil–Ulum ticket was leading in three sub-regions, namely in Greater Bandung, East Priangan, and West Priangan. This was expected as both Kamil and Ulum were popular regional leaders of Bandung and Tasikmalaya respectively. Furthermore, Kamil–Ulum also successfully broadened their electoral base across West Priangan, which was considered as a contested no-man's land (Nainggolan 2018). According to the same poll, Mizwar–Mulyadi were particularly strong in Karawang and the Greater Cirebon areas. The pair enjoyed overwhelming support in their stronghold due to Mulyadi's outstanding performance and approval rating as the regent of Purwakarta. Sudrajat–Syaikhu's electability were highest in the Jakarta hinterlands area of Depok, Bogor, and Bekasi, and they polled quite well in West Priangan and the Greater Bandung Area.

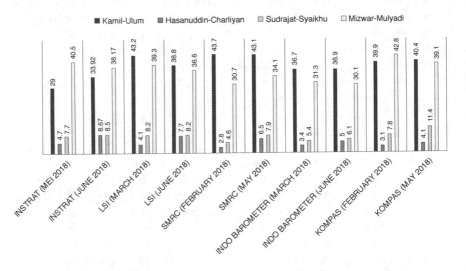

Figure 3.2 West Java gubernatorial election polling and official election results.

Table 3.2 2018 West Java gubernatorial election results at municipality and regency level

Regency/municipality	Sub-regions	Vote share			
		Kamil–Uluum (RINDU)	Hasanuddin–Charliyan (HASANAH)	Sudrajat–Syaikhu (ASYIK)	Mizwar–Mulyadi (2DM)
Bogor Regency	West Priangan	528,479 (23.6%)	319,189 (14.3%)	**801,322 (35.8%)**	590,882 (26.4%)
Ciamis Regency	East Priangan	**251,287 (36.4%)**	127,438 (18.4%)	179,232 (25.9%)	133,157 (19.3%)
Cianjur Regency	West Priangan	**338,346 (32.9%)**	101,525 (9.9%)	263,464 (25.6%)	326,547 (31.7%)
Cirebon Regency	Greater Cirebon	**306,712 (30.7%)**	204,861 (20.5%)	199,877 (20%)	289,093 (28.9%)
Garut Regency	East Priangan	**435,652 (36.2%)**	180,852 (15%)	249,580 (20.7%)	337,391 (28%)
Indramayu Regency	Greater Cirebon	**309,230 (41.2%)**	114,279 (15.2%)	121,757 (16.2%)	205,788 (24.7%)
Karawang Regency	Karawangan	227,146 (21.9%)	124,481 (12%)	279,176 (26.9%)	**407,526 (39.2%)**
Bandung Municipality	Greater Bandung	**656,090 (51.3%)**	111,190 (8.7%)	359,267 (28.1%)	153,323 (12%)
Banjar Municipality	East Priangan	**37,766 (34.1%)**	15,541 (14.1%)	21,407 (19.4%)	35,883 (32.4%)
Bekasi Megapolitan	Jakarta Megapolitan	353,556 (34.3%)	103,757 (10.1%)	**376,447 (36.6%)**	195,937 (19%)
Bogor Municipality	West Priangan	164,954 (33.2%)	47,947 (9.6%)	**173,995 (35%)**	110,337 (22.2%)
Cimahi Municipality	Greater Bandung	**135,268 (46.8%)**	21,132 (7.3%)	91,044 (31.5%)	41,681 (14.4%)
Cirebon Municipality	Greater Cirebon	**56,676 (35.3%)**	24,449 (15.2%)	41,119 (25.6%)	38,315 (13.9%)
Depok Municipality	Jakarta Megapolitan	246,992 (30.4%)	69,751 (8.6%)	**358,129 (44.2%)**	135,068 (16.7%)
Sukabumi Municipality	West Priangan	53,749 (32.3%)	20,579 (12.4%)	**59,410 (35.7%)**	32,889 (19.7%)
Tasikmalaya Municipality	East Priangan	104,402 (27.6%)	35,773 (9.5%)	**164,720 (43.5%)**	73,502 (19.4%)
Kuningan Regency	Greater Cirebon	**180,231 (31.5%)**	90,510 (15.8%)	168,892 (29.6%)	131,732 (23.1%)
Majalengka Regency	Greater Cirebon	186,892 (26.1%)	211,252 (29.5%)	166,873 (23.3%)	149,881 (21%)
Pangandaran Regency	East Priangan	75,500 (31%)	211,252 (29.5%) 83,478 (34.2%)	35,569 (14.6%)	49,292 (20.2%)
Purwakarta Regency	Karawangan	120,887 (24.3%)	33,206 (6.7%)	132,417 (26.6%)	**210,746 (42.4%)**
Subang Regency	Karawangan	217,827 (27.6%)	103,300 (13.2%)	117,844 (15%)	**346,216 (44.1%)**
Sukabumi Regency	West Priangan	296,823 (26.5%)	108,172 (9.7%)	**395,318 (35.3%)**	318,244 (28.5%)
Sumedang Regency	Greater Bandung	**253,744 (39.1%)**	82,862 (12.8%)	134,274 (20.7%)	178,590 (27.5%)
Tasikmalaya Regency	East Priangan	**363,470 (39.8%)**	99,230 (10.9%)	257,762 (28.2%)	193,059 (21.1%)
Bandung Regency	Greater Bandung	**743,156 (41.7%)**	146,913 (8.2%)	458,633 (25.7%)	435,221 (24.4%)
West Bandung Regency	Greater Bandung	**350,243 (40.1%)**	90,774 (10.4%)	220,790 (25.4%)	210,674 (24.1%)
Bekasi Regency	Jakarta Megapolitan	231,176 (20%)	100,637 (8.7%)	**489,097 (42.4%)**	332,224 (28.8%)
TOTAL VOTES		**7,226,254 (32.88%)**	2,773,078 (12.62%)	6,317,465 (28.74%)	5,663,198 (25.77%)

Source: Indonesian Election Commission (KPU) Final Tabulation, available at https://infopemilu.kpu.go.id/pilkada2018/hasil/penetapan/t1/jawa_barat

Note

Bold represents the candidate pair as declared the election winner in a particular municipality or regency.

2018 West Java gubernatorial election surprising results: key drivers

Despite concerns about a heated election following the 2017 Jakarta gubernatorial election, the West Java gubernatorial election turned out to be relatively smooth sailing, punctuated by identity and sectarian politics. Several factors helped explain this phenomenon – such as the relatively similar candidate background as well as relatively balanced nationalist–religious candidate pairs, which blunts the effect of smear campaigns (Warburton et al. 2018). More than 22.7 million voters came to polling stations – a turnout rate of 70 per cent, a better showing than the previous gubernatorial election's turnout rate of 65 per cent. Quick count results taken on the day of the election validated several polls predicting that Kamil–Ulum would win the highest vote share. The Election Commission's official tally announced on July made his victory official. Kamil garnered around 7.22 million votes (32.8 per cent), while his closest competitor gained about 6.31 million votes (28.74 per cent). The underdog Sudrajat–Syaikhu pair trounced all expectations by placing second. They bested one of the favourite pair (Mizwar–Mulyadi) and were only 900,000 votes behind Kamil – an incredible feat considering polls had demonstrated Sudrajat's low popularity.

As predicted by the poll mentioned above, Kamil–Ulum won by a landslide in Greater Bandung and dominated East Priangan. The pair also did quite well in urban centres in the province that supposedly supported PDI-P (Hasanuddin–Charliyan), even in the pair's home turf in Majalengka. Likewise, Mizwar–Mulyadi were only marginally successful in Mulyadi's home ground of Karawang sub-region, namely Purwakarta, Subang, and Karawang – losing much of the voter base they have previously attracted before the election. The dark horse Sudrajat–Syaikhu did especially well in sub-regions that were identified as PKS strongholds and more religiously conservative – the Jakarta Megapolitan Area and West Priangan sub-districts. Like Kamil–Ulum, the pair were notably successful in several urban centres and sub-urban electoral districts – often garnering the second most votes, which led them to overtake Mizwar–Mulyadi. The result leads us to ask to what extent did identity politics or other factors play a role in their surprising performance at the polls?

There are at least three variables that could help explain the astonishing result. The first was that Sudrajat–Syaikhu's stunt pulled at the debates and reverberated well with the electorate. By constructing a narrative that the 2018 West Java gubernatorial election was a preliminary to the 2019 presidential election, Sudrajat–Syaikhu were able to bring over Prabowo's supporters that had previously leaned towards Kamil or Mizwar. The exit-poll survey taken on election day by Saiful Mujani Research and Consulting (SMRC) shows that the retired general's popularity remains high in West Java. Around 51.2 per cent of West Java's electorate preferred him over president Jokowi if the presidential election were conducted simultaneously – indicating that there was a significant base of loyal Prabowo's voters that Sudrajat could rally. Just as PDI-P benefitted from the so-called 'Jokowi effect' in 2014, Sudrajat benefitted from the 'Prabowo effect', which was augmented by his popularity in the province. The full impli-cation of '*2018 Asyik Menang, 2019 Ganti Presiden*' tagline may never be truly understood, but nevertheless its effects are discernible.

Another critical element that played a major role in Sudrajat's performance was the eleventh-hour electioneering efforts by Gerindra and most importantly PKS, which begun to intensively campaign for Sudrajat about a month before the election. PKS' tardiness in picking up steam may have been one of the causes why Sudrajat's numbers in the polls were weak. Moreover, as this was a last-minute effort, the polls might not have captured the potency of PKS' party machinery. Nonetheless, Heryawan and PKS cadre was able to galvanise and boost the party's morale to campaign for Sudrajat by employing the party's deep network, which he had expanded and fostered during his tenure as governor (Pramono et al. 2018). He channelled a large sum of money to fund various campaign activities and logistical support to Sudrajat's campaign team (Warburton 2018). Apart from leadership and financial resources, Heryawan's efforts to secure endorsements from influential preachers at both the regional and national level bore fruit as they convinced the more religiously conservative Muslims to vote for Sudrajat. The endorsements basically propounded the narrative that the West Java gubernatorial election affected the interests of the Muslim community and that voting for Sudrajat–Syaikhu was a religious obligation. These messages were disseminated through popular social media platforms and reached a wide audience. As a result, the duo was able to split religious conservative voters, many of which formed a natural part of Mizwar's voter base. Given the similar-ities of Mizwar and Sudrajat voters' profiles, many of those who were persuaded by these endorsements went on to vote for Sudrajat instead of the other candidates.

The widespread slander levelled against Kamil and Mulyadi in the last weeks of the election also helped to whittle their voter base. Character assassination efforts against Kamil and Mulyadi largely targeted their piety and their devout-ness to Islam. Kamil was frequently painted as a secular, non-practising Muslim, LGBT-sympathiser, and a Shi'ite; whereas Mulyadi was accused as an idolater who practises mysticism. This organised slander campaign became more intense in the last leg of the campaign, particularly during the cooling down period, a few days before voting took place. Moreover, as the information was dissemi-nated through social media, the Election Supervisory Board was powerless to forestall them.

2019 simultaneous elections: identity politics in the West Java theatre

PDI-P was gunning to repeat its victory in 2014 in the 2019 legislative elections in 2019. A victory in West Java would help PDI-P to strengthen its grip in the national House of Representatives, as well as provincial parliaments, given that the province has the highest number of seats in the DPR (91 seats) – by virtue of the sheer size of its population. Though West Java is a predominantly Muslim majority and voter orientation is generally more religiously conservative, PDI-P had won the province in 1999 and 2014. Yet, PDI-P's prospects were tainted as the party endorsing Basuki Purnama – the former governor of Jakarta who was convicted of blasphemy charges against Islam. Subsequently, PDI-P, and other political parties that endorsed him, were stigmatised as anti-Islam. As a result of the Ahok fallout, PDI-P results were likely to be worse off compared to 2014. Gerindra and PKS could hope for a better showing judging from their performance in the gubernatorial election. If they could maintain their campaign machinery and maintain the momentum generated by gubernatorial election, the pro-Prabowo coalition had a decent shot of winning the legislative election in West Java.

The likelihood was that president Jokowi winning the West Java province in the presidential election was not very high, even though one poll posted a 60 per cent approval rating in the province (Hadi 2018). His relatively high approval rating in the province was supposedly the result of his efforts to support to infrastructure projects in West Java (at least 30 projects) under the National Strategic Project umbrella, namely the recently completed Kertajati International Airport in Majalengka and the Bogor–Ciawi–Sukabumi toll road. President Jokowi's preference to reside at the Bogor State Palace, rather than the Merdeka Palace in Jakarta, symbolically demonstrated his commitment to West Java. Moreover, president Jokowi campaign team had also enlisted the support of local notables, namely Solihin GP, Ginandjar Kartasasmita, and Agum Gumelar, to name a few, in order to garner support. His West Java regional campaign team also consisted of three pairs of gubernatorial candidates that ran in the 2018 West Java regional elections. Although Jokowi enjoyed a solid approval rating, the same poll indicated that his electability rating in West Java only stood at around 45 per cent. The disparity between approval rating and electability rating suggests that approval does not necessarily translate into electability.

Similar to the 2018 gubernatorial election, Jokowi's background made him vulnerable to accusations of religious impiety. His Islamic credentials were targeted, and he was said to be a descendant of a communist or a communist himself. These considerations mattered for West Javans in the context of the larger historical and social roots of political Islam in the province (Mudzakkir 2019). A survey by Indonesia Institute of Sciences (LIPI) found that half of its respondents believed that president Jokowi was not favourable to Islam, citing the recent criminalisation of several opposition-leaning religious scholars. On top of that, support from Ulum, now a part of Jokowi's campaign team, did not automatically translate into support from Miftahul Huda *pesantren* network. president Jokowi's electability rating was low in West Priangan and East Priangan, known to be religiously conservative regions (Rahadian 2018).

President Jokowi could not refurbish his image even with Kyai Ma'ruf Amin, then-chairman of the Council of Indonesian Ulema (MUI) and formerly Supreme Leader of the Nahdlatul Ulama as his running mate. Part of the political consideration in choosing Amin as his running mate was to ameliorate anti-Islam allegations levelled against Jokowi. Jokowi also tried to appease conservative Muslims by bringing up a plan to grant a conditional release for Abu Bakar Ba'asyir, the leader of Jemaah Islamiyah – a known radical Islam group. Despite these efforts, it appeared that president Jokowi's electability in West Java rating did not improve nor stop damaging rumours against him. In February 2019, after Jokowi announced Amin as his running mate, a viral video circulated showing a group of women using fearmongering tactics – Jokowi was portrayed as someone who would ban the call to prayer, the use of veil, and even allow same-sex marriages (Permadi 2019). The video was taken in Karawang, West Java. The relentless disinformation campaign was claimed to have lowered his electability rating in West Java by as much as 8 per cent (Ihsanuddin 2019).

Concurrently, Ma'ruf Amin was not able to energise Nahdlatul Ulama constituents in West Java and the influence of NU's central board in West Java was weaker than expected. While the majority of the Muslims in West Java share the same religious practices and customs as mainstream NU of Central and East Java, they do not necessarily follow their counterparts' political inclination. For example, some NU leaders in the East Priangan sub-region also serve as the head of local Islamic Defenders Front (FPI) and Hizb ut-Tahrir Indonesia (HTI), organisations known for strong anti-minority and religious conservative views. NU's structure as a loose confederacy of Islamic religious scholars and ulemas made it hard to mobilise the NU network as a vote-getter, especially in regions where NU do not have a strong presence. While NU *pesantrens* do exist all across the province such as Pesantren Cipasung Tasikmalaya, Pesantren Al-Masthuriyah Sukabumi, and Pesantren Al-Musaddadiyah Garut and in areas bordering Central Java, their reach and influence are limited. In 2018, the Indonesian Institute of Sciences (LIPI) also released a poll collected from 200 respondents, which showed that only 9 per cent of Muslims in West Java identified themselves as NU members, while the rest did not have any particular affiliation. Moreover, the influence of NU *kyai* in West Java, such as Kyai Nawar Mussad and Kyai Ilyas Ruhiat – both of whom are notable NU preachers – have waned as more and more Muslims seek counsels and religious advice from non-NU preachers (Nafi 2018).

In order to broaden Amin's appeal, president Jokowi's campaign team attempted to highlight his Sundanese ethnicity rather than his NU background. NU is strongly associated with traditional Javanese culture and prominent NU *kyais* are predominantly of Javanese descent and thus might generate some resistance from local population. Amin is originally from Banten, which was a part of West Java until it had become a separate province in 2000. Mulyadi, now the chairman of president Jokowi's West Java regional campaign team, utilised Amin's aristocratic lineage as the descendant of the last king of Sumedang Larang, a sixteenth-century Islamic kingdom in West Java. The narrative was that he would be the only ethnic-Sundanese since the late Umar Wirahadikusumah to hold one of the highest political offices in the country. This was an attempt to highlight Amin's ethnicity as a Sundanese and to address the aspirations for

Sundanese representation at the national leadership. Unfortunately, the plan was largely unsuccessful.

The majority of polls between December 2018 and April 2019 put president Jokowi ahead of Prabowo in West Java. A nationwide poll by the Centre for Strategic and International Studies Indonesia (CSIS) also showed that president Jokowi was leading in West Java. Meanwhile, polls by Roy Morgan Research in January and February 2019, as well as *Kompas* in October 2018 and March 2019, indicated that Prabowo was ahead of Jokowi in West Java. But these polls also indicated a high percentage of undecided voters. Moreover, the recent case of the West Java gubernatorial election showed that polling results could be inaccurate. Prabowo and his campaign team seemed confident that he could repeat the result of the 2014 presidential election in West Java, where he won by a landslide. Furthermore, the gubernatorial election showed that Gerindra's campaign machinery in West Java was well oiled and he had a loyal, if not fanatic, voter base. Moreover, Prabowo's campaign team had cultivated long-standing relations with notable clerics and various *pesantrens* since 2014, which are essential for voter mobilisation, and Gerindra's alliance with PKS enabled it to tap into PKS' networks driven by these factors, Prabowo and his campaign team diverted a majority of their focus and resources to challenge president Jokowi's stronghold of Central and East Java, leaving the campaign in West Java to his volunteers and ardent supporters at the grassroot levels.

2019 simultaneous elections in West Java: legislative and presidential elections

The outcome of the legislative elections in West Java reflected the continued dominance of secular–nationalist parties. Gerindra won both the national and provincial legislative elections, amassing more than 4.3 million and 4.1 million votes respectively, while PDI-P had to settle for second, garnering 3.5 million votes in both the national and provincial legislative elections. Gerindra's votes increased by 2 million in the national election, while PDI-P's votes decreased by 600,000. PKS enjoyed a strong showing garnering 3.2 million votes – an increase of 1.3 million. All in all, the result of the legislative elections in West Java showed a rebalancing of popular support in favour of the political parties in Prabowo's coalition, while some parties in president Jokowi's coalition experienced a decline in votes. This shift brought on some profound changes, especially in terms of local/regional politics. PDI-P, which previously dominated the provincial parliament, was now third in line and had lost the chairmanship of the provincial parliament. Gerindra and PKS had the largest and second-largest number of seats (25 and 21 respectively), while PDI-P maintained its seat count at 20. The implication is that Kamil may have to deal with a potentially hostile provincial parliament and obstruct his policy programmes. In the longer term, three parties in the provincial parliament – Gerindra, PKS, and PDI-P – are eligible to sponsor gubernatorial candidates without a coalition, thus diversifying the next gubernatorial race in 2023, provided that the stipulations of the election law persist. The complete breakdown of the legislative elections results is presented in Table 3.3.

The 2019 presidential election was a rehash of the 2014 elections. Prabowo amassed over 16 million votes while president Jokowi gained 10.75 million votes. Both improved their performance compared to their 2014 results. The only difference is that the margin between president Jokowi and Prabowo had increased in Prabowo's favour. President Jokowi's regional campaign team admitted that negative sentiment against Jokowi had festered in the past 5 years, making it an uphill task to persuade voters. Mulyadi further argued that religious sentiments and identity politics distracted voters from more pertinent economic issues (Ramdhani, 2019). The breakdown in Table 3.4 and Figure 3.3 shows that president Jokowi only won in several regencies and cities in West Java's North coast, a sub-region identified with more moderate religious views, as well as some cities and regencies directly bordering Central Java – PDI-P's traditional sphere of influence. The support of several *pesantren* leaders and local notables proved negligible and did not help president Jokowi to increase his standing in West Java significantly. Prabowo, on the other hand, dominated in most regencies and municipalities across different sub-regions of West Java, especially in sub-regions that have been identified to be more religiously conservative such as the Jakarta Megapolitan area, West Priangan, and East Priangan.

Table 3.3 2019 legislative election results – national parliament (DPR)

Political parties	2014 Legislative election vote share – House of Representatives (DPR)	Seats in DPR	2019 Legislative election vote share – House of Representatives (DPR)	Seats in DPR
Demokrat	1,931,014 (9.11%)	12	1,830,565 (7.49%)	11
Gerindra	2,378,762 (11.22%)	11	4,320,050 (17.69%)	25
Golkar	3,540,629 (16.71%)	17	3,226,962 (13.21%)	16
Hanura	1,160,572 (5.48%)	3	271,204 (1.10%)	–
NasDem	1,035,729 (4.89%)	5	1,213,414 (4.96%)	4
PAN	1,390,407 (6.56%)	4	1,690,821 (6.92%)	7
PBB	368,478 (1.74%)	–	236,304 (0.96%)	–
PDI-P	4,159,404 (19.63%)	20	3,510,525 (14.37%)	20
PKB	1,572,724 (7.42%)	7	1,896,257 (7.76%)	12
PKPI	119,748 (0.57%)	–	45,372 (0.18%)	–
PKS	1,903,561 (8.98%)	12	3,286,606 (13.46%)	21
PPP	1,631,804 (7.70%)	9	1,111,362 (4.55%)	3
PSI	N/A	N/A	401,835 (1.64%)	–
Garuda			114,894 (0.47%)	–
Perindo			695,083 (2.84%)	1
Berkarya			564,942 (2.31%)	–

Source: Indonesian Election Commission (KPU).

Table 3.4 2019 presidential election results in West Java province

Regency/municipality	Sub-regions	Jokowi–Amin	Prabowo–Uno
Bogor Regency	West Priangan	862,122	**2,035,552**
Ciamis Regency	East Priangan	303,323	**440,240**
Cianjur Regency	West Priangan	461,787	**775,354**
Cirebon Regency	Greater Cirebon	**103,878**	93,036
Garut Regency	East Priangan	412,136	**1,068,444**
Indramayu Regency	Greater Cirebon	**707,324**	282,349
Karawang Regency	Karawangan	584,682	**779,266**
Bandung Municipality	Greater Bandung	621,969	**867,945**
Banjar Municipality	East Priangan	**63,295**	55,732
Bekasi Municipality	Jakarta Megapolitan	617,907	**752,254**
Bogor Municipality	West Priangan	228,112	**399,073**
Cimahi Municipality	Greater Bandung	120,813	**214,452**
Cirebon Municipality	Greater Cirebon	**823,900**	449,455
Depok Municipality	Jakarta Megapolitan	464,472	**618,527**
Sukabumi Municipality	West Priangan	61,835	**139,106**
Tasikmalaya Municipality	East Priangan	302,132	**729,024**
Kuningan Regency	Greater Cirebon	252,373	**376,259**
Majalengka Regency	Greater Cirebon	346,980	**425,877**
Pangandaran Regency	East Priangan	**164,073**	96,943
Purwakarta Regency	Karawangan	155,863	**406,988**
Subang Regency	Karawangan	**537,114**	392,882
Sukabumi Regency	West Priangan	400,644	**1,012,116**
Sumedang Regency	Greater Bandung	310,579	**408,929**
Tasikmalaya Regency	East Priangan	111,785	**314,247**
Bandung Regency	Greater Bandung	778,826	**1,246,921**
West Bandung Regency	Greater Bandung	359,220	**649,988**
Bekasi Regency	Jakarta Megapolitan	593,424	**1,046.487**
TOTAL		10,750,568	**16,077,446**

Source: Indonesia's Election Commission (KPU).

Note
Bold indicates the presidential candidate who was declared election winner in a particular municipality or regency.

Conclusion

The 2018 West Java gubernatorial election and the 2019 simultaneous elections in West Java provided important insights regarding political and societal change in the province in post-Soeharto Indonesia. A wave of rising religious conservatism is fostered by a conducive democratic political environment that allows it to flourish. The visible signs – such as the persecution of Ahmadiyah sect followers, rising number of incidents of religious intolerance, and growing number of sharia or sharia-inspired regulations – were quite telling. Our analysis of the various elections held in West Java suggests that visible demonstrations of religious piety have become extremely important politically. Both the 2018 West Java gubernatorial elections and the 2019 presidential elections in West Java

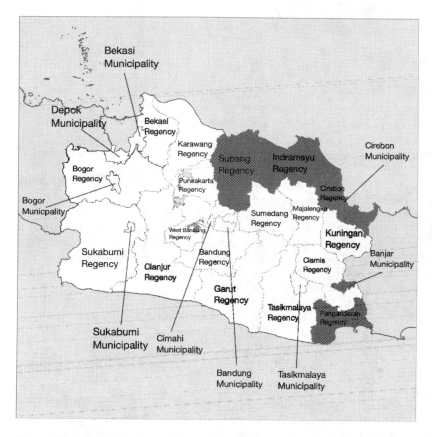

Figure 3.3 Regencies and municipalities in which each presidential candidates win.

demonstrated a common theme whereby candidates would strive to burnish their religious credentials through a myriad of ways – ranging from visiting and paying homage to local clerics to promising policy programmes that benefits the Muslim constituents. Profuse quantity of online slanders spread, primarily via social media and messaging applications, were evident in both cases. Given the far-reaching nature and high frequency of social media usage, these slanders were effective in disorienting the electorate.

Reflecting on a traditional saying of *Sunda itu Islam* (Sunda is Islam), one could argue that Islam is deeply rooted in the Sundanese community (Millie 2009, p. 5). A Sundanese proverb further depicts Sunda and Islam as *Gula Jeung Peueutna* (sugar and its sweetness) whereby the two elements cannot be separated from each other. Should false accusations undermine the piety of a candidate in the eyes of the voters, it will potentially erode their support base. Thus, identifying potential power brokers to protect and burnish the candidates' credentials also prove to be significant during the election. The candidates, however, cannot solely rely on the traditional power brokers, but also influential 'online' figures as false information tends to be easily disseminated on social media.

Bibliography

Ananta, A., E. Arifin, & L. Suryadinata. 2005. *Emerging Democracy in Indonesia*. Singapore: ISEAS-Yusof Ishak Institute.

Arifianto, A. 2016, 4 December. 'Islamic Defenders Front: An Ideological Evolution'. *RSIS Commentary*. Retrieved from https://dr.ntu.edu.sg/bitstream/10356/86891/1/CO17228.pdf.

Aspinall, E. 2013. 'Popular Agency and Interests in Indonesia's Democratic Transition and Consolidation'. *Indonesia*, Vol. 96: 101–121.

Bempah, R.T. 2018, 14 May. 'Sudrajat–Syaikhu Bawa Kaus "2018 Asyik Menang, 2019 Ganti Presiden", Debat Pilgub Jabar Berakhir Panas' ['Sudrajat–Syaikhu Brought T-Shirts Stating "2018 *Asyik* Won, 2019 Change the President", West Java Gubernatorial Debate Ended on a Tense Note'] *Kompas*. Retrieved from https://regional.kompas.com/read/2018/05/14/22420331/sudrajat-syaikhu-bawa-kaus-2018-asyik-menang-2019-ganti-presiden-debat.

Buehler, M. 2013. 'Subnational Islamization through Secular Parties: Comparing Shari'a Politics in Two Indonesian Provinces'. *Comparative Politics*, Vol. 46 (1): 63–82.

Buehler, M. 2016. *The Politics of Shari'a Law: Islamist Activists and the State in Democratizing Indonesia*. Cambridge: Cambridge University Press.

Caraway, T., & M. Ford. 2020. *Labor and Politics in Indonesia*. Cambridge: Cambridge University Press.

Dipa, A., & L. Aruperes. 2015, 14 November. 'Regent Enforces Tolerance'. *The Jakarta Post*. Retrieved from www.thejakartapost.com/news/2015/11/14/regent-enforces-tolerance.html.

Feith, H. 1957. *The Indonesian Elections of 1955*. Ithaca, NY: Cornell University.

Fikri, A. 2018, 8 January. 'Pengamat Duga Pencalonan TB Hasanuddin-Anton Charliyan Simbolik' ['Observers Thoughts the Nomination of TB Hasanuddin-Anton Charliyan is Just Symbolic'], *Tempo.co*. Retrieved from https://pilkada.tempo.co/read/1048247/pengamat-duga-pencalonan-tb-hasanuddin-anton-charliyan-simbolik/full&view=ok.

Formichi, C. 2012. *Islam and the Making of the Nation: Kartosuwiryo and Political Islam in Twentieth-Century Indonesia*. Leiden: KITLV Press.

Hadi, S. 2018, 21 June. 'Kalahkan Prabowo di Survei, Jokowi Rajin Blusukan ke Jawa Barat' ['Defeating Prabowo in Survey, Jokowi Often Goes on Unannounced Visitation in West Java'], *Tempo.co*. Retrieved from https://nasional.tempo.co/read/1099493/kalahkan-prabowo-di-survei-jokowi-rajin-blusukan-ke-jawa-barat/full&view=ok.

Hamayotsu, K. 2011a. 'Beyond Faith and Identity: Mobilizing Islamic Youth in a Democratic Indonesia'. *The Pacific Review*, Vol. 24 (2): 225–247.

Hamayotsu, K. 2011b. 'The Political Rise of the Prosperous Justice Party in Post-Authoritarian Indonesia'. *Asian Survey*, Vol. 51 (5): 971–992.

Hefner, R. 2012. 'Shari'a Politics and Indonesian Democracy'. *The Review of Faith and International Affairs*, Vol. 10 (4), 61–69.

Hindley, D. 1964. *The Communist Party of Indonesia: 1951–1963*. Berkeley, CA: University of California.

Horikoshi, H. 1975. 'The *Dar ul-Islam* Movement in West Java (1948–62): An Experience in the Historical Process'. *Indonesia*, 20: 58–86.

Ihsanuddin. 2017, 22 December. 'Prabowo Lobi PKS Duetkan Sudrajat–Syaikhu' ['Prabowo Lobbies PKS to Nominate Sudrajat–Syaikhu'], *Kompas*. Retrieved from https://nasional. kompas.com/read/2017/12/22/18494341/prabowo-lobi-pks-duetkan-sudrajat-syaikhu-di-pilgub-jabar.

Ihsanuddin. 2019, 2 March. 'Jokowi Mengaku Elektabilitasnya di Jabar Turun 8 Persen Karena Fitnah' ['Jokowi Admitted His Electability in West Java is Down by 8 percent due to Hoaxes'], *Kompas*. Retrieved from https://nasional.kompas.com/read/2019/03/02/11543581/ jokowi-mengaku-elektabilitasnya-di-jabar-turun-8-persen-karena-fitnah.

Junaidi, A. 2008, 17 April. Nationalism vs. Islamism in West Java Election? *The Jakarta Post*. Retrieved from www.thejakartapost.com/news/2008/04/17/nationalism-vs-islamism-west-java-election.html.

Kadir, S. 1999. 'The Islamic Factor in Indonesia's Political Transition'. *Asian Journal of Political Science*, Vol. 7 (2): 21–44.

Kramer, E. 2014. 'A Fall from Grace? "Beef-gate" and the Case of Indonesia's Prosperous Justice Party'. *Asian Politics and Policy*, Vol. 66 (4): 555–576.

Lanti, I., A. Ebih, & W. Dermawan. 2019, 19 July. *Examining the Growth of Islamic Conservatism in Indonesia: The Case of West Java*, RSIS Working Paper No. 322). Singapore: S. Rajaratnam School of International Studies. Retrieved from www.rsis. edu.sg/rsis-publication/idss/examining-the-growth-of-islamic-conservatism-in-indonesia-the-case-of-west-java/.

Marzuki, K. 2018, 25 June. 'The Race For West Java's Governorship: Some Preliminary Observations', *RSIS Commentary*. Retrieved from www.rsis.edu.sg/wp-content/ uploads/2018/06/CO18106.pdf.

Mietzner, M. 2011. 'Funding Pilkada: Illegal Campaign Financing in Indonesia's Local Elections', in Edward Aspinall & Gerry van Klinken (eds.), *The State and Illegality in Indonesia*. Leiden: KITLV Press, pp. 123–138.

Millie, J. 2009. *Splashed by The Saint: Ritual Reading and Islamic Sanctity in West Java*. Leiden: KITLV Press.

Mudzakkir, A. 2019, 5 January. 'Sulitnya Menaklukkan Banten dan Jawa Barat (The Difficulties to Conquer Banten and West Java)', *Tempo*. Retrieved from https://majalah. tempo.co/read/nasional/156888/sulitnya-menaklukkan-banten-dan-jawa-barat?.

Mujani, S., & R.W. Liddle. 2009. 'Muslim Indonesia's Secular Democracy'. *Asian Survey*, Vol. 49 (4): 575–590.

Nadlir, M. 2019, 1 January. 'Batal Dukung Deddy Mizwar di Pilkada Jabar, PKS Ungkap Pakta Integritas Ini' ['Changing Its Mind to Support Deddy Mizway in West Java Governor's Race, PKS Reveals This "Integrity Pact"], *Kompas*. Retrieved from https://nasional. kompas.com/read/2018/01/01/15432441/batal-dukung-deddy-mizwar-di-pilkada-jabar-pks-ungkap-pakta-integritas-ini.

Nafi, M.Z. 2018, 13 January. 'Asep Salahudin Jelaskan Anomali Nuansa NU di Jawa Barat' ['Asep Salahuddin Explains the Anomaly Regarding NU in West Java'], *NU Online*. Retrieved from www.nu.or.id/post/read/85184/asep-salahuddin-jelaskan-anomali-nuansa-nu-di-jawa-barat.

Nainggolan, B. 2018, 28 May. 'Ceruk "Tidak Bertuan" Menjadi Penentu' ['"Swing" Locations Becomes the Deciding Factor for West Java Elections'], *Kompas*. Retrieved from https://kompas.id/baca/polhuk/2018/05/28/ceruk-tidak-bertuan-menjadi-penentu/.

Nursanti, A. 2017, 19 November. 'Setelah Setya Novanto Ditangkap KPK, Wajar Jika Tiket Pilkada Golkar Berubah' ['After Setya Novanta was Arrested by KPK, It is Normal that Golkar's Choice for the Governor Changed'], *Pikiran Rakyat*. Retrieved from www.pikiran-rakyat.com/nasional/pr-01289447/setelah-setya-novanto-ditangkap-kpk-wajar-jika-tiket-pilkada-golkar-berubah.

Pamungkas, C. 2018. 'Gone but Not Forgotten: The Transformation of the Idea of Islamic State through Traditional Religious Authorities', *Masyarakat Jurnal Sosiologi*, Vol. 23 (2): 187–211.

Permadi, A. 2018, 23 March. 'Sudrajat-Syaikhu Janji Bangun Politeknik Berbasis Pesantren di Jabar' ['Syaikhu Promises to Build Pesantren-based Polytechnics in West Java'], *Kompas*. Retrieved from https://regional.kompas.com/read/2018/03/23/14012831/sudrajat-syaikhu-janji-bangun-politeknik-berbasis-pesantren-di-jabar.

Permadi, A. 2019. '3 Perempuan Terkait Video 'Jika Jokowi Terpilih, Tak Ada Lagi Azan' Ditahan di Polres Karawang' ['Three Women Linked to the Video "If Jokowi is Elected, There Will be No More Azan Calls" Were Arrested by the Karawang Police'], *Kompas*. Retrieved from https://regional.kompas.com/read/2019/02/26/11080301/3-perempuan-terkait-video-jika-jokowi-terpilih-tak-ada-lagi-azan-ditahan-di.

Power, T. 2018. 'Jokowi's Authoritarian Turn and Indonesia's Democratic Decline'. *Bulletin of Indonesian Economic Studies*, Vol. 54(3): 307–338.

Pramono, R.R., & W.A. Purnomo. 2018, 30 June. 'Laporan Utama – Lampu Kuning 2019' ['Cover Story: Yellow Light for 2019 Election'], *Tempo*. Retrieved from https://majalah.tempo.co/read/laporan-utama/155727/lampu-kuning-2019.

Rahadian, L. 2018, 13 November. 'Bisakah Jokowi–Ma'ruf Menang Pilpres di Jawa Barat' ['Can Jokowi–Ma'ruf Win in West Java Province?'], *Tirto*. Retrieved from https://tirto.id/bisakah-jokowi-maruf-menang-pilpres-di-jawa-barat-c9UH.

Ramdhani, D.I. 2019, 18 April. 'Jokowi–Ma'ruf Kalah Telak di Jabar, Ini Kata Dedi Mulyadi' ['Jokowi–Ma'ruf Were Trounched in West Java, This is What Dedi Mulyadi Said'], *Kompas*. Retrieved from https://bandung.kompas.com/read/2019/04/18/15573681/jokowi-maruf-kalah-telak-di-jabar-ini-kata-dedi-mulyadi.

Rikang, R.A. A. Prireza, & A. Fikri. 2017, 17 December. 'Rindu Reuni Koalisi DKI' ['DKI Coalition Parties Want a "Reunion" in West Java'], *Tempo.co*. Retrieved from https://majalah.tempo.co/read/154566/rindu-reuni-koalisi-dki&user=register.

Sarwanto, A. 2017, 27 October. 'Golkar Terbitkan SK Dukung Ridwan Kamil – Daniel Muttaqien' ['Golkar Issues a Decree Endorsing Ridwan Kamil – Daniel Muttaqin Candidacy'], *CNN Indonesia*. Retrieved from www.cnnindonesia.com/nasional/2017 1027161432-32-251651/golkar-terbitkan-sk-dukung-ridwan-kamil-daniel-muttaqien.

Sasongko, J.P. 2017, 18 December. 'Ketua DPP Golkar: Kami Tak Ingin Digantung Ridwan Kamil' ['Chairman of Golkar Party: We Do Not Want to be "Hanged" by Ridwan Kamil'], *CNN Indonesia*. Retrieved from www.cnnindonesia.com/nasional/20171218194414-32-263286/ketua-dpp-golkar-kami-tak-ingin-digantung-ridwan-kamil.

Soeriaatmadja, W. 2017, 18 September. 'Taking Religious Harmony as His Rallying Call', *The Straits Times*. Retrieved from www.straitstimes.com/asia/taking-religious-harmony-as-his-rallying-call.

Suryadinata, L. 2002. *Elections and Politics in Indonesia*. Singapore: Institute of Southeast Asian Studies.

Sutari, T. 2018, 27 June. 'Ridwan Kamil Klarifikasi Isu Pro LGBT Jelang Pencoblosan' ['Ridwan Kamil Clarifies Rumor that He Supports LGBT Rights Prior to Election Day'], *CNN Indonesia*. Retrieved from www.cnnindonesia.com/pilkadaserentak/nasional/20180627073428-32-309350/ridwan-kamil-klarifikasi-isu-pro-lgbt-jelang-pencoblosan?.

Sutisna, N. 2016. 'Purwakarta Regent Wins Award as "Human Rights Warrior"', Tempo. co. Retrieved from https://en.tempo.co/read/747807/purwakarta-regent-wins-award-as-human-rights-warrior.

Tanuwidjaja, S. 2010. 'Political Islam and Islamic Parties in Indonesia: Critically Assessing the Evidence of Islam's Political Decline'. *Contemporary Southeast Asia*, Vol. 32 (1): 29–49.

Temby, Q. 2018. 'Shariah, Dakwah, and Rock 'N' Roll: Pemuda Hijrah in Bandung', *New Mandala*. Retrieved from www.newmandala.org/shariah-dakwah-rock-n-roll-pemuda-hijrah-bandung/.

Warburton, E. 2018. 'West Java's 2018 Regional Elections: Reform, Religion, and the Rise of Ridwan Kamil', *ISEAS Perspective*, Issue 2018/42. Retrieved from www.iseas.edu.sg/images/pdf/ISEAS_Perspective_2018_42@50.pdf.

Warburton, E., D. Simandjuntak, & C. Setijadi. 2018. 'Indonesia's 2018 Regional Elections: Between Local and National Politics', *ISEAS Perspective*, Issue 2018/31. Retrieved from www.iseas.edu.sg/images/pdf/ISEAS_Perspective_2018_31@50.pdf.

4 The 2018 simultaneous regional elections and 2019 simultaneous national elections in East Java province

Alexander R. Arifianto

Introduction

Indonesia undertook its regional head election on 27 June 2018. Elections were held to elect provincial and local executives in 17 provinces, 39 municipalities, and 115 regencies throughout the Indonesian archipelago. For the 2019 simultaneous presidential and legislative election, the electorate voted for the president and members of Indonesia's national, provincial and local legislatures. The campaign period lasted 6 months from 13 October 2018 to 13 April 2019 while voting took place on 17 April 2019.

Due to the short time gap of 3 months between the 2018 regional election and the commencement of the campaign period for the 2019 simultaneous election, the 2018 regional election was seen as a barometer for the presidential election in 2019. This is a relatively novel development, as regional head elections tend to focus their campaigns on local issues. Electoral dynamics had changed significantly since then. During the 2017 Jakarta gubernatorial election, a number of hardline Islamist groups calling themselves the Defending Islam Movement, weaponised identity politics to serve political ends, engineered the defeat of ex-governor of Jakarta Basuki Tjahaja Purnama ('Ahok') in his re-election bid. It is now clear that the movement had targeted Ahok because he was a strong supporter of president Jokowi, the group's real target. The Defending Islam Movement sought to leverage on the anti-Ahok campaign to support retired Lieutenant General Prabowo Subianto, who was running against incumbent president Joko Widodo in the 2019 presidential election.

East Java is a province with a population of approximately 40 million residents and about 30 million eligible voters. As the second most populous city in Indonesia, the province is also economically advanced. It is considered one of the major centres for industrial manufacturing in Indonesia, especially around the Surabaya Metropolitan Area. Due to its economic significance, the East Java gubernatorial election is widely considered one of several key races during the 2018/2019 election cycle that is considered as a 'must-win province' for both Jokowi and Prabowo camps during the 2019 presidential election.

The voter demographic in East Java has historically favoured nationalist, *abangan* (Islamic syncretism with local Javanese beliefs) parties in cities and in

Mataraman (rural districts bordering East and Central Java) as well as traditionalist Muslim communities along the coast and in Madura Island. Thus, the province of East Java was highly favourable for president Jokowi's re-election campaign, since two major parties in his coalition – the Indonesian Democratic Party Struggle (PDI-P) and the National Awakening Party (PKB) affiliated with Nahdlatul Ulama (NU) – the largest Islamic organisation in Indonesia – have a reliable electoral base and a large number of dedicated cadres within the province. Although Jokowi managed to score a landslide election victory within the province, the path to victory was not as straightforward as portrayed in the mainstream media, since Prabowo Subianto and his supporters from the Alumni 212 group managed to put up a strong challenge in major cities like Surabaya as well as in deeply conservative Islamic areas like the Madura Island.

This chapter analyses the East Java elections in the following sections. The first section describes the historical and geographical electoral trends within the province. The second section is an analysis of the electoral dynamics between gubernatorial and presidential candidates in Java and the political parties that are supporting them. The third section describes how did identity politics played a role during the electoral campaigns in East Java. It details the role of Islamic groups, especially those who were part of the #2019ChangePresident (*#2019GantiPresiden*) movement, and their attempts to influence the election through a grassroot organising campaign where identity symbols were deployed to promote Prabowo's candidacy. The chapter ends with a general conclusion and future implications on what can be learned about identity politics and their implications during the 2019 election from our research in East Java.

History, geography, and socio-political demography of East Java

With a population of nearly 40 million, East Java province has one of the highest population densities, estimated at around 2,200 residents per square mile. The largest ethnic groups in the province are ethnic Javanese (approximately 80 per cent of the population) and ethnic Madurese (approximately 17 per cent). Ninety-six per cent of the province population are Muslims, while two-thirds of the Muslims of East Java are NU followers.[1] Until approximately three decades ago, East Java was home to millions of nominal Muslims (*abangan*) who subscribed to a more relaxed and culturally inflected practice of Islam. This preference was reinforced by the NU – the largest Islamic group in East Java – whose teachings propound a tolerant and syncretic interpretation of Islam in religious practices.

Administratively, East Java is divided into 38 districts and cities, making the province the second-largest province in Indonesia after West Java in terms of its administrative divisions. Consisting of 29 regencies (*kabupaten*) and 8 cities (*kota*), the province can be divided into 4 geographical sub-regions, each of them with their own socio-political characteristics:

1   The *Mataraman* (Western East Java) sub-region is the rural East Java district, which historically was part of the ancient Mataram Sultanate that ruled much of Central and East Java from the sixteenth to the eighteenth century. It extends from the Tuban and Lamongan regencies in the Northern coast of Java to the Pacitan and Trenggalek regencies on the Southern coast. This agricultural area is mainly populated by syncretic (*abangan*) Muslims. Given the relative closeness with the Mataram Sultanate and its remnants Yogyakarta and Surakarta Sultanate in Central Java, the local population tends to be less outspoken and more deferential to authority compared with the other East Java regions. Blitar – one of the largest cities in Mataraman – was the hometown of Indonesia's founding president Sukarno. As a result of these local dynamics, Mataraman was a stronghold of Sukarno's Indonesian Nationalist Party (PNI), which is known for its nationalist ideology. Today, it is a stronghold of the party's latest incarnation, the PDI-P.

2   The *Arek* region is the most urbanised sub-region of the province, where two of its largest cities – Surabaya (with a population of nearly 4 million people)[2] and Malang (with a population of approximately 900,000 people) – are located. It extends from the city of Surabaya and the Gresik regency on the Northern coast to the Malang regency on the Southern coast. A melting pot of different cultural, ethnicity, and religious traditions, the Arek region is the more cosmopolitan region of East Java. Its residents tend to be more outspoken in expressing their political views. The dominant parties in the Arek region are the nationalist PDI-P and the National Awakening Party (PKB) – a moderate Islamic party. However, more conservative Islamic parties like the Prosperous Justice Party (PKS – affiliated with the transnational Muslim Brotherhood movement) and the National Mandate Party (PAN – affiliated with Muhammadiyah – Indonesia's second-largest organisation) have become more influential in these urban areas. These are indicated by the fact they are picking up city council (DPRD II) seats in both Surabaya and Malang.

3   The *Pandalungan* or *Tapal Kuda* sub-region is the area located in the Western coastal regions of East Java, extending from the Pasuruan to the Banyuwangi regencies. This region is characterised by the large number of Islamic boarding schools (*pesantren*) established throughout the region, making it a more religiously pious (*santri*) part of the East Java province. Many of the Islamic schools are traditionalist Islamic-leaning schools linked to the NU.[3] The National Awakening Party (PKB) affiliated with NU tends to dominate local politics in the area, followed by the United Development Party (PPP) – another Islamic party that has a lot of members affiliated with NU. However, new Islamist parties like PKS are also gaining more regional council seats, thanks to the party's efforts to recruit children of prominent NU clerics (*kyai*) to run for regional council's office.

4   *Madura Island.* The large island off the coast of Surabaya has four regencies: Bangkalan, Sampang, Pamekasan, and Sumenep. The four regencies are among the poorest regencies within the province. Many residents earn

their livelihood by migrating to Java Island – especially to nearby Surabaya – or work as migrant workers overseas. This sub-region has become more religiously pious over the past 20 years. Most Islamic clerics of Madura would traditionally identify themselves as NU affiliates. However, lately, more conservative groups such as the Islamic Defenders Front (FPI) and PKS have gained more followers. Growing Islamic conservatism has been marked by the increased persecution of religious minorities such as the Shi'a Muslim community in Sampang, which forced the relocation of up to 500 Shiites from their homes to a refugee settlement nearby Surabaya, where they continue to live to this day (Miichi & Kayane 2020, Kayane 2020). Growing conservatism within the island was clearly reflected during the 2019 presidential election, with the overwhelming support for Prabowo among the Madurese voters, as shall be elaborated later in this chapter.

The dominance of PDI-P and PKB in regional politics in East Java can be seen from the number of provincial legislative (DPRD I) seats controlled by both parties. After the 2014 general election, PKB was the largest party represented in DPRD I, with 20 seats under its control, while PDI-P was the second-largest party with 19 seats. After the 2019 legislative election, PDI-P became the largest party in DPRD I, controlling 27 seats, while PKB held 25 seats.

The two parties' strong position in East Java politics aided Jokowi's re-election in 2019. The general picture is that the parties in the Prabowo coalition had a relatively modest presence in East Java (Gerindra, PAN, and PKS) compared to PDI-P and PKB. Hence, Jokowi's landslide victory during the 2019 election can be attributed to the strength of his coalition parties in East Java.

Table 4.1 Provincial legislation (DPRD I) seats in East Java (2014 vs. 2019)

Political party	Number of seats (2014)	Number of seats (2019)	Net change
National Awakening Party (PKB)	20	25	+5
Indonesian Democratic Party – Struggle (PDI-P)	19	27	+8
Gerindra Party	13	15	+2
Democratic Party	13	14	+1
Golkar Party	11	13	+2
NasDem Party	4	9	+5
National Mandate Party (PAN)	7	6	-1
Prosperous Justice Party (PKS)	6	4	-2
United Development Party (PPP)	5	5	0
Hanura Party	2	1	-1
Crescent Star Party (PBB)	0	1	+1
TOTAL	**100**	**120**	**20**

Source: Author's calculation.

East Java gubernatorial election

The relationship between the candidates and political parties

The 2018 East Java gubernatorial election was held to replace Soekarwo, the province's outgoing governor who had successfully completed two 5-year terms. He is a successful governor credited with modernising the province with investor-friendly policies to promote new investment and economic growth. During his tenure, Soekarwo promoted fixed regional minimum wage for companies operating in East Java and a more friendly investment climate in the province. As he sought to protect his political and economic legacy, it was widely believed that Soekarwo would have significant influence in choosing his successor as governor.[4]

Two candidates emerged as potential successors for Soekarwo: Saifullah Yusuf and Khofifah Indar Parawansa. Saifullah was the vice governor of East Java and was seeking to run for governor's office. Saifullah's running mate was Puti Guntur Soekarno, granddaughter of Indonesia's first president. They were backed by an influential coalition of parties including the Indonesian Democratic Party of Struggle (PDI-P), the National Awakening Party (PKB), the Great Indonesia Movement Party (Gerindra), and the Islamist Prosperous Justice Party (PKS).

Support for the Saifullah–Puti ticket was largely based on personal and familial ties. Besides the connection to Soekarno, Saifullah Yusuf is also the grandson of Bisri Syansuri, a co-founder of NU. This electoral combination was expected to win over voters of which two-thirds of the population are estimated to be affiliated with the NU. Meanwhile, Puti's familial connection to the PDI-P was thought to consolidate support from party loyalists, such as in the Mataraman sub-region on the border between East and Central Java – a traditional stronghold of the party.

Opposing them was Khofifah Indar Parawansa, the former Minister of Social Affairs under president Joko Widodo. She also served as Minister of Women Empowerment during the Abdurrahman Wahid presidency (1999–2001) and is a senior official within the NU, specifically chairwoman of the organisation's women's wing *Muslimat*. Khofifah had run unsuccessfully for the East Java governorship twice before in 2008 and 2013, losing both times to the Soekarwo–Saifullah team. Her running mate in 2018 was Emil Dardak, a 34-year-old former state-owned enterprise executive who served as the regent of Trenggalek, a rural region in the Southwest part of East Java, from 2014 to 2018. They were backed by a coalition consisting of the Golkar Party, the Democratic Party, the National Democratic Party (NasDem), and the National Mandate Party (PAN), among others. Khofifah's stint as Minister of Social Affairs in Jokowi's first term smoothed the process of obtaining endorsements from the local elites, as she was seen to have the president's blessing. Emil's youth and his credentials as a reformer during his time as Trenggalek Regent identified him as an emerging politician with ambitions for a possible future national office in the next 10 to 15 years.

Khofifah leveraged her status as an ex-Minister of Social Affairs and position as chairwoman of *Muslimat* to channel resources to assist her campaign, giving her a stronger financial advantage compared to her previous two gubernatorial campaigns.[5] She also requested *Muslimat* members to volunteer for her campaign, which helped her standing in NU-dominated areas in Northern East Java and Madura. Khofifah also received the unexpected endorsement of the outgoing governor Soekarwo, who chose to back her instead of Saifullah, his former vice governor and long-time running mate.[6] As a result, Khofifah's campaign benefitted from Soekarwo's strong network in the Mataraman region. As Puti and PDI-P were thought to have strong roots in the area, his endorsement turned the Mataraman area into a hotly contested battleground between the two candidates.

As the campaign went on, it became evident that the national-level political rivalry between president Jokowi and his opponent Prabowo Subianto was impacting the East Java gubernatorial race. This issue was that PDI-P (Jokowi's primary party ally) and Gerindra (Prabowo's political vehicle) were both backing the Saifullah–Puti ticket. A provincial PDI-P branch official we interviewed stated that many local party officials objected to having Gerindra and PKS join the Saifullah–Puti campaign, as they were not keen to collaborate with parties in Prabowo Subianto's coalition. However, they were overruled by national party officials close to PDI-P chairwoman Megawati Soekarnoputri.[7] The Gerindra East Java branch, while technically supporting the Saifullah–Puti campaign, committed more of its resources towards the upcoming presidential campaign, creating some doubt about the extent of their commitment to Saifullah's efforts.[8] Only the PDI-P and PKB parties – the main coalition members – devoted substantial resources, both financial and in terms of manpower, to the campaign.

While vote-buying will inevitably play a role in candidates' electoral strategies, it has become more difficult to do so for fear that candidates may be investigated by the Corruption Eradication Commission (KPK). As a result, informants have told us that more overt forms of vote-buying will only take place near the tail end of the electoral season. However, money politics is still expected to be significant in poor, rural areas where the two candidates are running neck-and-neck against each other – like the Madura Island and the Mataraman region. In these areas, senior politicians, power brokers, and Islamic religious leaders might play a role in influencing the voting preferences of undecided voters.[9]

Khofifah–Emil managed to beat Saifullah–Puti in the gubernatorial election with a margin of 54 to 46 per cent, winning in key sub-regions, including the Pandalungan (*Tapal Kuda*) sub-region of Northern East Java and in Madura Island. Both sub-regions are NU strongholds where Saifullah was expected to do well and where Khofifah had previously lost in her 2009 and 2013 gubernatorial campaigns. The Khofifah–Emil ticket also won in the Mataraman area (a PDI-P stronghold). While Puti Guntur is Soekarno's granddaughter, she spent much of her adult life in Jakarta and was a PDI-P MP from West Java, with little name recognition in East Java prior to her nomination as Saifullah's running mate.[10]

PDI-P officials blamed the pair's loss on Saifullah's decision to invite Gerindra and PKS to join his coalition, even though the two parties did not get along with PDI-P:

> Gus Ipul (Saifullah's nickname) wanted to play it safe, so he invited Gerindra and PKS to join his campaign, even though the rest of us did not approve of them joining due to their oppositional position against Jokowi. These two parties ended up stabbing us from the back [by secretly campaign against Puti] during the campaign's final days.[11]

They also blamed PKB for not spending all of its political and financial resources to support the campaign, as it wanted to maintain good relations with Khofifah, who is also a senior NU leader in East Java.[12]

Identity politics in the East Java gubernatorial campaign

East Java has experienced increasing Islamisation over the last three decades, as measured by the increasing number of observant East Javanese Muslims who attend mosque regularly and have gone on the Hajj pilgrimage, the number of new Islamic schools (*pesantren*) established in the province, and the number of Muslim women wearing veils (*hijab*). While growing Islamisation is particularly evident among upper-middle class professionals and university students in urban cities like Surabaya and Malang, Islam and identity politics did not play a major role in the East Java gubernatorial race.

The single most important reason why this paradoxical situation exists is because the NU remains the strongest socio-political force in the province, and its teachings are based on a moderate theological outlook. As perhaps two-thirds of East Java residents are NU followers, the organisation's moderate inclination is considered highly influential among the majority of Muslims living in the region. Both candidates had strong ties to NU, with Saifullah's family ties to its co-founder and Khofifah as chairwoman of *Muslimat*. This caused a split in the NU, with its political party the National Awakening Party (PKB) endorsing and campaigning for Saifullah, but *Muslimat* endorsing Khofifah and mobilising the NU women to vote for her.

Older NU clerics tended to back Saifullah–Puti because of the former's ties to NU's founder, while younger clerics tended to back Khofifah–Emil due to the duo's governing experience and Emil's credentials as a successful regent of Trenggalek.[13] Khofifah also received the backing of the National Mandate Party (PAN), which is affiliated with Muhammadiyah, Indonesia's second-largest Islamic organisation. PAN officials claimed that they spent lots of time campaigning on behalf of Khofifah.[14]

Hardline Islamist groups did not initially support either side during the gubernatorial election. Even though Surabaya was rocked by a series of terrorist attacks on 13 and 14 May 2018, they were one-off incidents unrelated to the gubernatorial election. Since both gubernatorial candidates came from pious

Muslim backgrounds and were senior figures within NU, there was no basis for hardline Islamist activists to doubt the religiosity of the candidates. However, towards the end of the campaign season, the Saifullah–Puti team began to face resistance from hardline Islamist groups due to her association with the PDI-P. In particular, Alumni 212 groups began to note that Puti was part of the PDI-P special campaign team that assisted Ahok during his failed re-election campaign in the 2017 Jakarta gubernatorial election.[15] They began to paint her as an 'un-Islamic' candidate and declined to vote for the Saifullah–Puti ticket.[16]

During the final weeks of campaigning there were social media 'black campaigns' regarding Puti's Islamic credentials and pictures were posted on social media alleging she had lived a 'hedonistic lifestyle' while she attended the University of Indonesia as an undergraduate during the early 1990s.[17] This negative campaigning convinced many Gerindra and PKS cadres that were backing Saifullah–Puti to switch their allegiance to Khofifah. It was believed that 60 per cent of Gerindra cadres and 50 per cent of PKS cadres decided to vote for the Khofifah–Emil ticket despite the two parties' official support for the Saifullah–Puti campaign.[18]

The 2019 presidential election in East Java

By August 2018, attention in East Java (as well as the rest of Indonesia) had shifted to the upcoming presidential and legislative elections scheduled to be held on 17 April 2019. Both governor-elect Khofifah and Saifullah immediately declared their endorsement for president Jokowi after the gubernatorial election was concluded. The coalitional divisions and the issues discussed during the campaign season, which began in mid-August, are quite identical with the issues nationally.

Similar to other provinces, East Java experienced significant polarisation between Jokowi and Prabowo supporters. Tensions became more acute in late August 2018 as the police broke up a #2019ChangePresident (#2019GantiPresiden) rally in Surabaya due to concerns that hardline Islamist groups such as the Islamic Defenders Front (FPI) and Hizb ut-Tahrir Indonesia (HTI) were organising the rally and had dispatched their supporters as rally participants. Despite this, tensions between Jokowi and Prabowo supporters in East Java have been milder because there are no real or latent identity issues that can be exploited by the Islamists.

The relationship between presidential candidates and political parties in East Java

In the 2019 election, Jokowi secured endorsements from notable political elites in East Java, including new governor Khofifah and her former opponent Saifullah. He was also endorsed by outgoing governor Soekarwo, even though he has traditionally been affiliated with the Democratic Party which, along with its chairman and former president Susilo Bambang Yudhoyono, has formally aligned with the Prabowo coalition. Sources close to Soekarwo explained that he was endorsing Jokowi for two reasons: 1) He wished to be considered as a cabinet minister if Jokowi won re-election, and 2) He wished to protect himself from a possible corruption investigation that may be launched into the alleged misappropriation of public funds conducted during his tenure as governor, most importantly, a scandal involving the provincial government-owned East Java Bank.[19] In addition, Jokowi was also endorsed by 32 out of 38 district heads (*Bupati*) and mayors from East Java. Thanks to the support from the province's political elite, Jokowi had a significant advantage over his challenger in East Java, which was very important given that its population of 42 million (the second most populous province in the country) constituted a significant voting bloc in the 2019 presidential election, and therefore was an integral part of Jokowi's re-election strategy.

However, a party's allegiance to a certain presidential candidate does not mean that party politicians will also endorse that candidate. Some politicians from Jokowi's coalition, especially among legislative candidates from the Golkar Party refused to back Jokowi because they considered him to be a political outsider who might threaten their political and economic interests.[20]

Golkar survived the fall of the Suharto regime in 1998 and has suffered from multiple splinters in recent years, as its former senior politicians like Prabowo Subianto, Wiranto, and Surya Paloh have all formed their own political parties. Now the party is facing another serious challenge from the new Working (*Berkarya*) Party of Tommy Suharto, Suharto's youngest son. The new party has recruited many grassroot-level Golkar cadres – particularly those with knowledge of voter mobilisation and fundraising – and they have switched over to Berkarya. As a result, Golkar insiders consider their party to be at its most vulnerable position since the 1998 *Reformasi*. To counter this development the party instructed its cadres and politicians running for the 2019 national and regional legislative elections not to publicly endorse Jokowi during their campaigns.[21]

A similar phenomenon was also seen among members of Prabowo's coalition. As East Java is considered the NU heartland and many of its followers are predicted to support Jokowi, politicians from other Islamic parties like PAN are under pressure to embrace strategies that will attract NU supporters. This requires them to take vague political positions so they would not be easily portrayed as supporting Prabowo.[22] Many PAN legislative candidates in East Java tend to de-emphasise their party's formal endorsement of Prabowo and in their public statements often express support towards Jokowi instead. For instance, a PAN provincial legislative candidate praised Jokowi's infrastructure projects and thought his choice of conservative NU cleric Ma'ruf Amin for vice president could appeal to young millennials in the same way as Sandiaga Uno, Prabowo's VP nominee despite Ma'ruf's age.[23] Another PAN national legislative candidate who ran in a predominantly non-Muslim district said he had de-emphasised religious issues in his campaign messages to focus on economic development and infrastructure issues, a major component of Jokowi's campaign messaging.[24]

Both secular and Islamic parties in East Java tend to recruit family members of prominent local Islamic clerics (*kyai*) due to the huge number of followers they have in numerous localities within the province. Our research finds these clerics are hedging their bets between the two presidential candidates by directing family members to become legislative candidates from various coalition parties so they can be aligned with both candidates. One prominent *kyai* from Lamongan District assigned his eldest child as a provincial legislative candidate from Gerindra Party (which supported Prabowo), while another son was running as a provincial legislative candidate for the NasDem Party (which supported Jokowi).[25] This was done as a 'hedging' mechanism for the *kyai* and his Islamic school (*pesantren*) so they so they would continue receiving state patronage regardless of who was elected president in April 2019.

In short, the above examples show that rank-and-file politicians of these parties do not always align with the official policy of their respective parties. They often align themselves with presidential candidates with more popular support within their legislative districts. Thus, they tie their own electoral chances with this presidential candidate, defying their own party's preferences.

Identity politics in the presidential election campaign in East Java

Once the gubernatorial election was over, identity politics began to take a more prominent role as the province geared up for the April 2019 election. Conservative and hardline Islamist groups became more active in mobilising their resources for the presidential election campaign compared to the gubernatorial election. Islamist groups were motivated by their desire to oust Jokowi from the presidency because he is perceived to be an 'un-Islamic president' who has failed to meet the demands of the Islamic community (*umma*). In August and September 2018 these Islamist activists organised two special clerical summits (*ijtima ulama*) that endorsed Prabowo Subianto to become their presidential candidate. Prabowo has mobilised a lot of volunteers from the ranks of Alumni 212 activists in battleground regencies considered crucial for him to score a victory in East Java. On many occasions his campaign has had volunteers in these regions for months, long before the Jokowi volunteers arrived.[26]

Jokowi's decision to appoint Council of Indonesian Ulama (MUI) general chairman Ma'ruf Amin as his vice-presidential nominee did not deliver Islamists to their side or weaken their opposition. This is because Ma'ruf is also a senior ulama from the NU, which historically has ideological differences with the more conservative Islamist ulama who participated in the Defending Islam Movement. Ma'ruf is also widely perceived by conservative and hardline Islamists as an elitist ulama who was easily co-opted by the Jokowi administration.[27] As a result, they persisted in their goal of defeating Jokowi in the April 2019 election. They devoted their time and resources to support Prabowo's candidacy against Jokowi in their respective regions and localities.

On 26 August 2018, a group of Islamist activists staged a #2019ChangePresident (*#2019GantiPresiden*) rally in the Surabaya city centre. Attended by thousands of activists, the rally was forcefully disbanded by the Surabaya police, with the assistance of youth militias such as *Banser* – affiliated with *Ansor* – Nahdlatul Ulama's youth wing, Pancasila Youth (*Pemuda Pancasila*), a militia loosely affiliated with Golkar Party, and the Indonesian National Marhaenist Movement (GMNI) affiliated with PDI-P. Officially, the police decided to disband the rally because it did not have the proper permits. However, it was widely believed the rally was disbanded because of concerns raised by community members that the rally and its participants could have disrupted law and order within the city had the rally been allowed to take place. There were concerns that as protestors consisted of activists from hardline groups such as FPI and HTI, the rally would spread ideas regarding the Islamic caliphate – considered a coup plot (*makar*) against the Indonesian state and which resulted in the ban on the HTI by the Jokowi administration in July 2017.

Rally organisers insisted that they were planning the protest because they wanted to replace Jokowi peacefully during the 2019 presidential election and did not plan to replace the Indonesian state with an Islamic state or caliphate. They said while many conservative and hardline activists were part of #2019ChangePresident movement, not all of the protestors were members of hardline groups and stated many middle-class families who do not emphasise their Muslim identity were also part of the group.[28] However, one cannot deny that Islamist groups played a important role in the #2019ChangePresident movement. A senior organiser of its Surabaya rally is also a provincial board member of the Indonesian Islamic Propagation Council (*Dewan Da'wah Islamiyah Indonesia* – DDII)[29] – a hardline group founded by former Masyumi chairman Mohammad Natsir when he was released from prison in 1967. Other rally organisers also stated they are members of Muhammadiyah, although they noted that they did not represent the organisation during the rally.[30] Therefore, it seems clear that conservative and hardline Islamist groups played a major role in anti-Jokowi activities such as #2019ChangePresident even if these activities were not organised in their official capacity.

Conservative Islamic activists also played a major role in anti-Jokowi campaigns and coalesced around Prabowo Subianto's candidacy. Many of these activists volunteered for the Prabowo campaign in East Java, spending many hours on get-out-the-vote efforts in areas considered as battleground areas. This included areas where conservative Islam had grown in recent years, including urban Surabaya and Malang (with many supporters of conservative Islamist parties like PKS and PAN), and in Madura Island (where FPI and its supreme leader Rizieq Shihab enjoys strong support). They mainly focused on canvassing activities – meeting with potential voters in their homes to convince them to switch their support from Jokowi to Prabowo. They were also very active on social media, as they believed that the mainstream TV media in Indonesia was implicitly supportive of Jokowi, while Prabowo supporters tended to obtain their information on current affairs online.

Islamist activists utilised their social media networks to raise funds for the Prabowo campaign. They also invested significant personal resources to support his campaign activities as the Prabowo campaign started running out of cash in 2018 and 2019. For instance, one of Prabowo's Muhammadiyah volunteer provided food and beverages for Sandiaga Uno's (Prabowo's vice-presidential partner) campaign activities in Probolinggo District and other Northern East Java coastline cities in December 2018. She raised funds to finance these expenses through pledges received via her Facebook page. The activist believed that raising her own funds and utilising them to fund the campaign is a better approach, as she could ensure that all the money raised is well spent. She claimed that her crowdsourced funding campaign had been relatively successful, as upper-middle class Muslim families give generously to Prabowo because of his Islamic credentials.[31]

The Prabowo campaign was able to make significant gains in the East Java province in the final month leading up to voting day. Indeed, he appeared to be running neck-to-neck with Jokowi in their electability ratings. Alumni 212 volunteers used both social media and support from some *kyai* to promote 'black campaign' narratIves against Jokowi. This includes rumours that he was formerly aligned with the illegal Indonesian Communist Party (PKI) and that he was not truly a pious Muslim. They also attacked Jokowi for failing to halt the decrease in the price of fish, salt, and other necessities important to the livelihood of fishermen and farmers living in the Pandalungan region within the province, and in Madura Island – regions that tend to be more religiously conservative compared to other East Java regions.

The Prabowo campaign also made a strong showing in cities like Surabaya, where volunteers affiliated with *Alumni 212* and *#2019GantiPresiden* movements campaigned in low to middle-class precincts considered to have many potential 'swing' voters for both camps. Conservative-leaning *kyai* who supported Prabowo also flexed their influence and networks. As stated by a senior Jokowi campaign volunteer, the kyais used a lot of identity-based rhetorics when they were making their case:

> [They] used rhetoric that 'Jokowi is a Communist,' 'Jokowi is from PDI-P,' and 'Jokowi is un-Islamic' to encourage voters to vote for Prabowo. Thanks to their efforts, many voters in these precincts are now becoming Prabowo's diehard supporters.[32]

Apparently, Jokowi campaign volunteers – who only began campaigning in these precincts nearly 2 months after the Prabowo's volunteers – encountered great difficulty in winning over prospective voters. According to the volunteer coordinator:

> [These] voters have now become hardcore Prabowo supporters. Nothing you say or do would have convinced them otherwise. They consider Prabowo to be Indonesia's savior, while they consider Jokowi as the devil incarnate who will destroy Islam and Indonesia.[33]

When asked on what would the Jokowi campaign do to turn the tide in these swing areas, she gave the following reply:

> There is only one way to turn the tide now. We need to flood these precincts with cash so they will be swayed to vote with us. These voters might be religious and supports Prabowo at their heart. However, giving them cash would have fulfilled their immediate need, hence many of them would end up voting for our side.[34]

Despite these challenges, Jokowi won a major victory in East Java province – winning nearly 66 per cent of all the votes cast – to Prabowo's 34 per cent. In Surabaya, Jokowi won almost 70 per cent of the vote to Prabowo's 30 per cent. The full breakdown of the candidates' performance can be seen in Table 4.2 while the sub-regional breakdown is found in Table 4.3.

As shown in Table 4.3, Jokowi managed to score a decisive victory in all East Java sub-regions except in Madura. Jokowi's victory in East Java can be explained by several factors. First, the alliance and synergy between PDI-P and PKB was a strategy tailored for East Java province. The two largest parties in East Java could pool their manpower and financial resources to support the Jokowi campaign. Since PDI-P dominates in the Mataraman region, PKB controls the Pandalungan region, and both parties are running evenly in the Arek region, the two parties were able to use their electoral advantage within these regions to deliver votes for Jokowi. Second, Jokowi's alliance with NU, as discussed by other observers (e.g. Fealy 2018, Aspinall 2019), convinced the majority of NU *kyais* from East Java to back his candidacy. This can be seen clearly in Jokowi's large electoral margins in regencies that are also NU strongholds like Jombang (77 per cent), Jember (65 per cent), and Pasuruan (61 per cent). NU's mobilisation was also an important factor in Jokowi's victory in East Java.

Beyond these two factors, however, there is a strong possibility that money politics also played a role in swaying prospective voters to Jokowi's side, particularly in swing precincts located in urban cities like Surabaya and Malang as well as in rural regencies where the candidates are running even like Bangkalan (Madura Island). The conversation with the senior Jokowi campaign volunteer earlier in this section indicated that patronage and material incentives could counter the Prabowo campaign's use of identity politics.

The only East Java region that overwhelmingly supported Prabowo was Madura. Two-thirds of the island's residents voted for Prabowo, despite Jokowi's attempt to win support from Madurese voters, for instance by removing toll fares for commuters utilising the Suramadu bridge that connects the island with Surabaya. Prabowo won 84 per cent votes cast in Pamekasan regency, 75 per cent of votes in Sampang regency, and 64 per cent of votes in Sumenep regency. He only lost in the Bangkalan regency, where Jokowi managed to win by 58 per cent of the votes. Prabowo's margin of victory in Madura Island was very decisive largely due to the solid support he received from senior Madura *kyais* who

Table 4.2 2019 presidential election results in East Java, by districts and cities

No.	District/city name	Region	Number of votes	% for Jokowi	% for Prabowo	Winner
1	Kediri (City)	Mataraman	182,946	78.71	21.29	Jokowi
2	Blitar (City)	Mataraman	94,746	77.74	22.26	Jokowi
3	Pasuruan (City)	Pandalungan	125,294	56.95	43.05	Jokowi
4	Mojokerto (City)	Arek	85,677	71.03	28.97	Jokowi
5	Madiun (City)	Mataraman	119,067	71.39	28.61	Jokowi
6	Batu (City)	Arek	136,758	74.06	25.94	Jokowi
7	Probolinggo (City)	Pandalungan	145,615	58.50	41.50	Jokowi
8	Nganjuk	Mataraman	673,132	80.40	19.60	Jokowi
9	Ngawi	Mataraman	593,038	78.11	21.89	Jokowi
10	Bojonegoro	Mataraman	834,426	67.22	32.78	Jokowi
11	Tuban	Mataraman	724,807	73.13	26.87	Jokowi
12	Lamongan	Arek	798,051	64.63	35.37	Jokowi
13	Gresik	Arek	758,822	66.72	33.28	Jokowi
14	Lumajang	Pandalungan	651,614	59.28	40.72	Jokowi
15	Pacitan	Mataraman	347,006	41.86	58.14	Prabowo
16	Ponorogo	Mataraman	588,732	71.68	28.32	Jokowi
17	Trenggalek	Mataraman	456,904	77.01	22.99	Jokowi
18	Tulungagung	Mataraman	677,894	81.83	18.71	Jokowi
19	Blitar (District)	Mataraman	740,847	85.21	14.79	Jokowi
20	Kediri (District)	Mataraman	1,024,981	82.50	17.50	Jokowi
21	Jember	Pandalungan	1,374,994	64.82	35.18	Jokowi
22	Banyuwangi	Pandalungan	984,660	72.22	27.78	Jokowi
23	Bondowoso	Pandalungan	491,564	43.51	56.49	Prabowo
24	Situbondo	Pandalungan	406,601	49.87	50.13	Prabowo
25	Probolinggo (District)	Pandalungan	710,469	60.70	39.30	Jokowi
26	Pasuruan (District)	Pandalungan	967,502	60.91	39.09	Jokowi
27	Sidoarjo	Arek	1,168,641	69.98	30.02	Jokowi

Continued

Table 4.2 continued

No.	District/city name	Region	Number of votes	% for Jokowi	% for Prabowo	Winner
28	Mojokerto (District)	Arek	696,768	76.30	23.70	Jokowi
29	Jombang	Arek	803,765	76.63	23.27	Jokowi
30	Madiun (District)	Mataraman	453,356	67.29	32.71	Jokowi
31	Magetan	Mataraman	422,421	67.71	32.29	Jokowi
32	Malang (City)	Arek	513,696	67.29	32.71	Jokowi
33	Malang (District)	Arek	1,565,242	75.33	24.67	Jokowi
34	Surabaya	Arek	1,603,405	70.16	29.84	Jokowi
35	Bangkalan	Madura	762,260	57.74	42.26	Jokowi
36	Sampang	Madura	757,786	24.70	75.30	Prabowo
37	Pamekasan	Madura	634,492	16.22	83.78	Prabowo
38	Sumenep	Madura	679,236	35.67	64.33	Prabowo
TOTAL	**East Java**		**24,672,915**	**65.79**	**34.21**	**Jokowi**

Source: Indonesian Election Commission (KPU).

Table 4.3   Results of East Java election (by sub-region)

Region	Number of districts/cities	Winner	Average vote (%)
Mataraman	15	Jokowi	73.7
Pandalungan	9	Jokowi	58.5
Arek	10	Jokowi	70.6
Madura	4	Prabowo	66.4
TOTAL	38	Jokowi	65.8

Source: Author's calculation.

had overwhelmingly backed him. The Madurese *kyais* – some of them have retained ties with the Islamic Defenders Front (FPI) and other hardline groups – tend to have more conservative theological outlook than other NU *kyais* living elsewhere in East Java.

Conclusion and implications

East Java was a major battleground province during the 2019 general election. Given its relatively homogeneous ethnic makeup (80 per cent Javanese) along with the predominance of PDI-P – the primary party backing Jokowi's presidency and NU – an Islamic organisation widely known for its moderate theology – within the province, it was perceived as the president's stronghold. Jokowi managed to win the province by nearly two-thirds of the popular vote over his challenger Prabowo Subianto. However, despite the long odds of winning in the province, Prabowo managed to pose a strong challenge against the president in East Java. With the backing of many Alumni 212 activists from the province, Prabowo launched his campaign utilising identity politics, portraying Jokowi as an 'un-Islamic' president. His campaigned gained plenty of support in urban areas like Surabaya and Malang and in more *santri* rural areas in the Pandalungan and Madura regions. In turn, Jokowi counter-attacked by unifying nationalists and moderate Muslims affiliated with NU that Prabowo and Alumni 212 activists were pushing for a radical agenda that ultimately could have turned Indonesia to become an Islamic state. Thanks to the strength of both PDI-P and NU – the former in the Mataraman region of East Java and the latter in the Pandalungan region – Jokowi managed to thwart Prabowo's effort to win in the province.

The East Java gubernatorial and presidential election campaigns were two completely different animals, especially when one compares the level of identity politics that were used in the two campaigns. The gubernatorial campaign was relatively quiet compared to other regional elections in Indonesia marked by massive polarisation and divisive identity politics. This is because both gubernatorial candidates came from pious Muslim backgrounds and have held long-term leadership positions within the moderate-leaning NU, the most dominant Islamic group within the province. Therefore, it would have been difficult for hardliners to question their Islamic credentials. This made the East Java gubernatorial election less contentious compared to other Indonesian regions like West Sumatra and West Java where it is the norm for conservative Islamist movements to be involved in regional politics. Gerindra and PKS did launch a last-minute identity-based campaign against Puti Guntur Soekarno, Saifullah Yusuf's running mate – despite the fact both parties were part of his political coalition. The subsequent defection of Gerindra and PKS cadres might have contributed to the pair's defeat in the gubernatorial race against Khofifah Indar Parawansa and Emil Dardak's pair. However, identity politics were relatively mute during much of the campaign, since both Saifullah and Khofifah are also senior NU leaders who did not resort to divisive identity-based campaign strategies.

However, the presidential election campaign saw the heavy usage of identity politics against Jokowi's candidacy. While conservative and hardline Islamists did not play much of a role during the gubernatorial election campaign, they fully mobilised in the run-up to the presidential election. Many staunch Islamists who were part of Alumni 212 campaign want to oust Jokowi from the presidency due to what they saw as Jokowi's lack of Islamic credentials. Many of them freely volunteer their time and resources to support Prabowo Subianto. However, while they managed to win strong support in urban areas as well as in strongly santri regions like Madura Island (where Prabowo won by more than two-thirds of the votes), they are not able to gain much traction in much of East Java, which is a stronghold of both PDI-P and NU. In addition to these mobilisational strengths, it was also strongly inferred – but not confirmed – that the Jokowi campaign might have resorted in utilising money politics in swing precincts like low–middle class neighbourhoods in Surabaya, where Alumni 212 volunteers initially managed to convince local voters to support Prabowo instead.

In conclusion, East Java remains a Jokowi stronghold due to the predominance of ethnic Javanese, PDI-P, and NU within the province. However, this should not be a source for complacency for both parties as they begin preparation for the 2024 general election. Prabowo did manage to win nearly one-third of the province's electorates – largely from the pockets of deeply religious voters in urban cities like Surabaya and in rural Pandalungan and Madura regions. As more East Java residents are becoming more deeply religious, they would be more likely to embrace the agenda of conservative Islamists to further Islamise Indonesia's state and society and elect candidates who share their goals. If PDI-P and NU continues to ignore the needs of these people, it is plausible that more of them would embrace these more religiously conservative movements rather than the moderate political platform embraced by the two groups.

Notes

1 Author's interview with Rusdiyanto, senior journalist, Jawa Pos Daily (Surabaya, 7 May 2018).
2 This figure is the estimated population of Surabaya Metropolitan Area, which includes City of Surabaya and surrounding regencies of Gresik and Sidoarjo.
3 Traditionalist Muslims – most of them are NU followers – are also characterised by their beliefs in several rituals and traditions – for instance ritual prayers for the dead

(*tahlilan*) and ceremonies marking the death anniversaries of a relative (*selametan*) that were rejected by modernists on the ground that these rituals are heretical Islamic teachings (*bid'ah*).

4 Author's interviews with Rusdiyanto (Surabaya, 7 May 2018) and with Dr Airlangga Pribadi, Faculty of Social and Political Sciences, Airlangga University and Advisor for Khofifah/Emil Dardak Campaign Team (Surabaya, 12 May 2018).

5 Author's interview with Rusdiyanto (Surabaya, 7 May 2018).

6 According to a PDI-P official, this is because Soekarwo questioned the competence of Saifullah to succeed him as governor, despite his decade of experience as a vice governor. (Author's interview with Hari Putri Lestari, vice president for Communications, PDI-P East Java province and candidate for East Java provincial legislative council, Surabaya, 31 October 2018).

7 Author's interview with Hari Putri Lestari (Surabaya, 31 October 2018).

8 Author's interview with Ira Darmayanti, vice president, Gerindra Party East Java province (Surabaya, 11 May 2018).

9 Author's interview with Rusdiyanto (Surabaya, 25 June 2018).

10 Some local PDI-P officials complained that Puti was a 'carpet-bagger' who came from Jakarta to run for deputy governor of a province she never lived in. They thought her candidacy robbed the opportunity from other potential PDI-P candidates from East Java who would have become a more attractive choice for PDI-P cadres and voters. (Author's interview with Hari Putri Lestari (Surabaya, 31 October 2018)).

11 Author's interview with Hari Putri Lestari (Surabaya, 31 October 2018).

12 Author's interview with Hari Putri Lestari (Surabaya, 31 October 2018).

13 Author's interview with Zainul Azhar As'ad, vice president for Spiritual Affairs, Golkar Party East Java province and spokesperson for the Khofifah/Emil team (Surabaya, 18 May 2018).

14 Author's interview with Khalid Fahmi, National legislative candidate, National Mandate Party (PAN) (Surabaya, October 28, 2018).

15 Author's interview with Rusdiyanto (Surabaya, 25 June 2018).

16 Author's interview with Hari Putri Lestari (Surabaya, 31 October 2018).

17 Author's interview with Hari Putri Lestari (Surabaya, 31 October 2018).

18 *Kompas* Daily exit poll released on 28 June 2018 (the day after the election was held).

19 Author's interview with Airlangga Pribadi (Surabaya, 8 May 2018).

20 Author's interview with Benny, Candidate for Surabaya city council, Golkar Party (Surabaya, 7 September 2018).

21 Author's interview with Benny (Surabaya, 7 September 2018).

22 Author's interview with Khalid Fahmi (Surabaya, 28 October 2018).

23 Author's interview with Arief Ajie, East Java provincial council candidate, PAN (Surabaya, 10 September 2018).

24 Author's interview with Khalid Fahmi (Surabaya, 28 October 2018).

25 Author's interview with Agus Iwan, East Java provincial council candidate, National Democrat (NasDem) Party (Surabaya, 19 September 2018).

26 Author's interview with Mila Machmudah, Coordinator, *#2019GantiPresiden Movement* in Surabaya and national legislative candidate from PAN (Surabaya, 27 December 2018).

27 Author's interview with Tjejep Yasin, vice chairman, Indonesian Islamic Propagation Council (DDII) East Java province (Surabaya, 10 September 2018).

28 Author's interview with Fahlesa Munabari, Lecturer, Faculty of International Relations, Budi Luhur University (Jakarta, 23 October 2018).

29 Author's interview with Tjejep Yasin (Surabaya, 10 September 2018).

30 Author's interview with Mila Machmudah (Surabaya, 27 December 2018).

31 Author's interview with Mila Machmudah (Surabaya, 27 December 2018).

32 Author's confidential interview with a senior Jokowi campaign volunteer coordinator (Surabaya, 13 March 2019).

33 Author's confidential interview (Surabaya, 13 March 2019).
34 Author's confidential interview (Surabaya, 13 March 2019).

Bibliography

Aspinall, E. 2019, 22 April. 'Indonesia's Election and the Return of Ideological Competition', *New Mandala*. Retrieved from www.newmandala.org/indonesias-election-and-the-return-of-ideological-competition/.

Fealy, G. 2018, 11 July. 'Nahdlatul Ulama and the Politics Trap', *New Mandala*. Retrieved from www.newmandala.org/nahdlatul-ulama-politics-trap/.

Kayane, Y. 2020. 'Understanding Sunni-Shi'a Sectarianism in Indonesia: A Different Voice from Nahdlatul Ulama under Pluralist Leadership', *Indonesia and the Malay World* (online first). Retrieved from https://doi.org/10.1080/13639811.2020.1675277.

Miichi, K., & Y. Kayane. 2020. 'The Political Aspirations of the Shi'ites in Indonesia: Response to the Sampang Incidents in 2011–12', *TRaNS: Trans-National and – Regional Studies of Southeast Asia*, Vol. 8 (1): 51–64. Retrieved from https://doi.org/10.1017/trn.2019.12.

5 *Aliran* politics, political *jihad*, and disappointment

Notes for Muslim Javanese in the pre- and post-2019 general election in Central Java

Syafiq Hasyim

Introduction

Javanese Muslims were a very important group in driving Joko Widodo and Ma'ruf Amin to victory in the 2019 presidential elections.[1] Two provinces in Indonesia, Central and East Java, are the main population centres for Javanese Muslims. Most of them theologically follow Nahdlatul Ulama and politically follow the Indonesian Democratic Party of Struggle (PDI-P, *Partai Demokrasi Indonesia Perjuangan*) or the National Awakening Party (PKB, *Partai Kebangkitan Bangsa*). For decades, Javanese Muslims have been key to the prominence of Nahdlatul Ulama as well as PDI-P in both Central and East Java. Along with West Java these are the most populous provinces in Indonesia and therefore they are critical to the electoral fortunes of Indonesian presidential candidates.

This chapter will investigate how Javanese Muslims participated and voted during the presidential election of 2019. It will highlight the Islamic religious narrative of Javanese Muslims and their choice for president and also examine some of the discontent that followed in the post-election period, as promises made by Jokowi–Ma'ruf to place Nahdlatul Ulama cadres in certain ministerial positions have gone unrealised.

This chapter is based on my short visit to Central Java in the period immediately prior to the 2019 election. During this fieldwork, I met and conducted interviews with various important Javanese Muslims in Central Java. I met with members of Nahdlatul Ulama including *kyais*, Nahdlatul Ulama's regional board members and the *pesantren* community. Besides the Nahdlatul Ulama community, I had conversations with members of the second-largest Muslim organisation in Central Java, Muhammadiyah. The Central Javanese regions where I conducted fieldwork were Demak, Jepara, Pati, Rembang, Tegal, Brebes, Purwokerto, Solo, and Yogyakarta. Supplementary information was also obtained from secondary sources like books and online media.

Anatomy of Javanese Muslims

Who are Javanese Muslims? Are Javanese Muslims considered an ethnic, linguistic, or geographical category? Javanese Muslims combine two important components of identity; the culture of Java and the belief and norms of Islam. The precise relation between culture and Islam is not an easy matter to discern, but they are both important in the creation of the Muslim Javanese identity. At times, the two can be in tension with one another. In addition to culture and Islam, Mark Woodward (2011) adds a further component – nationality. In the hierarchy of identity, Javanese Muslims often consider themselves first and foremost to be Javanese and Indonesian rather than Muslims. On the basis of this, the chapter follows a simple definition of Javanese Muslims as 'those who are ethnically Javanese and theologically Muslim and live in the areas of Central and East Java'.

In his book *The Religion of Java* Clifford Geertz (1976) categorised Javanese Muslims into three streams or *aliran*: *abangan*, *santri*, and *priyayi*. The term *abangan* referred to the peasant community who practiced Javanese syncretism. The term *santri* was used to refer to the trader-class, often living in urban areas and who tended to be more devout Muslims. And *priyayi* was applied to members of the Javanese bureaucratic and aristocratic class. Many have criticised Geertz's categorisation as no longer relevant given the complexity of social, political, and legal circumstances in Indonesia, as well as increased social and economic mobility. However, it is still possible to broadly identify these classifications running through elements of Javanese society, and many Javanese still self-identify according to these classes. Until recently, politics that used these three categories as their basis was called *politik* aliran (Hatherell 2019).

Until recently, Central Java was a province in which the presence of these *aliran*s was quite prominent, and the domination of *kaum abangan*, forming an important pillar of PDI-P support, remains very significant to this day. Owing to this support, including in 2014 and 2019, the PDI-P has consistently dominated elections in Central Java. In the general elections 2014, the PDI-P won 27 of parliamentary seats and in the general elections 2019 this nationalist party won 42 of parliamentary seats. Joko Widodo–Ma'ruf Amin won 77.29 per cent of the total votes cast in the presidential elections 2019 in Central Java.[2]

Central Java is considered as one of the main precincts in which *kaum abangan* reside (Muchtarom 1988, Daniels 2009) but there are also substantial numbers of *Nahdliyyin* – the followers of Nahdlatul Ulama representing the traditionalist *santri* stream – living in Central Java. There is no exact data about the number of Nahdlatul Ulama's followers but, religiously speaking, Nahdlatul Ulama is also the largest Islamic organisation in Central Java. This helps account for the significant presence of the PKB,[3] an Islam-based political party that is affiliated with Nahdlatul Ulama and popular in East Java. Districts in Central Java that have become bases for *kaum santri* include Demak, Jepara, Kudus, Kendal, Pekalongan, Rembang, Tegal, Brebes Temanggung, and Magelang. In these regions, a lot of big traditional Islamic boarding schools are established such as al-Anwar in Sarang, Api Tegal Rejo in Magelang, and many others.

Kaum priyayi are usually concentrated around the sites of current or former Javanese kingdoms such as Yogyakarta and Surakarta, although they can also be found in many urban settings. Different from previous times, contemporary *kaum priyayi* are now mostly working as civil servants or entrepreneurs. *Kaum santri* are much more visible in Central Java than *kaum priyayi* because of the successful spread of Islamisation among the *abangan* community (Ricklefs 2012). As more mosques, *pesantrens, madrasah*, and other Islamic centres are established in Central Java, the reach of the *kaum santri* is likely to grow and may come to challenge the dominance of the *kaum abangan* to some extent. For instance, although there are more followers of Nahdlatul Ulama in Central Java, Muhammadiyah, which represents the modernist *santri* stream, has built more schools, universities, and hospitals than Nahdlatul Ulama.[4]

Increasingly, however, it is becoming difficult to clearly differentiate between the different *aliran*. Since the presidential election in 2014, there has been a shift as the lines separating the three groups have begun to blur and blend together. This may be a result of the rapidly shifting economic and political circumstances that surround these three groups.

Many important social and political issues in Central Java reflect the mutually beneficial relationship between the *kaum abangan* and the *kaum santri*. The *kaum abangan* accommodate the cultural and religious identity of *kaum santri* on one hand and *kaum santri* also accept the presence of *kaum abangan* on the other hand. This mutual acceptance manifests not only in social and cultural spheres, but also in the political arena.

The governor of Central Java is Ganjar Pranowo, who is a member of the PDI-P and identifies with *kaum nasionalist-abangan*.[5] His vice governor is Taj Yasin, a member of Nahdlatul Ulama and PPP, a party associated with *santri*.[6] This indicates an important shift of *aliran* strictness. This is an interesting development because there has long been tension between *kaum santri tradisional* and *kaum abangan* in Central Java related to confrontations between Banser (the militia wing of Nahdlatul Ulama) and communist parties in the 1960s (Wieringa & Katjasungkana 2019). To reach the current position of mutual acceptance represents real progress.

Kaum priyayi, on the other hand, tend to build alliances with *kaum santri modernis* (modernist *santri*). Most modernist *santri* come from a Muhammadiyah background.[7] Their religious inclinations provide common ground between the groups. *Kaum priyayi* have a rational point of view and modernist *santri* have a purist view on religion. Neither group likes religious innovation (*bid'ah*) because it creates uncertainty in religion and undermines faith. Politically speaking, both groups are close to PAN, PKS, and PPP to some extent. However, there does not exist an absolute alliance between the two *aliran*, and their relationship can be nuanced and complicated.

The transformation of *abangan*

Is the *kaum abangan* transforming into a *santri* or *priyayi*? Or is the transformation happening in the opposite direction and *santri* are changing into *abangan* or *priyayi* in terms of their social, cultural, and religious inclination? One's position on this matter depends to some degree on how you define *abangan*. Harry J. Benda (1982) agreed with the way Geertz defined *abangan*, using it to refer to rural farmers who know very little Islamic teachings yet can be recognised as Muslims. Harsja W. Bachtiar (1985) took a different view from Geertz and Benda, arguing that Geertz misunderstood the definition of *abangan* in Javanese society and assumed they had no inclination to Islam at all, while in reality many *kaum abangan* do consider themselves as Muslims. Mitsuo Nakamura (2012) has helped revise and develop these categorisations especially in Geertz's placement of *abangan* in opposition to *priyayi*. Robert Hefner strengthens the implementation of theoretical frameworks of *abangan* in his many studies (Hefner 1985, 2000).

From my direct observation during my fieldwork (February–March 2019) in major areas of Central Java, *kaum abangan* tend to embrace some elements of traditionalist *santri* in their theological and political patterns of everyday life. The traditionalist *santri* – following the Geertz categorisation – are those who theologically and ideologically come from the Nahdlatul Ulama background. The *kaum abangan* of Surakarta, Pati, Banyumas, Wonosobo, and some others have indicated a shift of their cultural and religious leaning towards those practiced by traditionalist *santri*.

In Surakarta, for instance, there has been a dramatic change in the last 20 years in the religious behaviour of *kaum abangan*. There are now very few Muslims who do not go for prayer five times daily. Islamic expression is becoming more visible in the public sphere. A *Qur'an* and other Islamic texts are kept on the shelves of guest rooms at their houses.[8] More people are wearing the *jilbab* (veil) as part of their daily dress code, meaning the *abangan* is becoming less a nominal Muslim and more inclined towards the *santri* stream.

Generally speaking, most Muslims in Central Java are politically aligned with the secular and nationalist party (PDI-P), but this does not necessarily form an immovable part of their identity. Some regions long-identified with *kaum abangan*, like Solo and Sukoharjo, are now seeing the proliferation of Islamic schools, mosques, and social–religious activities – *Pengajian* and *Majlis Taklim*. Yet, as mentioned, despite increasing religiosity the PDI-P still dominates as the political party of Central Java. In Surakarta, for instance, most *abangan* gravitate towards Nahdlatul Ulama rather than Muhammadiyah, even though Muhammadiyah is also a strong Muslim organisation in Surakarta. This is because *kaum abangan* is closer in culture and politics to Nahdlatul Ulama than to Muhammadiyah. Importantly, the old rituals of *kaum abangan* – derived from Javanese tradition – can be Islamised through the tradition of Nahdlatul Ulama. From this, *kaum abangan* feel more comfortable going to Nahdlatul Ulama because their tradition is accommodated and respected.

The Islamisation of Javanese traditions is much harder to come by with Muhammadiyah, which is considered as a puritan organisation and rejects any localised traditions or rituals in Islam. The extended family of Jokowi in Surakarta who are associated with the *abangan* strain are, in their daily life, close to the tradition of Nahdlatul Ulama. They practice what the traditionalist *santri* practice in their daily rituals like holding *selametan* (Islamic ritual to commemorate their ancestors), *ziarah kubur* (visiting graveyard), and many others. On the basis of the abovementioned explanation, it is reasonable to expect that traditionalist *santri*-inclined *abangan* or Muslim Javanese would mostly support Jokowi–Ma'ruf.

When *priyayi* becomes more pious

The next question, to be discussed in this section, is whether the *priyayi*, like the *abangan*, are changing and if so in what way. Clifford Geertz described the *priyayi* as follows:

> *Prijaji* originally referred only to the hereditary aristocracy which the Dutch pried loose from the kings of the vanquished native states and turned into an appointive, salaried civil service. This white-collar elite, its ultimate roots in the Hindu-Javanese courts of pre-colonial times, conserved and cultivated a highly refined court etiquette, a very complex art of dance, drama, music, and poetry, and a Hindu-Buddhist mysticism. They stressed neither the animistic element in the over-all Javanese syncretism as did the *abangans*, nor the Islamic as did the *santris*, but the Hinduistic.
>
> (Geertz 1976, p. 7)

Yet despite their aristocratic, cultivated Hindu roots, Timothy Daniels (2009) has argued that culturally – particularly with regard to syncretic religious inclination – the *priyayi* are close in nature to the *abangan*. However, the *kaum priyayi* appear to be moving in the direction of *kaum santri* rather than towards the direction of *kaum abangan*. Being *santri* has been the general tendency of Indonesia's elite for the last three decades.

In the post-*Reformasi* era, the religious shift of *kaum priyayi* has been towards *kaum santri*. During the 1990s, in big cities like Jakarta they joined the clubs of *pengajian*, which were organised in five-star hotels. For instance, the Paramadina study club led by Nurcholish Madjid (Cak Nur, 1939–2005) was a very famous Islamic study club that *kaum priyayi* preferred to attend (Gaus 2010). The decline of Suharto changed the landscape of Indonesian Islam – during his rule it had been more inclusive, but afterward many groups became more intolerant (Hefner 1999, Elson 2001). In the beginning, these intolerant and more conservative groups did not attract the interest of *kaum priyayi* because their ideology was not compatible with the *santri* ideology. Within the past decade, however, *kaum priyayi* increasingly believe that the issue of social injustice that the Muslim community are facing now is perceived as a matter of Islam. They perceive that the poverty of the Muslim community is caused because their religion is Islam not because of economic and political issues.

Several major cities that are *priyayi* bases have begun to trend towards the *santri*. In the urban areas of Surakarta and Yogyakarta for instance the phenomena of *santrinisation* in the public sphere is noticeable in the daily activities of Muslim communities such as building Islamic schools and enforcing public morality. In this regard, the values of modernist *santri* are increasingly appearing in the public sphere. Islamic events are also often organised around the centre of *priyayi*'s dwelling zones in Central Java. The offices of several provincial governors and districts display Islamic symbols. Their administrators and bureaucrats follow the strict dress code of Sharia in their daily place of work.

However, the current *santrinisation* of *priyayi* is much more driven by the emergence of identity politics. To some extent, the families of *priyayi* at various levels have been involved in Islamic movements like *Aksi Bela Islam 212* (ABI 212, Action to Defend Islam). Some of them affiliate with Islamic political parties such as the United Development Party (PPP), National Mandate Party (PAN), and Prosperous Justice Party (PKS). They also promote a limited circle of study (*liqa'*) on the basics of Islam in Yogyakarta and Solo. In the 2019 presidential election, the majority of *kaum priyayis* who incline to modernist *santri* supported Prabowo and Sandiaga as president and vice-president. Muhammadiyah, the organisation most associated with modernist *santri*, endorsed Prabowo–Sandiaga. The leader of Muhammadiyah in Central Java stated that the electoral support of Muhammadiyah to Prabowo–Sandiaga was predicted to reach almost 70 per cent.[9]

Prabowo–Sandiaga were viewed *by the priyayis* as more inspiring figures for Islam than Jokowi–Ma'ruf. The feeling was that Jokowi–Ma'ruf would be against the interest of Islam as evident from previous Jokowi policies that targeted *ulama* as criminals like the case of Rizieq Shihab, Habib Smith, and others. Besides that, they stated that Jokowi–Ma'ruf were afraid of China. The issue of increasing Chinese investment and workers in Indonesia was a common narrative among them. Prabowo–Sandiaga were imagined as pluckier presidential and vice-presidential candidates who could fight against the economic domination of China, which was depicted as a serious danger to Islam in Indonesia.[10]

Besides the influence of the modernist *santri* narrative mentioned above, *kaum priyayi* were inclined to vote for Prabowo–Sandiaga due to a common perception among them that their leader should come from a similar class. Jokowi–Ma'ruf are not considered part of the *priyayi* group. Jokowi himself comes from the *abangan* background and Ma'ruf comes from the traditionalist *santri* background (Karni 2018). *Kaum priyayi* in general continue to view leadership in somewhat feudalistic terms.

Although many *priyayis* who follow the footsteps of modernist *santri* usually adopt liberal ideas, in the case of presidential elections they tend to adopt social class-based perceptions. Jokowi does not come from an aristocrat family and *priyayi* find this objectionable, as the *priyayi* class has traditionally been the leader-class of Indonesia. Based on the explanation above, the changing religious inclination of *kaum priyayi* towards modernist *santri* reflects a political preference for Prabowo–Sandiaga. It means that the religious tendency of *kaum priyayi* is closely related to their electoral choices.

The *santri* world

When Ma'ruf Amin, a prominent *santri* figure, was nominated as vice president the definition of *santri* become highly contested. As the general chairman of

MUI and head of Syuriah Nahdlatul Ulama (Sharia Consultative Body of Nahdlatul Ulama) Ma'ruf is an important *santri* figure. On the other hand, Prabowo's vice-presidential pick Sandiaga Uno also claims himself as *santri*. It is understandable when the word *santri* is used to categorise Ma'ruf Amin, but Sandiaga's use of the classification has a more political overtone. In this regard, Ma'ruf Amin is a real cleric playing a political role and Sandiaga is a politician who wants to be called *santri*.

To strengthen his claim, the Islamic political organisations backing Prabowo declared Sandiaga to be *santri*. The general leader of PKS, Shohibul Imam, made a public announcement that Sandiaga was '*santri-pos-Islamisme*' (post-Islamism *santri*).[11] When this caused some controversy, PKS tried to explain what they meant with '*pos-Islamisme*'. Suhudi Aliyun, coordinator of presidential candidacy for PKS, stated that it referred to a form of Islam focused more on the substantive than symbolic implementation of Islam. Aliyun stated that while symbols are important, substance is much more important and Sandiaga is a Muslim who embodied that principle.[12] It seems that the definition of *pos-Islamisme* introduced by Shohibul Imam is actually close to the use of the term in certain theoretical frameworks on 'post-Islamism' which has a deeper meaning in sociological and political discourse (Bayat 2007). In this theoretical framework, Islamic state is no longer important for the struggles of Islamist groups, but Islamic morality and sharia can be implemented in the form of nation state, and this might be the message that PKS wanted to give to the public at that time. In other words, Indonesian Muslim voters were persuaded by PKS not too much worried with the agenda of Islamic state because now the PKS has changed.

If we go back to Geertz's concept, the definition of *santri* clearly applies to those who have an intensive religious education background from *pesantren*. In this regard, *santri* means Islamic pupil and *pesantren* means an Islamic boarding school. Then Geertz divides *santri* into two large categories; traditionalist *santri* linked to Nahdlatul Ulama and modernist *santri* linked to Masyumi and Muhammadiyah backgrounds (Geertz 1976, Muchtarom 1988).

The participation of *kaum santri* in general elections in the history of Indonesia is not new; it has been an important political current since the beginning of democracy, and the electoral battle often reflects deeper religious tensions. The contestation between Masyumi and Nahdlatul Ulama as political parties in the general election of 1955 was actually a contestation between modernist *santri* and traditionalist *santri* (Noer 1973, Geertz 1976, Lev 2009). With the return of direct elections in recent years, the political contestation between traditionalist *santri* and modernist *santri* has resurfaced. The contestation is no longer taking place between Masyumi and Nahdlatul Ulama but between modernist *santri*-associated political parties and traditionalist *santri*-associated political parties.

Based on the importance the campaign placed on establishing Sandiaga's link with the *santri* stream to balance Ma'ruf Amin's *santri* links, it is clear that *kaum santri* are important political players in Indonesia. Based on this explanation, the definition of *santri* becomes wider and more political. This, however, is not totally acceptable among *santri*s themselves because it can denigrate the dignity of *kaum santri* and reduce them to mere political agents. Despite these objections, it appears that both campaigns felt it was important to associate with the *santri* stream in the 2019 election.

Political *jihad*

Broadly speaking, Jokowi–Ma'ruf drew their Javanese Muslim support from Nahdlatul Ulama, while Prabowo–Sandiaga drew their Javanese Muslim support from Muhammadiyah. As a civil society organisation, Nahdlatul Ulama is not explicitly a political party, but its members have the right to engage in politics (Fealy & Barton 1996; Kadir 1999, Bush 2009). Although the central headquarters (PBNU) of Nahdlatul Ulama did not issue a clear instruction to support Jokowi–Ma'ruf, Nahdlatul Ulama's support of Jokowi–Ma'ruf was obvious from the public statements made by elite members such as Kyai Said Aqil Siradj, the general chairman of Nahdlatul Ulama, who stated that '*warga* Nahdlatul Ulama' must support Jokowi.[13]

Central Java is the province with the second-largest number of Nandlatul Ulama members after East Java. This gives Nahdlatul Ulama substantial political influence. Most Nahdlatul Ulama figures in Central Java stated that supporting Jokowi–Amin was *harga mati* (non-negotiable).[14] From their perspective, supporting the ticket was similar to *jihad*. The support of Nahdlatul Ulama for Jokowi–Amin in Central Java was not just because Ma'ruf Amin was on the ticket but it also became an ideological matter.[15] Voting for Jokowi–Ma'ruf was framed as being similar to defending NKRI, the ideological foundations of Indonesia as a unitary state; in this framing, Prabowo–Sandiaga were portrayed as threatening the very ideological foundations of the state.

The supporters of Prabowo–Sandiaga in the perspective of Muslim Javanese of Nahdlatul Ulama in Central Java were portrayed as having an agenda to change the state form of Indonesia from NKRI to an Islamic state.[16] This was based on political narratives developed by supporters of Prabowo–Sandiaga that called for a system of political Islam like *NKRI Bersyariah* (Unitary State of Indonesian Republic which is based on sharia law) such as that promoted by *Front Pembela Islam* (FPI, Islamic Defenders Front) (Awas 2001, Jahroni 2008).[17] Leaders of Nahdlatul Ulama made a political calculation that if Prabowo–Sandiaga were to win and take the country in a more conservative direction, it might threaten their future as Nahdlatul Ulama has tried to establish itself as a moderate organisation.

Therefore, supporting Jokowi for a second term was an important goal for members of Nahdlatul Ulama. According to them, supporting Jokowi was analogous with the value of defending Indonesia as a unitary state. This did not contradict their own Islamic values, as NKRI includes protections for the rights of Muslims (*al-daruriyyat al-khamsah*).[18] The phrase '*NKRI harga mati*' therefore became a slogan reflecting the strong political alliance between Nahdlatul Ulama and Jokowi in Central Java.[19]

Besides the aforementioned argument, the support of Nahdlatul Ulama for Jokowi in Central Java was also related to the fact that Jokowi's religious practices were very close to the ritual tradition of Nahdlatul Ulama. In addition, the extended family of Jokowi, especially his late mother and sisters, are active in the activities of the Nahdlatul Ulama branch, especially with *Muslimat* (women wing of Nahdlatul Ulama) in Solo, Central Java.[20] The family has often organised *pengajian umum* and *tahlilan* long before Jokowi was president. This fact has helped convince Nahdlatul Ulama members in Solo that the family is genuinely devoted to the organisation, and not merely for political gain.

As mentioned before, while the followers of Nahdlatul Ulama mostly enthusiastically supported Jokowi, the followers of Muhammadiyah mostly supported Prabowo–Sandiaga. The general chairman of Central Java Muhammadiyah, Kyai Tafsir, states that approximately 70 per cent of Muhammadiyah members in this province supported Prabowo–Sandiaga.[21] This support was based on their assumption that Prabowo–Sandiaga gave more hope for the betterment of Islam not only in Java but also in Indonesia. According to them, during his first term Jokowi did a lot of things that were seen as attacks on the dignity of Islam in Indonesia – such as criminalisation of ulama – in order to win in the general elections.[22] The case of Rizieq Shihab (the spiritual leader of FPI) is often cited. However, there are simply fewer Muhammadiyah members in Central Java then there are Nahdlatul Ulama members. Thus, in the political battle between the traditionalist *santri* and modernist *santri* in the province, the victory went to the traditionalists.

The Ma'ruf Amin and Nahdlatul Ulama factor

Many observations state Nahdlatul Ulama was a more important component of Jokowi's success than Ma'ruf Amin. This statement is based on Jokowi's big losses in two important provinces: Banten and West Java.[23] Ma'ruf Amin was assigned by Jokowi to take responsibility to win in the provinces of Banten and West Java. This assignment was based on the possible capacity of Ma'ruf Amin to get support from Muslim communities in those two provinces. At the very least, it was thought perhaps Amin could get the support of Nahdlatul Ulama followers in West Java and Banten.

In the 2014 election Jokowi also lost both of those provinces, so the recruitment of Ma'ruf Amin for Jokowi was expected to improve his performance there. Banten is a place where Amin was born and he has family connections. Banten used to be part of West Java province but in the post-reform era was made into its own administrative territory. On the basis of this, assigning Amin to win in West Java was understandable due to the cultural and historical closeness between Banten and West Java.

More importantly, Banten is not only Amin's hometown, but he is also considered as a prominent ulama in the province. He built a big *pesantren* and sought to revive the legacy of Syaikh Nawawi al-Bantani, a historic ulama from Banten who passed away in Mecca. It is said in daily public conversation among the Banten community that Amin was the grandchild of Syaikh Nawawi al-Bantani (Hurgronje 2007). In the end, though, Ma'ruf Amin was unable to improve Jokowi's chances in West Java and Banten, as voters from both provinces voted overwhelmingly for Prabowo. In Central Java and East Java, meanwhile, Jokowi received large vote shares even without Ma'ruf making a personal effort to win there. This shows us that Ma'ruf Amin is not a very important factor in attracting the Muslim Javanese of Nahdlatul Ulama.

From the perspective of Javanese Muslims of Nahdlatul Ulama, the appointment of Ma'ruf Amin as Jokowi's vice-presidential candidate was understood as a bonus for Nahdlatul Ulama. However, it seems that the fundamental reason that Javanese Muslims of Nahdlatul Ulama supported Jokowi was not because of Amin, but because the central headquarters of Nahdlatul Ulama in Jakarta indicated support for Jokowi. On the basis of this, it means that the Nahdlatul Ulama factor is much more dominant than the Ma'ruf Amin factor. However, it should also be recognised that the position of Ma'ruf Amin as the vice-presidential candidate is an additional value for *nahdliyyin*.

The choice of Ma'ruf Amin as the vice-presidential candidate was perceived by Jokowi's opponent as a negative factor. Ma'ruf Amin was understood by the Muslim Javanese of Muhammadiyah as evidence of Jokowi's preference towards Nahdlatul Ulama. The Muhammadiyah community felt that if Jokowi was serious about getting support from other Islamic organisations, he would not have chosen Ma'ruf Amin. The appointment of Ma'ruf Amin demonstrated the character of Jokowi as a leader who has big political ambitions. With regard to this, the position of Ma'ruf Amin as the vice-presidential candidate of Jokowi blocked possible support from other Islamic groups for voting Jokowi.

As the leader of MUI, Amin actually has a long history of working together with other Muslim groups considering MUI is the meeting point of many Islamic organisations in Indonesia. The problem is that when Amin was chosen by Jokowi, he was chosen because of his capacity as the general leader (*Rais Am*) of Syuriah Nahdlatul Ulama. This was evident from the statement of PBNU and also the role of Muhaimin Iskandar as the general chairman of PKB as well as Rommahurmuzy (Gus Rommy) as the general chairman of PPP in getting Ma'ruf Amin on the ticket.[24]

Jokowi was originally leaning towards another Nahdlatul Ulama-affiliated candidate, Mahfud MD. But after lobbying from Muhaimin and Gus Rommy Jokowi appointed Amin because he was very concerned with securing the full support of these political parties and Nahdlatul Ulama for his re-election campaign. On the basis of this, it can be concluded that the main factor for Javanese Muslims was not Ma'ruf, but Nahdlatul Ulama.

Expectation and disappointment

Javanese Muslims expected that if Jokowi won then Nahdlatul Ulama would reach a new prominence in the government. In addition to Ma'ruf Amin as vice president, Nahdlatul Ulama also expected one of their cadres would be appointed as Minister of Religious Affairs, in addition to other ministerial positions in the Jokowi cabinet. This was seen as their reward for helping deliver millions of votes in Central and East Java.

In the end, Jokowi did not give that ministerial position to a Nahdlatul Ulama cadre, instead naming Fahrur Razi (retired general and coordinator of Bravo 5) the new Minister of Religious Affairs. Soon after the announcement, the central headquarters of Nahdlatul Ulama in Jakarta expressed disappointment. Although Jokowi had asked the PBNU for a name of candidates, and was provided with a list of around ten names, he ultimately did not select anyone from the list.[25] This has created some tension and feelings of disappointment between Jokowi and Nahdlatul Ulama leadership. PBNU felt that Jokowi had intentionally forgotten the contribution of Nahdlatul Ulama and their critical support for his victory in the presidential elections of 2019.

Kyai Said Aqil Siradj now has changed his position and become critical of Jokowi. Kyai Said criticism of the new cabinet composition is something that Jokowi did not expect. As part of PBNU's disappointment with Jokowi, Kyai Said extends his criticism not only in regard to the position of Minister of Religious Affairs but also related to other political and economic issues. In a 26 December 2019 speech, Kyai Said accused Jokowi of doing more to serve the interest of the oligarchy – including the military and his party, the PDI-P – than the interest of the people. Kyai Said explicitly stated that those who have money are the ones chosen by Jokowi as his ministers.[26] This is a particularly harsh criticism of Jokowi because it comes from one of his main political allies, the general chairman of PBNU.

The Nahdlatul Ulama organisation has also shown disappointment in Ma'ruf Amin. It was expected that he would provide Nahdlatul Ulama with direct access to the levers of state power, but so far this has not been the case. Many Nahdlatul Ulama elites expected that Amin would play a role like Jusuf Kalla – Jokowi's vice president 2014–2019 – who was very active and innovative when he was vice president. Yet public evaluation of 100 days of his vice-presidential performance was negative.[27]

This negative performance results from his minimal experience and capacity working in the state bureaucracy, and that he has focused too much on his own affairs, inner circle, and group and has done little to advance the interests of Nahdlatul Ulama. So far Amin has been closer to his circle and group at MUI than at PBNU. Many of his staff are recruited from MUI. However, all these circumstances can change with Amin because he still has more time to change in the future.

Concluding remarks

The politics of *aliran* appear to be shifting, but still constitute an important part of Indonesian elections. The streams of *abangan*, *santri*, and *priyayi*, introduced by Geertz, have apparently begun to undergo a shift in their theological alignment, but not in their political behaviours. PDI-P remains very strong in the *abangan* zone in Central Java while Islamic parties such as PPP, PKB, and PKS remain strong in their *santri* zones.

The emergence of identity politics has contributed to the *santrinisation* of both *abangan* and *priyayi*, but their evolution is not fixed and tends to follow certain social and theological patterns. Most of the *kaum abangan* have mutual acceptance with the traditionalists *santri* organisations like Nahdlatul Ulama and most *priyayi* have mutual acceptance with modernist *santri* like Muhammadiyah and PKS. As these streams increasingly coalesce around the *santri*, it is expected to narrow the polarisation and gap caused by electoral politics.

Although Nahdlatul Ulama became a strong supporter of Jokowi–Ma'ruf during the 2019 election, it does not guarantee that their support will continue unbroken. The extent of Nahdlatul Ulama's continued support for Jokowi will depend, to some degree, on what reciprocal political benefits they receive. So far, Nahdlatul Ulama has been disappointed in Jokowi's failure to appoint a Nahdlatul Ulama cadre as Minister of Religious Affairs and Ma'ruf Amin's apparent preference for prioritising MUI rather than Nahdlatul Ulama issues. While the coalition Jokowi built with Nandlatul Ulama helped ensure a big victory in Central Java, the future stability of this coalition remains uncertain.

Notes

1 See Pepinsky 2019.
2 BeritaSatu.com 2019.
3 *Kompas.com* 2019.
4 The estimation of Nahdlatul Ulama followers is 36.5 per cent and that of Muhammadiyah followers are 5.4 per cent. This data is from Hasinuddin Ali's personal blog (2017).
5 Detiknews.com 2018a.
6 Detiknews.com 2018b.
7 Interview with the general chairman of Central Java Muhammadiyah, Ahmad Tafsir, March 2019.
8 Interview with Sukemi, supervisor of student dormitory of MAN PK (Madrasah Aliyah Negeri Program Khusus), Solo.
9 Interview with the leader of Muhammadiyah of Central Java, March 2019.
10 Focus group discussion with Muhammadiyah figures at Rector of Muhammadiyah University of Purwokerto (UPM), March 2019.
11 Tempo.co 2018a.
12 Ibid.
13 Tempo.co 2018b.
14 Interview with board member of NU Tegal Branch, Tegal, March 2019.
15 Interview with Nahdlatul Ulama figure in Tegal, March 2019.
16 This narrative was commonly introduced by Nahdlatul Ulama figures that I had met during my fieldwork in Central Java.
17 Detiknews.com 2019.
18 NU Online 2015.
19 Ibid.
20 Interview with the board member of NU Solo branch, March 2019. See also Tribunnews 2019a.
21 Interview with him on at Muhammadiyah office of Central Java, Semarang, March 2019.
22 Interview with the Muhammadiyah activist in Tegal, Central Java, March 2019.

23 Tempo.co 2019.
24 Detiknews.com 2018c.
25 Confidential interviews with PBNU officials, January 2020.
26 Tribunnews.com 2019b.
27 Tempo.co 2020.

Bibliography

Ali, H. 2017, 19 January. 'Menakar Jumlah Jamaah NU and Muhammadiyah', ['Measuring the Number of NU and Muhammadiyah Followers'] (personal blog). Retrieved from https://hasanuddinali.com/2017/01/19/menakar-jumlah-jamaah-nu-dan-muhammadiyah/.

Awas, I. 2001. *Risalah Kongres Mujahidin I dan Penegakan Syariah Islam* ['Summary of The First Mujahiddin Congress: Formation of Islamic Syariah']. Jakata, Indonesia: Wihdah Press.

Bayat, A. 2007. *Making Islam Democratic: Social Movements and the Post-Islamist Turn.* Stanford, CA: Stanford University Press.

Benda, H.J. 1982. *The Struggle of Islam in Modern Indonesia.* Leiden: Springer.

Bachtiar, H.W. 1985. 'The Religion of Java: A Commentary.' In I. Achmad, S. Sharon & Y. Hussain (eds.). *Readings on Islam in Southeast Asia.* Singapore: Institute of Southeast Asian Studies.

BeritaSatu.com. 2019, 13 May. 'Menang Telak di Jateng, PDIP "Meriahkan" Gedung Dewan' ['After a Landslide Won in Central Java, PDIP "Reddened" Local Assemblies']. Retrieved from www.beritasatu.com/politik/553812/politik/553812-menang-telak-di-jateng-pdip-merahkan-gedung-dewan.

Bush, R. 2009. *Nahdlatul Ulama and the Struggle for Power within Islam and Politics in Indonesia.* Singapore: Institute of Southeast Asian Studies.

Daniels, T. 2009. *Islamic Spectrum in Java.* London: Routledge.

Detiknews.com. 2018a, 8 January. 'Shalawat Iringi Pernikahan Ganjar-Yasin di PPP Jateng' ['Shalawat Prayer Accompanies the Marriage between Ganjar-Yasin at PPP Central Java Headquarters']. Retrieved from https://news.detik.com/berita-jawa-tengah/d-3805181/shalawat-iringi-pernikahan-ganjar-yasin-di-ppp-jateng.

Detiknews.com. 2018b, 10 March. 'Relawan Perempuan, Santri, dan Pemuda Gabung ke Ganjar -Yasin' ['Female Volunteers, Santri, and Youths Join the Ganjar-Yasin Team']. Retrieved from https://news.detik.com/berita-jawa-tengah/d-3909381/relawan-perempuan-santri-dan-pemuda-gabung-ke-ganjar-yasin.

Detiknews.com. 2018c, 10 August. 'Gerilya Cak Imin dan Rommy untuk Ma'ruf' ['Cak Imin and Rommy's Guerilla Warfare to Support Ma'ruf']. Retrieved from https://news.detik.com/x/detail/investigasi/20180810/Gerilya-Cak-Imin-dan-Rommy-untuk-Maruf/.

Detiknews.com. 2019, 24 August. 'Habib Rizieq Bicara NKRI Bersyariah di Milad FPI: Pancasila Bukan Pilar Negara' ['Habib Rizieq Discusses NKRI Bersyariah in FPI Anniversary: Pancasila Is Not the Foundation of the State']. Retrieved from https://news.detik.com/berita/d-4679056/habib-rizieq-bicara-nkri-bersyariah-di-milad-fpi-pancasila-bukan-pilar-negara.

Elson, R.E. 2001. *Suharto: A Political Biography* (Vol. 13). Cambridge: Cambridge University Press.

Fealy, G., & Barton, G. (Eds.). 1996. *Nahdlatul Ulama, Traditional Islam and Modernity in Indonesia.* Mebourne, Australia: Monash Asia Institute, Monash University.

Gaus, A. 2010. *Api Islam Nurcholish Madjid: Jalan hidup seorang visioner* [Nurcolish Madjid's Islamic Fire: A Visioner's Way of Life]. Jakarta, Indonesia: Kompas Publishers.

Geertz, C. 1976. *The Religion of Java*. Chicago, IL: University of Chicago Press.

Hatherell, M. 2019. *Political Representation in Indonesia: The Emergence of the Innovative Technocrats*. London: Routledge.

Hefner, R.W. 1985. *Hindu Javanese: Tengger Tradition and Islam*. Princeton, NJ: Princeton University Press.

Hefner, R.W. 1999. Islam and Nation in the Post-Suharto Era. In A. Schwarz & J. Paris (Eds.), *The Politics of Post-Suharto Indonesia*. Washington, DC: Council of Foreign Relations.

Hefner, R.W. 1985. *Hindu Javanese: Tengger Tradition and Islam*. Princeton, NJ: Princeton University Press

Hefner, R.W. 2000. *Civil Islam: Muslims and Democratization in Indonesia*. Princeton, NJ: Princeton University Press.

Hurgronje, S.C. 2007. *Mekka in the Latter Part of the 19th Century*. Amsterdam: Brill.

Jahroni, J. 2008. *Defending the Majesty of Islam: Indonesia's Front Pembela Islam, 1998–2003*. Bangkok, Thailand: Asian Muslim Action Network.

Kadir, S.A. 1999. *Traditional Islamic Society and the State in Indonesia: The Nahdlatul Ulama, Political Accommodation and the Preservation of Autonomy*. Ph.D. Dissertation, University of Wisconsin–Madison.

Karni, A.S. 2018. *Biografi Singkat Kiai Ma'ruf Amin, Mufti, Ahli Siyasah dan Penggerak Ekonomi Syariah* [Kiai Ma'ruf Amin: A Short Biography – *Mufti, Siyasah* Expert, and A *Syariah* Economy Thinker]. Jakarta: Stif Syentra.

Kompas.com. 2019, 12 March. 'Pemilu 2019 Cak Imin Pasang Target PKB Peringkat Ke Dua Di Jateng' ['Cak Imin Targets PKB as the Second Largest Party in Central Java in the 2019 General Election']. Retrieved from https://regional.kompas.com/read/2019/03/12/23040 681/pemilu-2019-cak-imin-pasang-target-pkb-peringkat-2-di-jateng.

Lev, D.S. 2009. *Islamic Courts in Indonesia: A Study in the Political Bases of Legal Institutions*. Jakarta, Indonesia: Equinox.

Muchtarom, Z. 1988. *Santri dan Abangan di Jawa* [Santri and Abangan in Java]. Yogyakarta: INIS Publishers.

Nakamura, M. 2012. *The Crescent Arises Over the Banyan Tree: A Study of the Muhammadiyah Movement in a Central Javanese Town, C. 1910-2010*. Singapore: Institute of Southeat Asian Studies.

Noer, D. 1973. *The Modernist Muslim Movement in Indonesia, 1900–1942*. Oxford: Oxford University Press.

NU Online 2015, 3 May. 'Ini Alasan NKRI Harga Mati Bagi NU' ['This is the Reason Why NKRI is Non-Negotiable for NU']. Retrieved from www.nu.or.id/post/read/ 59266/ini-alasan-nkri-harga-mati-bagi-nu.

Pepinsky, T. 2019, 28 May. 'Religion, Ethnicity, and Indonesia's 2019 Presidential Election *New Mandala*'. Retrieved from www.newmandala.org/religion-ethnicity-and-indonesias-2019-presidential-election/.

Ricklefs, M. 2012. *Islamisation and Its Opponents in Java: A Political, Social, Cultural and Religious History, C. 1930 to the Present*. Singapore: National University of Singapore Press.

Tempo.co. 2018a, 11 August. 'Sandiaga Uno Disebut Santri Post-Islamisme, Begini Penjelasan PKS' ['Sandiaga Uno is Given Title a "Post-Islamism *Santri*", The Following is PKS Explanation']. Retrieved from https://nasional.tempo.co/read/1116076/ sandiaga-uno-disebut-santri-post-islamisme-begini-penjelasan-pks/full&view=ok.

Tempo.co. 2018b, 14 August. 'Said Aqil Siradj: Warga NU Dukung Pasangan Jokowi–Ma'ruf Amin' ['Said Aqil Siradj: NU Community Are Supporting Jokowi–Ma'ruf Amin Pair']. Retrieved fromhttps://nasional.tempo.co/read/1116993/said-aqil-siradj-warga-nu-dukung-pasangan-jokowi-maruf-amin/full&view=ok.

Tempo.co. 2019, 22 April. 'Jokowi Kalah di Banten, Tim Ma'ruf Amin Dinilai Tak Maksimal' ['Jokowi Lost in Banten Province, Ma'ruf Amin Team is Viewed Not Effective']. Retrieved from https://pilpres.tempo.co/read/1197900/jokowi-kalah-di-banten-tim-maruf-amin-dinilai-tak-maksimal.

Tempo.co. 2020, 28 January. '100 Hari Jokowi, Kiprah Ma'ruf Amin Dianggap Belum Siginifikan' [Jokowi's First 100 Days: Ma'ruf Amin's Accomplishments Is Not Considered Significant']. Retrieved from https://nasional.tempo.co/read/1300572/100-hari-jokowi-kiprah-maruf-amin-dianggap-belum-signifikan.

Tribunnews.com. 2019a, 27 January. 'Yenny Wahid Sebut Jokowi Keluarga Besar Muslimat NU, Ungkap Ibunda Jokowi yang Rajin Ikut Pengajian' ['Yenny Wahid Said Jokowi Family are Muslimat NU Members, Reveals Jokowi's Mother is a Member of NU-Sponsored Prayer Group']. Retrieved from https://jatim.tribunnews.com/2019/01/27/yenny-wahid-sebut-jokowi-keluarga-besar-muslimat-nu-ungkap-ibunda-jokowi-yang-rajin-ikut-pengajian.

Tribunnews.com. 2019b, 27 December. 'Kritik Pemerintahan Jokowi, Ketum PBNU Said Aqil Sebut Negara Dikuasai Orang-Orang Punya Duit' ['Criticising the Jokowi Administration, PBNU Chairman Said Aqil Siradj States that Indonesia is Being Run by 'Wealthy Oligarchs']. Retrieved from www.tribunnews.com/regional/2019/12/27/kritik-pemerintahan-jokowi-ketum-pbnu-said-aqil-sebut-negara-dikuasai-orang-orang-punya-duit, viewed on 22 January 2019.

Wieringa, S., & Katjasungkana, N. 2019. *Propaganda and the Genocide in Indonesia: Imagined Evil*. London: Routledge.

Woodward, M. 2011. *Java, Indonesia and Islam*. Heidelberg and New York: Springer.

6 The 2018 simultaneous regional elections and 2019 simultaneous national elections in North Sumatra

Different facades of identity politics

Tiola and Adhi Primarizki

Introduction

Since democratisation and decentralisation were instituted in Indonesia in 1999, the province of North Sumatra (*Sumatera Utara*) had served as an important electoral battleground for national politics. While provinces such as West and Central Java tend to comprise of a more homogeneous population with Javanese Muslims as predominant, North Sumatra provides a more complex mix of ethnicities and religions. Spanning over 33 regencies, North Sumatra is Indonesia's fourth most populous province with a population of 14.4 million. While Islam is still the dominant religion in the province (at 66.09 per cent), Muslims are generally dispersed along the East Coast area. There is a significant non-Muslim population that includes Protestant Christians at 27.03 per cent. They mostly reside in the West Coast area and the Nias Islands. The Batak is the biggest ethnic group in North Sumatra, comprising of different sub-ethnic groups and religions, including Christianity and Islam as the two most common religions adhered to. The Javanese is the second-largest ethnic group in North Sumatra, who are predominantly *santri* or pious Muslims and are spread out in the plantation area in the East Coast. Identity politics in the province does not only revolve around religion and ethnicity but can also be found in particular regions such as the Toba Bataks or the Karo Bataks where identity is tied to the land.

North Sumatra hosts the largest number of eligible voters in the island of Sumatra with 9.8 million people, dwarfing other provinces in the island, including South Sumatra (6.2 million), West Sumatra (3.7 million), and Aceh (3.5 million). Thus, a political win in the province meant a significant step towards securing victory at the national level. North Sumatra is also the economic belt of Sumatra Island, and its high growth rate ensures that the province remains one of the richest in Indonesia.[1] Given all these factors, North Sumatra is certainly a critical province due to its high population and economic output, but also one of the most complex, due to the presence of a heterogeneous mix of ethnicities and religions distributed distinctively within the province – a configuration that is easily galvanised via identity politics.

The existing literature on North Sumatra, and its capital city of Medan, have provided much context on the blatant use of identity politics in the province (Aspinall et al. 2011, Mukin & Damanik 2018, Simandjuntak 2018). Our examination of the region's electoral dynamics in the run up to the 2019 presidential elections re-investigates the role of identity politics to provide a fresh perspective – we argue that it is used by all candidates in the election to determine certain electoral outcomes. While previous discussions focused solely on regional elections alone, this chapter examines both kinds of elections, in this case the 2018 simultaneous regional elections and the 2019 presidential elections.

To a large extent, specific forms of identity politics that were utilised during the regional elections were replicated in the presidential elections for the province. Voters in the East Coast area, consisting mostly of Javanese Muslim immigrants, were roused by the need to vote for pious Muslim candidates. They were thus inclined by preference and design to vote for candidates that promoted conservatism and exclusivity. In the 2018 elections, they voted for the Edy Rahmayadi–Musa Rajekshah pair. Edy was a former military unit commander while Musa was a prominent member of a youth organisation. Rhetoric that verged on emphasising religious identity were utilised during their campaign. Subsequently, in the 2019 presidential election, most voters in the East Coast voted overwhelmingly for the Prabowo–Sandi pair, using a similar strategy that focused on religious identity.[2]

The next section delves into the history of electoral dynamics in North Sumatra, beginning with the province's first direct gubernatorial elections in 2008 until that of the latest simultaneous regional elections of 2018. This will be followed by an overview of the candidates in the 2018 gubernatorial elections and the 2019 presidential elections. The chapter will subsequently discuss the polarising narratives utilised by candidates and political parties both in the 2018 and the 2019 elections. The results of both elections will be further broken down and analysed at the district level in finer detail so as to demonstrate aspects that identity politics and other vitiating factors play. The chapter concludes by looking at the wider implications of identity politics for future elections in North Sumatra and Indonesia.

Historical, demographical, and geographical trends in North Sumatra

The Regional Development Board of North Sumatra had divided the province into four regions in the 1980s: the West Coast Region, the Mountain Region, the East Coast (North) Region, and the East Coast (South) Region (Barlow and Thee 1988). The West Coast region covered 37 per cent of the province's territory, and consisted of districts in Nias, Sibolga, and Central and South Tapanuli. This region was the least developed and only comprised of 18 per cent of North Sumatra's population. The Mountain region consisted of regencies surrounding Lake Toba, including North Tapanuli, Simalungun, Dairi, and Karo, and the Pematang Siantar regencies. Like the West Coast, the Mountain region was also not very well developed in terms of infrastructure. On top of this, this region struggled with issues of deforestation and declining water levels in Lake Toba. Meanwhile, the East Coast regions were the most densely populated – the East Coast (North) alone hosted 42 per cent of the province's population although it only made up 15 per cent of North Sumatra's territory. The regions mainly consisted of Medan – the province's capital, as well as Deli Serdang, Langkat, Binjai, and Tebing Tinggi. This region was the most developed in North Sumatra, with major plantations and developments (Barlow and Thee 1988). It continues to be the case today, with Medan, Deli Serdang, and Langkat ranked as the province's top income generators, significantly dwarfing some other regencies (North Sumatra Statistics Agency 2018).

In terms of community and identity groups, North Sumatra is often divided into the West Coast (which covers the above West Coast and Mountain regions) and the East Coast. This divide goes back decades and was enabled by the flow of migrations from Java to the plantation area in the East Coast. For instance, South Tapanuli, Mandailing, and Angkola (collectively known the Southern Batak) – which lie in the Southern part of North Sumatra but are part of the East Coast cluster due to religious and cultural affinity – are distinguishable from the Toba Batak areas in the West Coast, particularly in the conversion of its population to Islam in the middle of the nineteenth century. Meanwhile, in the West Coast, such as in the North Tapanuli area, the local population had converted to Christianity (Smail 1968). The East Coast of Sumatra was utilised for tobacco, palm oil, and rubber plantations, with Javanese being brought to work in the plantations and contributing to the large Javanese Muslim population in the area. The West Coast area, on the other hand, has a majority Christian Batak community.

Unlike other provinces in Indonesia, no political party had attained significant dominance in North Sumatra. In 2008, North Sumatra held its first direct gubernatorial elections, in which the Syamsul Arifin – Gatot Pujo Nugroho pair gained victory. The pair was supported by a number of Islamic parties, notably the United Development Party (PPP), the Prosperous and Justice Party (PKS), and the Crescent and Star Party (PBB).[3] President Susilo Bambang Yudhoyono (2004–2014) later dismissed Syamsul from his governorship due to a corruption case conviction in 2012.[4] Gatot then replaced Syamsul as governor of North Sumatra. In 2013, Gatot ran as a gubernatorial candidate with Tengku Erry Nurady, a former regent of North Sumatra's Serdang Bedagai (2005–2013), as deputy governor candidate. Gatot and Nurady gained support from PKS and the Hanura Party. He however did not finish his gubernatorial term as he was then convicted of misappropriating social aid funds (*bansos*) in 2016 (Detik 2016).

The North Sumatra gubernatorial elections were held a year after the 2017 Jakarta gubernatorial elections and closely trailed events and politics in Jakarta, particularly the 212 movement.[5] In fact, Jakarta's former deputy governor and deputy governor candidate Djarot Saiful Hidayat ran as a gubernatorial candidate for North Sumatra in 2018, together with Sihar Sitorus, a non-Muslim.[6] Edy Rahmayadi, a former Strategic Reserve Army Command (Kostrad) Commander (2015–2018) and Commander of Bukit Barisan Territorial Command (overseeing the North Sumatra area), won the election. Together with his running mate Musa Rajekshah, a local businessman, the pair was nominated by Gerindra, Hanura, PKS, the National Democrat Party (NasDem), and the National Mandate Party (PAN). The pair also received support from the Indonesian Unity Party (Perindo), PBB, Garuda, Demokrat, and the National Awakening Party.

Identity politics however was not absent from the 2018 North Sumatra regional elections. Deasy Simandjuntak, an expert on North Sumatra politics, noted that identity politics were prevalent in both Muslim-majority districts, which overwhelmingly voted for the all-Muslim pair (Edy and Musa), and Christian-majority districts, which voted for the Djarot and Sihar pair (Simandjuntak 2018). While religion was often utilised, the concept of tying people to their place of birth and region, known colloquially as the 'son of the soil' (*putra daerah*) was also utilised heavily to bring in more votes. These strategies that were employed were intended to challenge Djarot's campaign as he is not a localised Javanese and possessed no significant attachment to the province. His opponent, Edy Rahmayadi, heavily promoted himself as a 'son of the soil' who is proud of his Sumatran and military roots as the former commander of the Bukit Barisan Territorial Command (Mukin & Damanik 2018).

The results of the presidential election in North Sumatra nonetheless derives much less traction from the kind of identity politics that was successfully utilised for the gubernatorial election. Support from Islamic parties was no guarantee that a particular candidate pair would win. While Susilo Bambang Yudhoyono (SBY) had managed to win two consecutive victories in 2004 and 2009 in the province through the strong support of Islamic parties, such a trend had ceased in 2014 when Joko Widodo (Jokowi) won in the province. Jokowi had won on the back of only one Islamic party – the National Awakening Party (PKB). Meanwhile, his opponent, Prabowo Subianto had support from four Islamic parties (PAN, PKS, PPP, and PBB). In contrast to the regional elections, we found that securing the support of Islamic parties contributed little towards ensuring victory in the presidential elections in North Sumatra. This phenomenon will be discussed in greater detail in the following sections on the narratives and results of the 2018 simultaneous regional elections as well as the 2019 presidential elections.

Identity politics in the 2018 regional elections and the 2019 presidential elections

The 2018 North Sumatra regional elections and the 2019 general elections were held in close succession, respectively in June 2018 and April 2019, or about 10 months apart from each other. The campaign for the 2019 elections officially began in September 2019, 3 months after the regional elections were held. The short timeframe had created avenues for competing political parties to employ similar strategies and target similar groupings of people in the two elections, albeit with some modifications. The dynamics, strategies, and identity politics employed in the 2018 and 2019 elections are discussed in the following sections.

The 2018 regional elections: cultivation of identity politics

On 27 June 2018, North Sumatra, along with 16 other provinces, held simultaneous elections to choose the governor and deputy governor for the period of 2018 to 2023 (Prasetia 2017). The candidates consisted of two pairs: Lieutenant General Edy Rahmayadi and Musa Rajekshah; and that of Djarot Saiful Hidayat and Sihar Sitorus. Rahmayadi was formerly the chief of the Army Strategic Command (*Komando Strategis Angkatan Darat*, Kostrad) while Rajekshah is a local businessman who was active in a local youth organisation known as the Pancasila Youth. His opponent, Djarot Saiful Hidayat, was the deputy governor of Jakarta when Basuki Tjahaja Purnama or Ahok was governor; while Sihar Sitorus is the son of a local businessman and politician. All candidates, except for Sihar Sitorus, were Muslims.

At the start of the campaign, J.R. Saragih and Ance Selian – a candidate pair – had also declared their willingness to run. However, the Indonesia Electoral Commission (KPU) decided that they did not qualify as the authenticity of Saragih's education certificates were held in doubt (Hantoro 2018). On the other hand, the Edy Rahmayadi–Musa pair (also known as 'Eramas' or 'golden era' in Indonesian), had a clear advantage in terms of the number of political parties who supported them. As mentioned before, they were endorsed by a coalition of six parties, which held 60 per cent of seats in the North Sumatra Legislative Council (*Dewan Perwakilan Daerah Sumatera Utara*). The pair also received support from the Demokrat Party, which initially supported the Saragih–Selian pair. The Party however switched to supporting the Rahmayadi–Musa pair after Saragih's failure to run in the elections. The Djarot–Sihar pair was only endorsed by two political parties, the Indonesian Democratic Party of Struggle (PDI-P) and the United Development Party (PPP), making up 20 per cent of the North Sumatra Legislative Council (Sasongko 2018). Law No. 10/2016 on Regional Elections require that gubernatorial candidate hopefuls be endorsed by a political party, or a coalition of political parties, which carry at least 20 per cent of the seats at the regional legislative council or a total of 25 per cent of votes in the previous legislative elections (Susilo 2018). This means that the Djarot–Sihar pair only secured the bare minimum of seats to run.

During the campaign period, the Rahmayadi–Musa pair had apparently adopted the use of both religion and regional identity as a strategy. The pair targeted Djarot's outsider status in order to dissuade the local Javanese population from voting for their opponent. This strategy had proven successful in bringing them victory. Apart from his identity as a Muslim with Sumatran origins, Edy Rahmayadi's strong-man image was also linked to his military career. He began his military career in 1985, after graduating from the Indonesian Military Academy, leading various platoons and companies in the Army's Elite Special Forces (Kopassus) and the Army Strategic Command (Kostrad). His career took off in 2014, when he became commander of the 1st Kostrad Infantry Division. In the following year, he returned to Sumatra and became the commander of the Bukit Barisan Military Command. Subsequently, after only a few months in

Bukit Barisan, he was appointed as commander of Kostrad. He then resigned to run for the governor's office (Retaduari 2017). Such a background proved advantageous for Rahmayadi in the electoral race. In addition, serving time at the Bukit Barisan Military Command had helped build up a strong alliance with various Muslim communities. He also supported the building of a local mosque and enjoyed close relations with Muhammadiyah, one of Indonesia's largest Islamic organisations.

Meanwhile, his deputy gubernatorial candidate, Musa Rajeckshah, also known as Ijeck, had a more varied background. He comes from a family of Malay businessmen, known by the name of Hanif Shah. The family enjoyed strong ties with Muhammadiyah through the Haji Hanif Foundation – a foundation owned by Haji Hanif, Ijeck's father. Haji Hanif was also heavily involved in Muhammadiyah mosques and charities throughout North Sumatra, providing a firm network for Edy and Ijek to tap into. They own huge businesses in North Sumatra and had affiliated themselves with a right-wing youth organisation called the Pancasila Youth. Members of the Pancasila Youth are known to be involved in notorious activities like debt collection and for a long time were considered a vigilante group working under former president Suharto (Wagstaff 1999).

Ijeck, however, tried to hide his affiliation with the Pancasila Youth by associating himself with the Indonesian Red Cross (*Palang Merah Indonesia*, PMI) in which he was chairman (Eramas 2018). Djarot's running mate, Sihar Storus, also had unsavoury links. A well-known business mogul, Sihar is Batak Christian and is supported by the Youth Workers Association (Ikatan Pemuda Karya), a rival organisation to the Pancasila Youth. Paired with Djarot, a well-known ex-deputy governor of Jakarta, Sihar did not have the same negative image as that of Ijeck.

The Djarot–Sihar pair had been promoting the subsidised healthcare programme (*Kartu Sehat*) and education programme (*Kartu Pintar*) in their campaigns. They were focused on being pragmatic and technocratic in their campaigns. However, that did not stop the Rahmayadi–Musa pair from utilising identity politics in their campaigns to counter these programmes. These include appeals to Muslim exclusivism in which banners were displayed to remind the general Muslim population not to vote for a non-Muslim. Here, Sihar stood out as he is clearly a non-Muslim. Nonetheless, it had implications for Djarot as well. Djarot was associated with the Ahok campaign and, although Muslim, he is generally seen as a lackey of Ahok, a Chinese Christian who was implicated for blasphemy. Djarot's PDI-P support did not put him in good stead either as the PDI-P is perceived to be a majority non-Muslim party in the province. In 2013, the PDI-P had put forward Effendi Simbolon as a Batak Christian candidate as a gubernatorial candidate against Gatot Pujonegaoro and Tengku Erry Nuradi, two candidates that had openly campaigned along Islamic lines, set the foundation of projecting the PDI-P as an enemy of Islam.

The Djarot–Sihar pair however were also perpetrators of identity politics. While the Rahmayadi–Musa pair targeted the Muslim-majority coastal regions of Langkat, Medan, and Binjai, the Djarot–Sihar pair placed emphasis on North

Tapanuli, which has a majority a Christian population. They tried to consolidate the seven biggest Batak sub-ethnic groups of the Simalungun, Karo, Dairi, and South Tapanuli by appealing to the Christian religion as a unifying factor. To the Batak Christians, Djarot was a welcome presence to the hardline coastal Islamic conservative candidates and was accepted readily by them, even though he was neither Christian or from the province.

Despite largely aligning themselves with Christian voters, Djarot did not cease to neglect the Muslim voter base. He relied on the United Development Party (PPP), an Islamic party with strong ties to the PDI-P, to help secure votes from the Muslim population. The PDI-P had agreed to support PPP's candidate Taj Yasin, son of Kyai Haji Maimun Zubair, as deputy governor in the Central Java gubernatorial election, and this had provided the basis for PPP's support for the Djarot–Sihar pair (Nurita 2018). The support that the PPP had guaranteed however did not translate into actual votes for the pair. PPP strongholds, such as South Tapanuli, Mandailing Natal, and Tanjung Batu, had mostly voted for the Rahmayadi–Musa pair. This demonstrated that voters tended to be swayed less by political parties and more by local religious leaders.

During the 2018 gubernatorial election, the 212 event was an important galvanising factor for the consolidation of the conservative Muslim vote in the province. The KPU and the Election Supervisory Agency (Bawaslu) had noted this phenomenon and had taken measures to discourage the use of identity politics. Most notably, in mid-May 2018 – only a few days before the start of the fasting month (Ramadhan) – Bawaslu issued a letter that banned candidates from taking advantage of the religious month for campaign purposes. Among others, candidates and party machines were banned from holding religious gatherings with campaign messages. Candidates were also banned from distributing prayer booklets with campaign messages and from delivering Ramadhan and Eid greetings in printed and electronic medias throughout the month. However, their efforts had resulted in resentment from conservative Muslims in North Sumatra.[7] Shortly after Bawaslu issued the letter, protests were held in front of their office by the North Sumatra Muslim Alliance – a local branch of Muslim Alliance and an Islamist group linked to the 212 movement. Some members of the group had even entertained the fact that Bawaslu enacted the policy in favour of the Djarot–Sihar pair. In fact, many Islamic clerics felt that the Agency was not objective and was intentionally obstructive.

In the run up to voting day on 27 June 2018, campaigns were heated and religious and ethnic rhetoric were used by both sides to shore up votes. A mass prayer event had been organised and led by Abdul Somad, a North Sumatran celebrity preacher known for his popular YouTube videos, to support the Rahmayadi–Musa pair. This event was attended by other key Islamic figures such as Tengku Zulkarnain, a popular Sumatran preacher, and the former Chief of the Indonesian Military, Gatot Nurmantyo, who was also supporting the Rahmayadi–Musa pair. In many cases, preaching was adamantly political, with the imams utilising religious rhetoric to side with the Rahmayadi–Musa pair who are Muslims.[8] In addition, while Muhammadiyah as a mass organisation was careful not to take sides, in a bid to curb speeches that transgress the line of politics, it had instituted heavy penalties and sanctions for those who crossed the line, including excommunicating preachers from the local Muhammadiyah leadership. Such penalties however did not amount to much as religious congregations were common and people tended to discuss politics outside the mosques in study groups. Galvanised by events in Jakarta, many also contributed to charity and personally campaigned for their favourite candidates. Islamic leaders who opposed the Muhammadiyah rulings had even formed an entirely new association called *Kembang Surya* such that they do not flout the sanctions. In this association, they actively campaigned and promoted the Rahmayadi–Musa pair.

A respected *ustadz* from Java who is based in North Sumatra and a founder of *Kembang Surya*, revealed that the Javanese elites within the province were undecided between which pair of gubernatorial candidates.[9] According to him, the Rahmayadi–Musa pair were solid in terms of Islamic credentials, while the Djarot–Sihar pair had the advantage of having an ethnic Javanese as a candidate. Nonetheless, it seemed that in this case, religious identity trumped that of ethnic identity in terms of preference. There were fears that if Djarot were to get elected as governor, his running mate Sihar, who is Christian, might have a greater chance of running for governor in the next elections. The previous governor of the province, Gatot Pudjonegoro, is Javanese and is currently serving a prison sentence due to corruption. This gave even less credence for voters to vote along ethnic rather than religious lines. This is notwithstanding the fact that the Muslim community in North Sumatra, especially the Javanese, are also very much conservative. Djarot is seen as too 'abangan' or less pious, especially in his last electoral defeat when running with Ahok in Jakarta.

After months of campaigning, around 64.2 per cent of the 9.05 million eligible voters turned up at voting booths throughout the province (Muhardiansyah 2018). This was considered a relatively high participation rate, compared with the 2013 regional election where the participation rate was only 48.5 per cent (Detik 2013). The Rahmayadi–Musa pair emerged as the winner, gaining 57.58 per cent of the vote. On the other hand, the Djarot–Sihar pair gained 42.42 per cent of the vote (*Kompas* 2018). The breakdown of votes at the city and district levels showed a strong correlation between voters' choices and their ethno-religious background. The Djarot–Sihar pair gained significant votes in areas where there was a majority Batak Christian population, including that of the Samosir region, where 95.9 per cent voted for the pair. Other regions that voted overwhelmingly for the pair included Toba Samosir (93.7 per cent) and the Nias Islands (88.2 per cent). The pair also won huge margins in the West Coast districts of North Tapanuli, Central Tapanuli, and Sibolga. Meanwhile, the Rahmayadi–Musa pair managed a landslide win in the East Coast area, including South Tapanuli, Padang Sidempuan, and Mandailing Natal.

In an interview that was conducted with a *Kompas* journalist, it was noted that such a result was expected – that the Rahmayadi–Musa pair would win overwhelmingly in the East Coast.[10] According to her, the people residing on the East Coast tend to be more conservative and Islamic in their political choices. In contrast, the population residing in the West Coast is perceived to be more liberal in thinking, partly because of the migrant culture of the Bataks. She felt that the Djarot–Sihar pair had made a tactical mistake in focusing most of their campaigns on the West Coast Area – an easy win for them – rather than the East Coast. Hendra Harahap, a lecturer at the University of North Sumatra, echoed the journalist's opinion that the Djarot–Sihar pair should have paid more attention to voters from the East Coast.[11] In fact, by concentrating efforts on regions which are a shoo-in, the Djarot–Sihar pair had further isolated themselves from the larger conservative Muslim base. Specifically, the Djarot–Sihar pair had made a mistake by switching from a strategy of campaigning on practical matters of programmatic healthcare and education to participating in the same kind of identity politics akin to their rivals.

Fortunately, the politics of identity did not pervade all regions in the province. According to Rano Hutasoit, a *Metro Siantar* journalist, there were attempts made by groups related to the 212 movement to influence voters to vote for the Rahmayadi–Musa pair but backfired in Pematang Siantar district.[12] According to him, the people of Siantar were dismissive of Jakarta's brand of politics being forced upon their district. Many were already weary of the identity politics being exploited constantly. Siantar's population included an almost a balance mix of Muslims (43.9 per cent) and Christian Protestants and Catholics (51.25 per cent) (Statistics Indonesia 2016). As demonstrated in Table 6.1, in the 2018 regional elections, the Djarot–Sihar pair won 62.3 per cent of the votes. Additionally, during the 2019 elections, the Jokowi–Ma'ruf pair won 73.85 per cent of the votes. This figure demonstrates that some Muslim voters voted for candidate pairs that were portrayed to be more 'moderate'.

The 2019 presidential election: replication of primordial strategy

This section explores the electoral dynamics of the 2018 gubernatorial elections and the 2019 presidential election by mapping voting configuration in the two elections utilising data from Statistics Indonesia (*Badan Pusat Statistik*/BPS) for religious composition and population. Data from the General Elections Committee of Indonesia (*Komisi Pemilihan Umum*/KPU) is also utilised. North Sumatra is a significant province as fierce contestations took place between the Jokowi–Ma'ruf pair and the Prabowo–Sandi pair for the presidential election. Jokowi–Ma'ruf managed to grab 52.32 per cent of total votes while Prabowo–Sandi managed 47.68 per cent. While the margin seemed to indicate a tight race between the two pairs, competition at the sub-district level (municipalities and regencies) showed greater nuance. It was only in the Serdang Bedagai Regency that the vote gap between Jokowi and Prabowo came under 5 per cent (see Table 6.2).

Table 6.1 2019 North Sumatra gubernatorial elections results by city/district

City/district	Vote share (%)		Majority	
	Eramas	Djoss	Religion	Ethnicity
Samosir	4.10	95.90	Christian	Batak Toba
Sibolga	46.50	53.50	Islam	Mandailing
Humbang Hasundutan	6.20	93.80	Christian	Batak Humbang
Toba Samosir	6.30	93.70	Christian	Batak Toba
Karo	15.70	84.30	Christian	Batak Karo
Pakpak Bharat	39	61	Christian	Batak Pakpak
Dairi	18.40	81.60	Christian	Batak Dairi
Simalungun	47.90	52.10	Christian	Batak Simalungun
Pematang Siantar	37.70	62.30	Christian	Batak Simalungun
North Tapanuli	8.70	91.30	Christian	Batak Toba
Central Tapanuli	22.90	77.10	Christian	Batak Toba and Mandailing
Gunung Sitoli (Nias Islands)	17	83	Christian	Nias
Nias (Nias Islands)	11.80	88.20	Christian	Nias
Nias Utara (Nias Islands)	17.80	82.20	Christian	Nias
Nias Barat (Nias Islands)	22.90	77.10	Christian	Nias
Nias Selatan (Nias Islands)	24.30	75.70	Christian	Nias
Medan	60.60	39.40	Islam	Malay–Javanese
South Tapanuli	76.20	23.80	Islam	Angkola and Mandailing
Padang Lawas	83.20	16.80	Islam	Angkola and Mandailing
Tebing Tinggi	70.20	29.80	Islam	Malay
Labuhan Batu	75.70	24.30	Islam	Malay
Labuhan Batu Selatan	68.50	31.50	Islam	Malay
Labuhan Batu Utara	71.60	28.40	Islam	Malay
Deli Serdang	64.20	35.80	Islam	Malay and Batak Karo
Binjai	75.60	24.20	Islam	Malay-Javanese
Padang Lawas Utara	78.30	21.70	Islam	Angkola and Mandailing
Mandailing Natal	89.10	10.90	Islam	Mandailing
Serdang Bedagai	69.50	30.50	Islam	Malay–Javanese
Asahan	75.10	24.90	Islam	Malay
Padang Sidempuan	84.40	15.60	Islam	Angkola dan Mandailing
Langkat	71	29	Islam	Malay
Batu Bara	71.70	28.30	Islam	Malay
Tanjungbalai	80	20	Islam	Malay

Source: Indonesian Electon Commission (KPU).

Other regencies in North Sumatra displayed a huge gap either in the areas that Jokowi won and vice versa. While the Jokowi–Ma'ruf pair won in all Christian-majority sub-districts, they did not fare as well in others. The pair won only in one Muslim-majority city, which was Sibolga. Nonetheless, Sibolga's population was much lower (at 87,000) compared to larger cities like Medan and Deli Serdang with populations of more than 2 million. Not surprisingly, the Prabowo–Sandi pair secured a clean-sweep in Muslim-dominated areas (see Table 6.2).

Rampant use of identity politics by both sides contributed to the polarised results of the presidential elections in North Sumatra. As for the performance of political parties, things were not so straightforward. Table 6.2 shows political

Table 6.2 2019 presidential elections result and 2019 local legislative election winners

City	Vote share (%)		Largest votes in the 2019 Local Legislative Elections
	Jokowi–Ma'ruf	Prabowo–Sandi	
Samosir	98.07	1.93	PDIP
Sibolga	58.89	41.11	Nasdem
Humbang Hasundutan	95.49	4.51	PDIP
Toba Samosir	95.79	4.21	Golkar
Karo	92.08	7.92	PDIP
Pakpak Bharat	68.83	31.17	Demokrat
Dairi	89.53	10.47	Golkar
Simalungun	68.13	31.87	Golkar
Pematang Siantar	73.85	26.15	PDIP
Tapanuli Utara	94.08	5.92	PDIP
Tapanuli Tengah	75.21	24.79	Nasdem
Gunung Sitoli (Nias Islands)	85.40	14.60	PDIP
Nias (Nias Islands)	92.53	7.46	Demokrat
Nias Utara (Nias Islands)	87.16	12.84	Golkar
Nias Barat (Nias Islands)	93.34	6.66	PDIP
Nias Selatan (Nias Islands)	93.86	6.14	PDIP
Medan	45.66	54.34	PDIP
Tapanuli Selatan	37.33	62.67	Gerindra
Padang Lawas	11.61	78.39	Golkar
Tebing Tinggi	44.22	55.78	Golkar
Labuhan Batu	34.65	65.35	Golkar
Labuhan Batu Selatan	41.39	58.61	PAN
Labuhan Batu Utara	41.86	58.14	Golkar
Deli Serdang	45.76	54.24	Gerindra
Binjai	35.88	64.12	Golkar
Padang Lawas Utara	29.15	70.85	Golkar
Mandailing Natal	17.53	82.47	Gerindra
Serdang Bedagai	48.19	51.81	Gerindra
Asahan	39.98	60.02	Gerindra
Padang Sidempuan	21.44	78.56	Golkar
Langkat	41.93	58.07	Golkar
Batu Bara	42.60	57.40	PDIP
Tanjungbalai	37.85	72.15	Golkar

Source: Indonesian Election Commission (KPU).

parties wins in the local legislative elections in the various cities and regencies. The Jokowi–Ma'ruf pair of coalition parties won in most of the cities where incumbent candidates gained victory, except for Pakpak Bharat and Nias regencies in which the Democrat Party, officially part of the Prabowo–Sandi pair camp, secured the largest amount of votes.

Interestingly, coalitions under the Prabowo–Sandi pair only gained the largest vote in the local legislative elections in 6 out of 17 cities where the pair had won. The PDI-P, the main supporting party of Jokowi, even managed to win Medan and Batu Bara. According to Deasy Simandjuntak, this is due to the fact that candidates only campaigned for themselves even though they may be affiliated with either presidential candidate pair.[13] This would have, in reality, minimised whatever coattail effect[14] it may have on certain political parties. North Sumatra's Eastern and Western coastal regions split between Muslim-majority and Christian-majority certainly had an effect.[15]

Another thought-provoking element is the result of the 2018 gubernatorial elections at the city and regency level. The patterns mirrored the 2019 presidential elections in terms of the electoral configuration at the national level. A member of the Democrat Party's 2018 Regional Elections Campaign Team (*Tim Pemenangan Pilkada 2018*) revealed in an interview with the authors that political parties used their experiences with the 2018 regional elections as a gauge for 2019.[16] This partly explains why Djarot was fielded as a PDI-P candidate in North Sumatra after having failed in his run as deputy governor candidate in Jakarta in 2018.

Having the fourth-largest population in Indonesia, which is diverse both ethnically and culturally, North Sumatra province is seen by many as a crucial province to capture for the 2019 presidential elections. The decision to field Djarot as a gubernatorial candidate in North Sumatra may seem like a tactical mistake – Djarot was formerly a regent from Blitar and had no connections to North Sumatra. Closer examination of the tactics of the PDI-P however revealed that the party had relied too much on Jokowi's success in Jakarta as a template for Djarot while neglecting the unique political configuration of North Sumatra.

Djarot's identity as Javanese had an enormous part to play in why he was fielded in the province as well. The Javanese is the second-largest ethnicity (33.4 per cent) in North Sumatra after the Batak (44.8 per cent) (Ananta et al. 2015) while the PDI-P is one of the largest parties in North Sumatra, especially in the West Coast region which has a Batak Christian majority.[17] Both Jokowi and Djarot had also worked with Ahok in the gubernatorial race in 2017 and 2014 respectively and many Bataks in Jakarta, particularly the Batak Tapanuli ethnic group, had voted for the Ahok–Djarot pair in the 2017 Jakarta gubernatorial elections (Khadafi 2017).

Nonetheless, Djarot's close association with Ahok proved to be a liability in North Sumatra, especially after Ahok was sentenced to jail for blasphemy. Despite the loss, Djarot's entry into North Sumatran politics was seen as a yardstick for the eventual electoral performance of the presidential candidate pair of Jokowi and Ma'ruf, under the auspices of PDI-P.[18]

This was due to the fact that the political landscape and configuration of North Sumatra, being quite distinct from that of Jakarta in terms of the distribution of Muslim-majority and Christian-majority regions, proved to be the main reason for the loss of the Jokowi–Ma'ruf pair and a win for the Prabowo–Sandi pair (see Table 6.2). The Christian-majority regions had overwhelmingly voted for Jokowi, like how they voted for Djarot and the opposite took place for the Prabowo–Sandi pair.

While the Jokowi–Ma'ruf pair did not end up winning the province, its vote share was larger than that of the Djarot–Sihar pair. One of the main reasons for this was a significant increase in voters' participation. The Indonesian Election Commission noted a total of 73.24 per cent participation in the 2018 gubernatorial elections for North Sumatra. The percentage of voter participation actually increased to 79.91 per cent for the 2019 presidential elections. In addition, the number of registered voters had also increased from 9.05 to 9.8 million.[19] Ma'ruf Amin's background as a respected conservative Nahdlatul Ulama (NU) cleric was also important and probably had an impact on the conservative Islamic vote in the province.[20]

The above discussion had demonstrated similarities and nuances between the 2018 gubernatorial elections and that of the 2019 presidential elections for North Sumatra. The results of the 2018 gubernatorial elections were seen as a barometer to gauge the electability of the presidential candidate pairs in 2019. Although Jokowi managed to eventually secure a victory in the province, his voter base had dropped from 55.24 per cent in 2014 to 52.32 per cent in 2019. Second, Islamic political parties had less of an influence when it came to national-level politics in the province. Lastly, the loss of the Gerindra Party in areas where Prabowo won showed that the coattail effect did not always work. Political parties might decide to dissociate from a particular candidate if the party determines that the candidate is a liability to its electoral interest.

Conclusion

The 2018 North Sumatra gubernatorial election and the 2019 simultaneous elections demonstrated the significance of identity politics in explaining voters' preference in the province. While religious rhetoric was employed to galvanise votes gained from the momentum of the 212 movement in Jakarta, these were not the only strategies that were adopted. A lot also rested on the unique ethnic configuration of the province, especially the cleavages between Muslim-majority and Christian-majority areas, which allowed for a 'son of the soil' kind of rhetoric to emerge. Both Djarot and Jokowi secured a high margin of votes in Christian-dominated areas. Candidates running under the PDI-P banner won in only one majority Muslim region, Sibolga, which is less populated than bigger cities like Medan. On the other hand, the Prabowo–Sandi pair was victorious in Muslim-majority cities and regencies. This was reflective of the victory of the Rahmayadi–Musa pair who won the gubernatorial election in 2018. Although Djarot and Jokowi are both ethnically Javanese, this was not a crucial vitiating factor in bringing in votes for the province.

Table 6.3 Comparison between 2018 gubernatorial elections and 2019 presidential elections

City	Largest religion	2018 North Sumatra Gubernatorial Elections		2019 Presidential Elections	
		Djarot–Sihar (%)	Eddy–Musa (%)	Jokowi–Ma'aruf (%)	Prabowo–Sandi (%)
Samosir	Christian	95.90	4.10	98.07	1.93
Sibolga	Islam	53.50	46.50	58.89	41.11
Humbang Hasundutan	Christian	93.80	6.20	95.49	4.51
Toba Samosir	Christian	93.70	6.30	95.79	4.21
Karo	Christian	84.30	15.70	92.08	7.92
Pakpak Bharat	Christian	61	39	68.83	31.17
Dairi	Christian	81.60	18.40	89.53	10.47
Simalungun	Christian	52.10	47.90	68.13	31.87
Pematang Siantar	Christian	62.30	37.70	73.85	26.15
Tapanuli Utara	Christian	91.30	8.70	94.08	5.92
Tapanuli Tengah	Christian	77.10	22.90	75.21	24.79
Gunung Sitoli (Nias Islands)	Christian	83	17	85.40	14.60
Nias (Nias Islands)	Christian	88.20	11.80	92.53	7.46
Nias Utara (Nias Islands)	Christian	82.20	17.80	87.16	12.84
Nias Barat (Nias Islands)	Christian	77.10	22.90	93.34	6.66
Nias Selatan (Nias Islands)	Christian	75.70	24.30	93.86	6.14
Medan	Islam	39.40	60.60	45.66	54.34
Tapanuli Selatan	Islam	23.80	76.20	37.33	62.67
Padang Lawas	Islam	16.80	83.20	11.61	78.39
Tebing Tinggi	Islam	29.80	70.20	44.22	55.78
Labuhan Batu	Islam	24.30	75.70	34.65	65.35
Labuhan Batu Selatan	Islam	31.50	68.50	41.39	58.61
Labuhan Batu Utara	Islam	28.40	71.60	41.86	58.14
Deli Serdang	Islam	35.80	64.20	45.76	54.24
Binjai	Islam	24.20	75.60	35.88	64.12

Continued

Table 6.3 continued

City	Largest religion	2018 North Sumatra Gubernatorial Elections		2019 Presidential Elections	
		Djarot–Sihar (%)	Eddy–Musa (%)	Jokowi–Ma'aruf (%)	Prabowo–Sandi (%)
Padang Lawas Utara	Islam	21.70	78.30	29.15	70.85
Mandailing Natal	Islam	10.90	89.10	17.53	82.47
Serdang Bedagai	Islam	30.50	69.50	48.19	51.81
Asahan	Islam	24.90	75.10	40	60
Padang Sidempuan	Islam	15.60	84.40	21.44	78.56
Langkat	Islam	29	71	41.93	58.07
Batu Bara	Islam	28.30	71.70	42.60	57.40
Tanjungbalai	Islam	20	80	37.85	72.15

Source: Indonesian Statistical Agency (BPS) and Indonesian Election Commission (KPU).

For the case of North Sumatra, identity politics had been the norm. This had led to a greater polarisation among the electorate. A better approach would be to campaign on the basis of practical issues such as that of healthcare, economy, and education. In addition, we observed that legislative candidates in the East Coast area opted to campaign for themselves and avoided promoting and using Jokowi as they were afraid it would jeopardise their credentials. Here we can see that the attack that targeted Jokowi's Islamic credentials showed that campaigning under the president would be a liability, thus decreasing their chances of being elected. However, further research, possibly through in-depth interviews with parliamentarians and local party members, is required to explain such a phenomenon. We can also use this circumstance as a case study to examine the impacts of the coattail effect theory in the study of Indonesian politics.

Notes

1 North Sumatra gained the highest economic growth (5.22 per cent) among other provinces in Sumatra in 2019.
2 Encouraging people to vote only based on religious considerations and attacking religious credentials of other candidates are the most common methods of primordial sentiments utilisation in electoral campaign.
3 Gatot is PKS cadre and held PKS' regional representative office.
4 The court found Syamsul guilty of corrupting Langkat Regency's regional budget (APBD) when he was a regent there (1999–2008). See Detik (2012).
5 The 212 event was a rally held on 2 December 2016 (hence the numerical '212' tag), where thousands of people rallied to central Jakarta to demand the ousting of then Jakarta governor Basuki 'Ahok' Tjahaja Purnama for allegedly insulting Islam. The protestors mainly consisted of Salafi modernist and conservative traditionalist Muslim networks. Some of them, usually referred as the '212 alumni', remain active in highlighting practices and activities that they perceive as 'anti-Islam', and publicly protest against them.
6 Djarot was Jakarta's deputy governor (2014–2017) and Ahok's running mate. The smear campaign targeted Ahok, a Chinese descendant and non-Muslim.
7 There was a widespread speculation that Bawaslu leadership was biased. Some speculated that the head of Bawaslu in Medan, who was the son of Jumiran Abri, a senior member of PDI-P in North Sumatra, was determined to curb support for the Eramas pair.
8 Interview with a Lecturer at Faculty of Islamic Studies, Muhammadiyah University North Sumatra (Medan, 28 June 2018).
9 Interview with a former regional leader of Muhammadiyah in North Sumatra, who was also the spearhead of Kembang Surya (Medan, 27 June 2018).
10 Interview with a *Kompas* journalist (Medan, 28 June 2018).
11 Interview with Hendra Harahap, Lecturer, University of North Sumatra (Medan, 19 June 2018).
12 Interview with Rano Hutasoit, Journalist, Metro Siantar (Medan, 22 June 2018).
13 Authors' interview with Deasy Simandjuntak, Associate Fellow at The Institute of South East Asian Studies – Yushof Ishak Institute, Singapore, 8 January 2020.
14 Coattail effect refers to the impact of a particular presidential candidate to his party when winning (Crockett, 2003).
15 Authors' interview with Deasy Simandjuntak (8 January 2020). Many of citizens in those Muslim-majority cities have resentment towards PDI-P as the party is perceived as a non-Muslim party. This circumstance can be a venue for study on the coattail

effect in presidential elections, particularly through survey methodology. While Jokowi's positive coattail effect seemed working in the non-Muslim regions, there was little indication of the reverse impact to PDI-P in the Muslim-dominated areas.

16 Authors' interview with a member of Democrat Party's 2018 Regional Elections Campaign Team (Tim Pemenangan Pilkada 2018), Jakarta, 1 November 2019.

17 Authors' interview with Deasy Simandjuntak (8 January 2020).

18 However, the Eramas pair and Prabowo did not pursue the same experiment, though they also realised the importance of winning in North Sumatra to create a foothold to win the national elections.

19 For the 2019 elections, the KPU initially acknowledged 9.4 million voters. Later the number was revised into 9.8 million. See KPU.go.id and Jawa Pos 2018.

20 Authors' interview with Deasy Simandjuntak (8 January 2020).

Bibliography

Ananta, A., E.N. Arifin, M.S. Hasbullah, N.B. Handayani, & W. Pramono. 2015. *Demography of Indonesia's Ethnicity.* Singapore: ISEAS.

Aspinall, E., S. Dettman & E. Waburton. 2011. 'When Religion Trumps Ethnicity: A Regional Election Case Study from Indonesia', *South East Asia Research*, Vol. 19 (1): 27–58.

Barlow, C. & K.W. Thee. 1988. *The North Sumatran Regional Economy: Growth with Unbalanced Development.* Singapore: Institute of Southeast Asian Studies.

Crockett, D.A. 2003. 'Samson Unbound: Opposition Presidents and the Failure of Party Leadership', *The Social Science Journal*, Vol. 40 (3): 371–383.

Detik. 2012, 1 November. 'Korupsi, Syamsul Arifin Resmi Dicopot Sebagai Gubernur Sumut' [North Sumatra's Governor Syamsul Arifin Sacked for Corruption Charges']. Retrieved 1 January 2020, from Detik: https://news.detik.com/berita/2079184/korupsi-syamsul-arifin-resmi-dicopot-sebagai-gubernur-sumut.

Detik. 2013, 15 March. 'Tingkat Golput dalam Pilgub Sumut Lebih dari 50 Persen' [Voter Turnout in North Sumatra Gubernatorial Election Less Than 50 Percent']. *Detik News.* Retrieved from https://news.detik.com/berita/d-2195547/tingkat-golput-dalam-pilgub-sumut-lebih-dari-50-persen.

Detik. 2016, 24 November. 'Korupsi Dana Bansos, Gatot Pujo Divonis 6 Tahun Penjara' [Gatot Pujo Sentenced to 6-year Imprisonment for Corrupting Social Aid Fund]. Retrieved 3 January 2020, from Detik: https://news.detik.com/berita/d-3353772[/korupsi-dana-bansos-gatot-pujo-divonis-6-tahun-penjara.

Eramas. 2018. 'Profil Musa Rajekshah' [Musa Rajekshah's Profile]. Retrieved from https://eramas.id/musa-rajekshah-ijeck/profil-musa-rajekshah/

Hantoro, J. 2018, 19 March. 'Mengurai Kasus Dokumen Palsu JR Saragih' [JR Saragih's Forged Documents Explained]. Retrieved from https://fokus.tempo.co/read/1070930/mengurai-kasus-dokumen-palsu-jr-saragih.

Jawa Pos. 2018, 14 November. 'DPT Meningkat, KPU Sumut Yakin Partisipasi Pemilih Tembus 77,5 Persen' [North Sumatra KPU Confident Voter Turnout to Reach 77.5 percent as Number in Final Voters List Increased]. Retrieved 10 January 2020, from JawaPos: www.jawapos.com/nasional/pemilihan/14/11/2018/dpt-meningkat-kpu-sumut-yakin-partisipasi-pemilih-tembus-775-persen/.

Kompas.com. 2018, 11 July. 'Infografik: Peta Kemenangan Pilkada Sumatera Utara 2018' [Infographic: Map of Election Results of 2018 North Sumatra Regional Election], *Kompas.* Retrieved from https://nasional.kompas.com/read/2018/07/11/16345571/infografik-peta-kemenangan-pilkada-sumatera-utara-2018.

Khadafi, A. 2017, 20 April. 'Faktor Agama Menentukan Kemenangan Anies-Sandiaga' [Religious Factors Determine Anies-Sandiaga's Victory]. Retrieved 9 January 2020, from Tirto: https://tirto.id/faktor-agama-menentukan-kemenangan-anies-sandiaga-cm79.

Muhardiansyah, Y. 2018, 9 July. 'Partisipasi pemilih di Sumut melonjak, KPU klaim sosialisasi berhasil' [Voter Turnout in North Sumatra Surged, KPU Claimed Socialization Worked], *Merdeka*. Retrieved from www.merdeka.com/politik/partisipasi-pemilih-di-sumut-melonjak-kpu-klaim-sosialisasi-berhasil.html.

Mukin, B.A., & M.R. Damanik. 2018. 'Demografi Politik Sumatera Utara: Analisis Pilihan Politik Masyarakat Berdasarkan Persebaran Penduduk, Agama dan Etnis Dalam Pemilihan Gubernur Sumatera Utara Tahun 2018 di Kota Medan' [Demographics of Politics in North Sumatra: Analysis of People's Political Preferences based on Population Distribution, Religion and Ethnicity in the 2018 North Sumatra Regional Election in Medan]. *Jurnal Geografi*, Vol. 10 (2): 129–144.

North Sumatra Statistics Agency. 2018. 'Anggaran Pendapatan Asli Daerah Kabupaten/Kota Menurut Jenis Pendapatan' [Revenue Budget of Regency/City Based on Type of Revenue]. Retrieved from https://sumut.bps.go.id/statictable/2020/01/29/1629/anggaran-pendapatan-asli-daerah-kabupaten-kota-menurut-jenis-pendapatan-ribu-rupiah-2018.html.

Nurita, D. 2018, 10 January. 'PPP: Ada Barter Politik dengan PDIP di Pilgub Sumut dan Jateng' [PPP: Political Trade-Offs Took Place with PDIP in Regional Elections in North Sumatra and Central Java], *Tempo*. Retrieved from https://nasional.tempo.co/read/1049238/ppp-ada-barter-politik-dengan-pdip-di-pilgub-sumut-dan-jateng.

Prasetia, A. 2017, 20 April. 'Ini 171 Daerah yang Gelar Pilkada Serentak 27 Juni 2018' [List of 171 Regions Holding Simultaneous Regional Elections on 27 June 2018], *Detik*. Retrieved from https://news.detik.com/berita/d-3479819/ini-171-daerah-yang-gelar-pilkada-serentak-27-juni-2018.

Retaduari, E.A. 2017, 5 December. 'Pangkostrad Letjen Edy Rahmayadi Mundur dari TNI', *Detik News*. Retrieved from https://news.detik.com/berita/d-3756451/pangkostrad-letjen-edy-rahmayadi-mundur-dari-tni.

Sasongko, J.P. 2018, 10 January. 'PPP Sepakat Koalisi PDIP Dukung Djarot-Sihar di Pilkada Sumut' [PPP Agrees to Join PDIP's Coalition to Support Djarot-Sihar in North Sumatra Regional Election], *CNN Indonesia*. Retrieved from www.cnnindonesia.com/nasional/20180110120356-32-267854/ppp-sepakat-koalisi-pdip-dukung-djarot-sihar-di-pilkada-sumut.

Simandjuntak, D. 2018, 1 October. 'North Sumatra's 2018 Election: Identity Politics Ruled the Day', *ISEAS Perspective*, Issue: 2018 (60): 1. Retrieved from www.iseas.edu.sg/images/pdf/ISEAS_Perspective_2018_60@50.pdf.

Smail, J.R.W. 1968. 'The Military Politics of North Sumatra: December 1956–October 1957', *Indonesia*, Vol. 6 (October): 128–187.

Statistics Indonesia. 2010. 'Penduduk Menutut Kelompok Umur dan Agama yang Dianut, Kota Pematang Siantar (Population Based on Age Group and Religion, Pematang Siantar).' Retrieved from https://sp2010.bps.go.id/index.php/site/tabel?tid=320&wid=1273000000

Susilo, M. 2018, 12 January. 'Ada 13 calon tunggal di Pilkada 2018, mengapa dan bagaimana jika kolom kosong menang?' [What Would Happen If 'Empty Column' Wins Against 13 Sole Candidates in 2018 Regional Elections], *BBC Indonesia*. Retrieved from www.bbc.com/indonesia/indonesia-42647891.

Wagstaff, J. 1999, 25 May. 'Indonesian Youth Group Seeks To Shed Its Bad-Boy Reputation', *The Wall Street Journal*. Retrieved from www.wsj.com/articles/SB927576795912883254.

7 West Sumatra in the 2019 general election

The past in shaping the region's identity

Adri Wanto and Leonard C. Sebastian

Introduction

On 17 April 2019, up to 193 million Indonesians voted for a president, vice president, and legislatures across the country. For the first time in Indonesia's history, the presidential and parliamentary elections were held on the same day. There were 809,500 polling stations, which were run by around 6 million temporary election workers. Each polling station catered for 200 to 300 voters. Indonesian voters chose from more than 250,000 candidates for 20,538 legislative seats at five levels of government over a period of just 6 hours across hundreds of islands in the country. The people were presented with five different ballot papers: grey for the president and vice president, yellow for the People's Representative Council (DPR), red for the Regional Representative Council (DPD), blue for the relevant provincial legislature (DPRD *provinsi)* and green for the relevant district or municipal legislature (DPRD–*kabupaten* or *kota*). An Australian think-tank – the Lowy Institute – called it 'one of the most complicated single-day elections in global history'.[1]

For the presidential race, essentially, the 2019 election was a rematch between two political rivals. In the bitterly divisive 2014 presidential election, Jokowi defeated his challenger Prabowo by a margin of 6 per cent. Meanwhile, in the 2019 election, Jokowi defeated Prabowo by 5 per cent. The coalitions behind both presidential candidates were broadly similar to the 2014 presidential election. Jokowi and Ma'ruf were supported by nine parties, representing about 60 per cent of the seats in the national legislature (DPR), while Prabowo and his partner, former Jakarta deputy governor Sandiaga Uno, were supported by five political parties.

Jokowi came from humble beginnings but is a new political phenomenon in Indonesia. His popularity has been meteoric since his emergence as the successful mayor of Solo. He rose to national prominence as a political figure by winning the Jakarta gubernatorial election in 2012. During the 2014 presidential election, Jokowi campaigned on a 'man of the people' and an anti-corruption platform, promising to tackle poverty and to stamp out nepotism and intolerance. Under his leadership the economy has grown steadily, the poverty rate has fallen, and some key infrastructure projects have been finalised including a much-needed mass rapid transit network in the capital, Jakarta.

Representing the opposition, Prabowo teamed up with Sandiaga Uno, a wealthy former investment banker who was briefly deputy governor of Jakarta. Prabowo is closely associated with the traditional political elite. He is the son of Soemitro Djojohadikoesoemo, one of the leaders of the 1957–1958 PRRI/Permesta rebellion during which disgruntled leaders in several provinces in Sumatra and Sulawesi formed a revolutionary republic to challenge central government rule during the Sukarno era. He was previously married to the daughter of former dictator, General Suharto, who ruled Indonesia with an iron fist for three decades. Prabowo has been dogged by allegations of being complicit in human rights abuses committed during the Suharto era, though he has maintained his innocence. Having spent many years overseas, he made his political comeback in 2009. In the 2014 presidential election he campaigned on an anti-poverty platform, saying he wanted to reduce unemployment and create new jobs.

On 21 May 2019, the Indonesian Election Commission (KPU) announced incumbent president Jokowi as the winner of the 2019 presidential election. Jokowi won in 21 of 34 provinces while Prabowo won 13 provinces, most of which were in Sumatra. Java and Sumatra are the two islands with the largest population in Indonesia. These two islands were the key to winning the electoral battle since the number of votes from these two islands comprises 78 per cent of the total votes.

Much of Jokowi's support was gathered from Central and East Java provinces where he also won a significant margin in 2014. In addition, he also won a plurality of votes in provinces with a significant number of non-Muslim voters, including North Sumatra, West Kalimantan, North Sulawesi, Bali, East Nusa Tenggara, Papua, and West Papua. Meanwhile, Prabowo won in provinces viewed by observers of having a tendency towards growing Islamism over the past decade.[2] The provinces where Prabowo won in 2019 include West Java, Aceh, Banten, West Sumatra, South Sumatra, South Kalimantan, and South Sulawesi. A significant number of his supporters are members of religiously observant and conservative groups. Many of them participated in the Defending Islam Movement (also known as '212') against Basuki Tjahaja Purnama, the former governor of Jakarta, in 2016 and 2017.

Some scholars have argued that the 2019 general election brought about a greater polarisation of Indonesian society based on religious and ethnic cleavages.[3] The argument is based upon the fact that the election was perceived one-dimensionally as a contestation between the Javanese heartland and Eastern Indonesia's minority enclaves who supported Jokowi versus the religiously conservative province of West Java and the Muslim-dominated islands of Sumatra, Sulawesi and Kalimantan who supported Prabowo.[4]

This argument is supported by the lowest and the highest vote share for Jokowi–Amin (JA) in 2019 versus Jokowi–Kalla (JK) in 2014, as seen among the various provinces. In the 2019 presidential election, the result indicates a growing evidence of a hardening religious cleavage across the country. In the province of Aceh, a Muslim-majority population, Jokowi gained only 14.41 per cent of the votes. Meanwhile, in the predominantly Hindu province of Bali,

Jokowi gained some 92 per cent of the votes. For some scholars, this trend pointed to an increasingly polarised Indonesian society based on religion, where Prabowo's campaign appealed to Muslims and Jokowi's to non-Muslims.[5] A similar pattern was also discernible in other largely Christian provinces such as East Nusa Tenggara and North Sulawesi.

Although it is logical to make the argument that religion was a prominent factor as political preference in the 2019 presidential election[6] – a claim made by Aspinall and others – this argument has to be examined closely, by taking into account facts from Indonesia's historical past.[7] Prabowo Subianto won significant votes in the provinces that rebelled against the Sukarno regime from 1945 to 1965, like Aceh, Riau, South Kalimantan, West Sumatra, West Java, and North Sulawesi. Meanwhile Jokowi won in the provinces with a strong nationalist base. Against this backdrop, our chapter aims to examine the role of religious factors in the 2019 election weighing it against Indonesia's historical political events from 1945 to 1965.

The research questions to be addressed are: Can religious factors explain this polarisation of voter behaviour in Indonesia or are there other variables that need to be investigated explaining the causes behind Jokowi's defeat in the Muslim-majority provinces of the outer islands? If the religious factor was truly a prominent political preference during 2019 presidential election, then Jokowi's decision to choose Kyai Ma'ruf Amin – a prominent Muslim scholar – as his vice-presidential candidate works against such a logic as Ma'ruf was virtually ineffective when it comes to garnering support from the predominantly Islamic province of West Sumatra and other outer island provinces. Is it a mere coincidence that Prabowo Subianto won overwhelmingly in provinces that rebelled against the Sukarno regime, while Jokowi won convincingly in the nationalist-based provinces?

To answer these questions, the research will focus on West Sumatra as a case study. The province of West Sumatra, the home of the Minangkabau ethnic group, was selected because it was considered a province that had the lowest number of votes for Jokowi in both the 2014 and 2019 Indonesian presidential elections. Similarly, West Sumatra was a province where voter preferences in the 2019 election did not experience a significant change compared to the election results in 2014. Most importantly, West Sumatra is the birthplace of the PRRI–Pemesta rebellion during the era of Sukarno.

Although Jokowi won in provinces with a significant number of non-Muslim voters and Prabowo won in the majority Muslim provinces, it is premature to assume that the politicisation of religion is the only factor that brought about the polarisation of Indonesian Muslims in the 2019 presidential election. Based on our research in the province of West Sumatra, we conclude that the role of historical narratives, ethnicity, and religion in the identity formation of the West Sumatran people influenced people's perception of the presidential candidates during the 2014 and 2019 general elections.

The data for this study are primarily based on fieldwork conducted from November 2018 to January 2019. When obtaining information related to this topic, in-depth interviews were conducted with cadres and political party elites at the provincial and regional level, religious organisations, local leaders, and scholars in West Sumatera Province.

Indonesia's democracy at a crossroads

Viewed from the perspective of procedural democracy,[8] since the collapse of Suharto's regime, Indonesia has undergone a massive transformation, especially with regard to its political structure. For instance, elected officials such as the president, governors, regents (*bupati*), and mayors are restricted to only two terms in office. The party system of Indonesia has also experienced significant changes. The three-party system that was dominated by Golkar (Golongan Karya, also known as Functional Groups) for almost 26 years had been replaced by a multi-party system. In the 1999 general election, Indonesia witnessed the emergence of new political parties. Forty-eight new political parties[9] campaigned during the first free and fair democratic election since 1955. In the 2004, 2009, and 2014 general elections, 24, 38, and 12 political parties competed respectively.[10] During the 2019 general elections, 16 political parties competed.

In contrast to the pre-Jokowi narrative of Indonesia as a successful case study of democratisation, the Economist Intelligence Unit's (EIU) recently released an annual democracy index downgrading Indonesia's democracy since scoring began in 2006. The 2019 index places Indonesia in 64th position out of a total of 167 countries with a score of 6.48. According to the index, Indonesia is now plunging downwards towards the bottom of the index's category of 'flawed democracies'.[11] Some analysts have argued that political Islam had played an increasingly pervasive role, threatening Indonesia's democracy.

In today's Indonesia, loyalty to religiously and ethnically based politics is still very high. For many Indonesian Muslims, voting for a pious Muslim candidate in the 2014 and 2019 presidential elections was important. Many Muslims believe that religion serves an important factor for the election. Hence, many Indonesians vote for their presidents, provincial and local chief executives, and parliamentary representatives based on their perception of a candidates' religiosity and ethnic background. In the case of West Sumatra, this situation was aggravated by the painful historical narrative of oppression during the post-independence period that continues to haunt the memories of the local population. To a certain extent, this historical narrative has become a prominent factor in the identity formation of the Minangkabau people.

In 1956, Indonesia's first president, Sukarno, was faced with a major challenge from several regional commanders well on their way to becoming warlords who demanded autonomy for their respective regions. After mediation failed, Sukarno removed the dissident commanders from their positions. As a consequence, in 1958, elements of the Indonesian military rebelled against the rule of president Sukarno. In February 1958, dissident military commanders in Central Sumatra (Colonel Ahmad Hussein) and North Sulawesi (Colonel Ventje Sumual) established the Revolutionary Government of the Republic of Indonesia

(PRRI)–Permesta Movement, which was aimed at overthrowing the Sukarno regime.[12] They were joined by many civilian politicians from the Masyumi Party, like Muhammad Natsir, a prominent Minangkabau political figure.[13]

By 1960, the PRRI–Permesta rebellions were successfully repulsed by the Indonesian Armed Forces (TNI) and all of its leaders were arrested and imprisoned. Following the collapse of the Sukarno regime, the New Order imposed a repressive military order that curbed civic freedoms. During his reign from 1966 to 1998, Suharto managed to supress all forms of alternative political identities, especially those that are based on religion. However, the Reform Order that came into being in 1998 created the opportunity for all ideologies to promote their ideas and the ideological cleavages once suppressed during the Suharto era emerged once again. Ironically, it aided in returning the country back to its polarised state again, similar to the era from 1945 to 1965.

The issue of religion became prominent once again during the campaign for the 2014 and 2019 presidential elections. Identity politics, particularly religious-based ones, had gradually become prominent in Indonesian elections since 1999. The politicisation of religion had created the assumption that one candidate pair represented Islamic political interests better than the other. In addition to the religious factor, we argue that the polarisation of Indonesian society in the 2014 and 2019 elections is a continuation of the '*aliran* politics' (*politik aliran*) that was prevalent from 1945 to 1965, before the arrival of Suharto's New Order regime.

Jokowi, who had previously faced protests from hardline Islamic groups during the 2016/2017 Defending Islam rallies, then opted to ban Hizb ut-Tahrir – a pan-Islamist political organisation that believes Muslims should unite to form a global caliphate. This further concretised the perception that he was anti-Islam. Soon after, numerous Islamic groups, especially from conservative and hardline camps, gave their support to Prabowo Subianto. While secular in his personal lifestyle and orientation, Prabowo nevertheless panders to Islamist sentiments. To counter accusations of being anti-Islam, Jokowi chose a traditional Muslim cleric, Ma'ruf Amin, as his running mate. However, this strategy did not increase the number of votes for Jokowi.

Mirroring a trend in predominately conservative Muslim provinces, and confirmed in the election results, the Joko Widodo–Ma'ruf Amin pair lost to the Prabowo Subianto–Sandiaga Uno pair in Sumatra. Meanwhile, in non-majority Muslim provinces like North Sumatra, Jokowi won by a small margin. Prabowo won 85.59 per cent in Aceh, 85.91 per cent in West Sumatra, 61.27 per cent in Riau, 62.21 per cent in Jambi, 58.32 per cent in Bengkulu, and 50.11 per cent in South Sumatra. Meanwhile, Jokowi won 52.32 per cent in North Sumatra (non-majority Muslim province) and 59.34 per cent of the vote in Lampung where many are immigrants from Java. In the Riau Islands, where Indonesian Chinese and Javanese populations are high, Jokowi won 54.19 per cent. Jokowi also won 63.23 per cent in Bangka Belitung, which has a similar demographic background to that of the Riau Islands. The 2014 and 2019 presidential election results show that the election process has intensified into latent conflict between groups associated by religion and ethnicity. This polarising trend is not an exception to Indonesia. Research shows that newly democratic countries – especially those with plural and divided societies – are always prone to the intensification of identity-based politics and conflicts.[14]

The case of West Sumatra

Following the fall of the Suharto regime, the PDI-P was increasingly seen in unfavourable terms in West Sumatra. In the 1999 elections, although the PDI-P gained majority seats in parliament, it won a mere two national legislative seats in West Sumatra (out of a total of 14 seats). In the 2004 and 2009 elections, the PDI-P failed to gain a single seat at the national level representing West Sumatra. Only during the 2014 election did the PDI-P regained two legislative seats.[15] This situation was short-lived however. The PDI-P did not manage to win a single DPR–RI seat in the 2019 election.

For the case of the presidential election, candidates running for president and vice president under the aegis of the PDI-P found very little support among the dominant Minangkabau community (see Table 7.1). During the 2004 election, when the PDI-P nominated Megawati Soekarnoputri and Hasyim Muzadi as the presidential candidate pair, they lost in the province. The 2004 election was the first direct presidential/vice-presidential election after the fall of the Suharto regime. In the final round, the Megawati–Hasyim pair only received 16 per cent of the votes while the Susilo Bambang Yudhoyono–Jusuf Kalla pair received 84 per cent of the votes from West Sumatra.

Likewise, during the 2009 election, the PDI-P, which nominated the Megawati Soekarnoputri–Prabowo Subianto presidential candidate pair, failed to win a majority of votes in West Sumatra. The pair only received 5.9 per cent of votes. Meanwhile, the Susilo Bambang Yudhoyono–Budiono pair received 79.91 per cent and the third pair comprising of Jusuf Kalla and Wiranto received 14.2 per cent of the votes. This negative trend for PDI-P continued for the 2014 election, when the PDI-P nominated Joko Widodo paired with Jusuf Kalla. Even though Kalla's wife was of Minangkabau ethnicity, this was not enough to attract support from the electorate in the province. The Widodo–Kalla pair only gained 23.1 per cent of the votes compared to that of Prabowo Subianto and Hatta Rajasa who won 76.9 per cent of the votes.[16] Similarly, for the 2019 presidential election, Jokowi only received 14.08 per cent of the votes.

At the provincial level of legislative elections, the PDI-P's performance was also less than stellar in the province. In the 1999 elections, despite the party's popularity at the national level, the PDI-P only gained 5 provincial legislative seats in West Sumatra from a total of 49 DPRD seats available at that time. This negative trend continued in the 2004 elections where the PDI-P gained only four provincial legislative seats from the 55 legislative seats available. In the 2009 elections, the acquisition of PDI-P seats for the provincial legislative in West Sumatra again declined, with only 3 seats out of the 55 legislature seats available. In the 2014 elections, although 4 seats were gained, the increase did not mean anything significant considering that the availability of provincial-level

Table 7.1 National PDI-P DPR seats and vote for candidates supported by PDI-P

Election (year)	1999	2004	2009	2014	2019
DPR-RI (National Legislator)	2 Seats	0 Seats	0 Seats	2 Seats	0 Seat
Support to the presidential candidates from PDI-P	The President and vice president not yet elected directly by voters.	Megawati Sukarnoputr–Hasyim Muzadi: 16%	Megawati Sukarnoputr–Prabowo Subianto: 5.9%	Joko Widod–M. Jusuf Kalla: 23.1%	Joko Widod–Ma'ruf Amin: around 14%

Source: Indonesian Election Commission (KPU).

Table 7.2 Provincial legislative seats acquisition by PDI-P in West Sumatra

Election year	1999	2004	2009	2014	2019
PDI-P seats in the provincial legislative of West Sumatra	5	4	3	4	3
Total seats of provincial legislative of West Sumatra	49	55	55	65	65

Source: West Sumatra Provincial Legislature (DPRD I).

legislative seats in West Sumatra grew to 65 seats. The number of PDI-P seats in the provincial legislative in West Sumatra differed significantly from the national legislative seats in the 2014 elections (see Table 7.2).

Identity politics' historical roots

Based on our fieldwork in West Sumatra, we observed three main factors that explained the Joko Widodo electoral defeat in the region in both the 2014 and 2019 presidential elections. First, there was a deliberate negative campaign against Jokowi accusing him of being part of or close to the PKI while, alleging that he is of Chinese descent, even questioning Jokowi's Islamic credentials. Second are factors relating to Jokowi's coalition partners who nominated him as a presidential candidate, namely PDI-P, NasDem, PKB, and PKPI. Public acceptance of these four parties in almost every general election in West Sumatra remained weak. Third, the majority of the West Sumatra's community (or *adat*) leaders, such as *Ninik–Mamak* and *Datuak* supported Prabowo Subianto due to sentimental historical factors relating to his father's participation in the PRRI movement.

On 17 September 2018, ten local government heads (two mayors and eight regents) in West Sumatra pledged their support for Joko Widodo to run for a second presidential term. While this triggered a debate within Minangkabau society[17] this declaration did not have any influence when it came to increasing the number of votes for Jokowi–Ma'ruf Amin in the region. Regardless of the political perspectives of these elites, there were fundamental differences between them and West Sumatran political society.

For political elites like regents and mayors, president Jokowi was viewed as a successful president whose policies improved the general welfare of the Indonesian people, including West Sumatrans. For this reason they supported Jokowi to be re-elected for a second term. In addition, the regional heads also judged Jokowi on his development efforts in the province. During his 4-year term, Jokowi made five trips to West Sumatra.[18] There were also several infrastructure development projects initiated by the central government to improve the welfare of the Minangkabau people.

Yet on the other hand, for a larger proportion of the Minangkabau community, there is also the narrative circulating that Jokowi is a lackey or subordinate of the PDI-P, the party led by Megawati Sukarnoputri, daughter of

Sukarno who was Indonesia's first president. Based on our interviews with religious leaders and traditional (*adat*) leaders during fieldwork, anything related to Sukarno was still considered taboo due to his crackdown on the PRRI movement from 1958 to 1961 which left a deep and indelible wound in the Minangkabau body politic. Azhar Datauk Marajo, a tribal leader from Ampek Angkek, Bukittinggi, highlighted the psychological wounds that still remained raw till now:

> I saw with my own eyes, the central army [the Minangkabau people were then called Sukarno's army] lead hundreds of people in small groups around the Jam Gadang (Clock Tower) monument. Although, I didn't see what they did to those people, I heard multiple shots from the Clock Tower. I was 10 years old when the incident took place.[19]

Many felt that the central government had also betrayed the trust of some PRRI leaders who wanted to collaborate. According to Azhar, some PRRI leaders were persuaded by the Sukarno government to negotiate but instead found themselves arrested and sent to prison. During this incident, thousands of Minangkabau people were victims of reprisals by the Indonesian Army.[20] Following the defeat of PRRI, there was an exodus of Minangkabau people from Sumatra to other regions in Indonesia. The humiliation and trauma of the defeat rocked the self-esteem and dignity of the Minangkabau people, despite the fact that many of Indonesia's pre-Independence leaders were Minangkabau.[21] This traumatic historical narrative continues in the memories of a number Minangkabau public figures. As a result, the acceptance of the Minangkabau community with anything affiliated or associated with Sukarno and the ideology he promoted, including his political party, is still relatively low.

Historical factors contributed significantly to the low number of votes for Joko Widodo in West Sumatra in the 2014 and 2019 elections. Sukarno, Indonesia's first president, imprisoned Muhammad Natsir, a Minangkabau religious and political figure, for his involvement in the PRRI uprising in 1958.[22] Natsir believed that Indonesia should be a federal state and opposed the nationalists in Java like Sukarno who supported the republican cause. To cite Gusti Asnan, a professor from Padang's Andalas University:

> Jokowi was supported by the PDI-P. This election is relatively similar to that of the Sukarno era. Sukarno was then leading the PNI (Indonesian National Party). On the other hand, Prabowo is a representative of his father, Soemitro Djojohadikusumo who was pro-PRRI.[23]

When we interviewed Datuk Majo Kayo – an indigenous community leader in West Sumatra – he similarly asserted that the PDI-P had close relations with the PNI and also Christian groups in which, during the Sukarno administration, the PNI was viewed as complicit in the imprisonment of Muhammad Natsir and the renowned Muslim scholar and Masyumi politician Buya Hamka.

The victory of the PDI-P is the victory of the Christians and the left-wing movement, which in the Sukarno era was represented by the Indonesian National Party (PNI). They were the ones who imprisoned Natsir and Hamka. It later evolved into the PDI-P now led by Megawati, daughter of Sukarno.[24]

The PRRI uprising from 1958 to 1961 continues to influence the political behaviour of some Minangkabau people who live in West Sumatra province today. The PRRI rebellion began a disgruntlement over Sukarno's downsizing of the Republic of Indonesia Armed Forces' (*Angkatan Perang Republik Indonesia*, APRI) Banteng Division, leaving in place only one brigade. This decision was made abruptly without any consultation with the unit's soldiers. The officers and soldiers of the Banteng Division felt unappreciated considering that they had to struggle and risk their lives for Indonesia's independence. Conditions deteriorated with both the welfare of the soldiers and the local population neglected due to poor government policy regarding how the allocation of the benefits of independence would be provided for by the central government.

As a result of these problems, some military officers took the initiative to form a regional military council called the Struggle Council (*Dewan Perjuangan*) and at the same time stated their refusal to acknowledge the legitimacy of the Djuanda-led government. On 9 January 1958, military and civilian leaders held a meeting in Sungai Dareh, West Sumatra. The meeting formulated a statement demanding that president Sukarno return to the orthodox constitutional position and dismantle all policies and actions that violated the 1945 Constitution.

Sukarno rejected this demand which then led to Lieutenant Colonel Ahmad Hussein proclaiming the establishment of the Revolutionary Government of the Republic of Indonesia (PRRI) on 15 February 1958 with Syafruddin Prawiranegara as its prime minister.[25] The Sukarno government response was to crush the PRRI movement with military force and then split Central Sumatra province into three regions, namely West Sumatra Province, Riau, and Jambi. As a result of these divisions, the province of West Sumatra had never been allowed to celebrate the province's anniversary. This wound inflicted by the central government remained in the hearts of the majority of the Minangkabau people.

This situation had been taken advantage of by political parties, especially Islamic parties like the National Mandate Party (PAN, *Partai Amanat Nasional*) – with Muhammadiyah its primary supporter – and the Prosperous Justice Party (PKS, *Partai Keadilan Sejahtera*). Today, the province of West Sumatra is a key operating hub for the PKS. There were two administrative periods when the governor of West Sumatra was affiliated with the PKS. The current mayor of Padang is also from the same party. However, for the legislative elections, this province has been dominated by parties with a relatively secular orientation. For instance, the Golkar Party won the legislative elections in 1999 and 2004, while the Democrat Party won in the 2009, and the 2014 election. Six political parties, namely PDI-P, Golkar, Gerindra, Democrat Party, PKS, and PPP gained two seats each at the national legislative level.

At the opposite end of the spectrum, Prabowo's father, the late Soemitro Djojohadikusumo, was part of the PRRI leadership. He held the appointment of Trade and Communications Minister in the government of prime minister Syafruddin Prawiranegara. When Prabowo Subianto became the principal challenger to Jokowi in both the 2014 and 2019 presidential elections, a majority of the Minangkabau people, identifying his father's commitment to the PRRI cause, pledged their support to him. The contestation during the 2014 and 2019 elections revived all the bitter memories long held by the Minangkabau people concerning the history and outcomes of the PRRI rebellion.

West Sumatrans attitudes towards Jokowi, PDI-P, and *Islam Nusantara*

In addition to these historical factors, a majority of the Minangkabau people believe that Jokowi's policies regarding Islam was detrimental and in contradiction with Minangkabau culture and its traditional philosophy which was '*adat bersandi syarak, syarak bersandi Kitabullah*' (traditions are built based on religion and religion founded on the Al-Quran). This proved to be a stumbling block for Jokowi and the PDI-P to gain political support from the Minangkabau community.

Jokowi's support for the *Islam Nusantara* concept was also opposed by the West Sumatran Islamic scholars. The death knell for Jokowi took place when leaders of the Council of Indonesian Ulema (MUI) of West Sumatra issued a joint ruling to reject the Islam Nusantara concept. The decision made on 21 July 2018 outlined eight reasons for the rejection of Islam Nusantara:

1   *Islam Nusantara* will create problems that would invite useless debates and neglects the challenges and important issues faced by Muslims. Even the term *Islam Nusantara* can bring confusion and disorientation for people when understanding Islam.
2   The concept of *Islam Nusantara* has resulted in the stunting and narrowing of the scope of Islam that should be a blessing for the entire universe (*rahmatan lil'alamiin*) and for all humanity (*kaaffatan linnaas*).
3   If the term *Islam Nusantara* means *wasattiyah* hospitality (proportional and balance in justice) as well as tolerance, it is not a special character of Islam in a particular area but is considered *munazziyat* (privileges), a very basic Islamic teaching. Therefore, labelling '*Nusantara*' in front of Islam has the potential of dividing Muslims, creating a negative perspective of the religion in other regions.
4   *Wasatiyyah, samhah*, justice, *aqliy*, and other values characterised within the concept of *Islam Nusantara* are only a segment and feature of Islam that cannot be separated from other values such as *rabbaniyyah, ilahiyyah, syumuliyyah, mumayyizat.* By doing this, it will only cause confusion in the understanding Islam while diminishing Islam from its perfection.
5   If *Islam Nusantara* is understood by preaching which refers to the teachings and approaches of *Wali Songo* on the island of Java, this could have a

serious impact on the integrity of the nation, because in various regions within Indonesia, there are scholars with a different approach to that of *Wali Songo*. Imposing the teachings of *Wali Songo* throughout Indonesia would mean downplaying the role of scholars who spread Islam in other regions that have other diverse characteristics.

6   If the cultural approach put forward is characteristic of the concept of *Islam Nusantara*, then it is not the monopoly of *Islam Nusantara* but has become a common character of *da'wah* (or proselytisation) in various regions of the world. Islamic attitudes that combined traditional and cultural approaches have been applied clearly in the study of *Ushul Fiqh*. Even West Sumatran clerics with a long experience of preaching in the province have adopted various cultural approaches. They have even arrived at a joint commitment towards the 'Marapalam Pledge', its philosophy upheld by the Minangkabau people until today: '*Adat Basandi Syara', Syara' Basandi Kitabullah, Syara' Mangato, Adat Mamakai*'. Even though the Minangkabau people have arrived at the point of togetherness, none of the Minangkabau Islamic scholars had added the label Minangkabau with that of Islam.

7   If the meaning of *Islam Nusantara* is that of a tolerant, non-radical Islam confronting conditions in the Middle East today, then it is an accusation against the violent teachings that originate from the Middle East. This is viewed as a threat to the *ukhuwwah Islamiyyah* among Muslims in the world, because the struggle carried out by some Muslims who are oppressed in Palestine cannot be labelled as radicalism or intolerance. Muslims in Palestine should receive our sympathies, as we see them as no different when our forebears fought for Indonesia's independence.

8   Given these reasons, we, the West Sumatera Council of Indonesian Ulema, state without any doubt that the concept of *Islam Nusantara* is not welcomed in the Land of the Minangkabau (West Sumatra). For us, the name of Islam has is perfect by itself and no label needs to be attached to it.

Islam Nusantara was a concept devised by the Nahdlatul Ulama (NU), the largest Islamic organisation in Indonesia. However, NU itself does not have adequate support in West Sumatra compared to its strong influence on the island of Java, particularly Central and East Java. NU's lack of influence in West Sumatra is the result of historical factors going back to when it officially withdrew from the Masyumi Party in 1952, then under the leadership of Muhammad Natsir. The withdrawal of NU from Masyumi took place after Masyumi changed its leaders from Sukiman Wirjosandjojo to Muhammad Natsir during the organisation's 1952 congress.

Some of the policies of president Jokowi that were considered detrimental to Islam were certainly a source of serious concern for the Minangkabau people. Among this was the issuance of government regulation in lieu of law, (*Peraturan Pemerintah Pengganti Undang-Undang*, Government Regulation in lieu of Law, Perppu) No. 2 of 2017, which has been enacted into Law No. 5 of 2018 concerning Civil Society Organisations (*Perppu Ormas*). The rationale for the government to issue the *Perppu Ormas* was a perception that an emergency situation had existed due to the prevalence of mass organisations whose activities were considered contrary to Pancasila and whose adherence to 'radical ideas' endangered the integrity of the country.

Several organisations rejected the *Perppu Ormas*, and these included religious groups like Muhammadiyah, the Islamic Community Association (PUI), *Mathalaul Anwar*, *Persatuan Islam (Persis)*, and the Indonesian Islamic Propagation Council (DDII). These Islamic organisations believed that that the *Perppu Ormas* would threaten their existence and their members lamented that their struggle to uphold Islamic law in Indonesia would be threatened. The banning of *Hizb ut-Tahrir Indonesia* (HTI) was seen as a flagrant attempt at undermining democratic freedoms. For this reason, these organisations requested that the government abort the implementation of the *Perppu*. However, NU supported the *Perppu Ormas* – one of the few Indonesian Islamic Organisations to do so.

Although their arguments for the rejection of the law differ, the main reasons for the denunciation from these groups are the same, namely that the 'emergency' conditions that form the basis for the issuance of the *Perppu Ormas* were considered weak and baseless. In addition, the *Perppu Ormas* is deemed contrary to the values of democracy and human rights, specifically related to the freedom of association and assembly and is considered contrary to the Constitution. The dissolution of mass organisations carried out by the government (executive power) and not through the courts as seen in the issuance of *Perppu Ormas* thus ignored the principle of checks and balances allowing for potential abuses to take place.

From a democratic perspective, the dissolution of mass organisations by the government and not through the judicial mechanism is a step backwards, mirroring the approach adopted by Suharto's New Order when dealing with mass organisations through the use of Law No. 8 of 1985, which at that time became a powerful tool in the hands of the government for the dismantling of mass organisations.

Thus, the politics behind the issuance of the *Perppu Ormas* (Law No. 5 of 2018) is certainly difficult to separate from the increased political temperature during and after the Jakarta elections. One of the important events that preceded the issuance of the *Perppu* was the large-scale protest by Muslims against Basuki Tjahaya Purnama (Ahok) as governor of Jakarta in relation to his alleged blasphemy case of that time. The controversy surrounding these accusations of blasphemy led to Ahok's defeat in the Jakarta elections. Regardless of the disturbing political dynamics leading to polarisation during the Jakarta elections, there was seemingly no agenda or plan for the government to take stock of the possible repercussions and to revise the Civil Society Organisation Law No. 17 of 2013.

Another factor that added a negative sting to perceptions of the Jokowi administration among the Minangkabau people, was his political proximity to Ahok. As former mayor of Jakarta, Jokowi certainly had a close relationship with Ahok who became his successor. Even though Jokowi did not openly express his support for Ahok during the Jakarta elections, most Minangkabau people believed that Jokowi's preference was for Ahok to be elected as governor of Jakarta. A commonly held perception was that the issuance of the *Perpu Ormas* which was followed by the disbandment of Hizb ut-Tahrir Indonesia (HTI) – seen as a form of political acquiescence by the authorities to balance the ledger following the imprisonment of Ahok for 2 years. The common theme of Jokowi's favouritism of Ahok was evident in an interview with Agus Susanto, a field coordinator at the 212 demonstration from Bengkulu:

> Indeed, since the beginning of the Ahok case, we Muslims see President Jokowi as not being neutral, with his inclination to protect Ahok, a non-Muslim more. Even though Jokowi is perceived to be fair and indiscriminate by not explicitly protecting Ahok, it is only an attempt at camouflage. Jokowi is anti-Islam. The proof is that Jokowi issued a law to dissolve HTI.[26]

Chairman of the Jabodetabek Civil Society Organisation and Islamic Alliance Habib Kholilullah bin Abu Bakar Al Habsyi Al Hasani, in his assessment of the purpose for the issuance of Government Regulation in Lieu of Law No. 2 of 2017 concerning Mass Organisations in the aftermath of Ahok defeat in the Jakarta election, claimed that the *Perppu Ormas* was political revenge that contradicted Indonesia's Constitution. He stressed the anti-Pancasila nature of *Perppu Ormas* because it undermined the human rights of the Indonesian people.[27]

This theme of Joko Widodo's proximity to Ahok being a factor in the Minangkabau community's rejection of Jokowi can also be seen in an article written by Miko Kamal, a legal practitioner in Padang. Writing in the *Padang Ekspres*, he claimed that Jokowi not only supported Ahok in the election for the governor of Jakarta in 2017 initially, but also protected him when Muslim disquiet over his alleged blasphemy of the Al-Maidah verse 51 came to the surface. Miko explicitly wrote:

> the West Sumateran people did not choose the Jokowi–Kalla presidential pair as a manifestation of their sense of responsibility to their brothers and sisters in Jakarta who will be led by someone who is not in line (religiously) with them. Most of the West Sumateran people actually adhere to that of the Al Imran Verse: 28 and QS: Al Maidah Verse: 51. For the Minangkabau people who are not migrants (not migrating because they are still useful in the village), I feel they are not comfortable with Ahok's and Jokowi's actions during and after the presidential election ...[28]

Although the legal case against Ahok case was prosecuted and he was charged in court for blasphemy, this action did not necessarily negate the view that Jokowi had protected a 'religious blasphemer'. The issuance of the *Perpu Ormas* was viewed as an opportunity for Joko Widodo's government to stifle the pace of Islamic groups' political movements, which in turn could precipitate a prolonged crisis pitting these groups against the government. The Jokowi government has repeatedly been under immense pressure from Islamic groups culminating in the large-scale demonstration against Ahok. As a result, the *Perppu Ormas* is viewed as a tool for the government to threaten and curb its political opponents from Islamic groups. Among the several Islamic organisations, HTI contributed significantly to each of the protests. Meanwhile, for pro-democracy groups, the issuance of the *Perpu Ormas* is a return to the manner when Suharto utilised the *Undang-undang Subversi* or the 1963 Anti-Subversion Law to emasculate political opposition.

Table 7.3 summarises our interviews in West Sumatra and shows the circulation of news items, some of which were fabrications devised to exacerbate tensions between Jokowi and conservative Muslims.

Anti-Islamic perceptions of Joko Widodo were also constructed following a statement made by Trimedya Panjaitan, the leader of the law team of the Jokowi–Kalla pair, at the PDI-P headquarters, Jakarta on 4 June 2014. Trimedya stated that the Joko Widodo–Jusuf Kalla government (Jokowi–JK) would ban all regional regulations based on Islamic law (*Perda Syariah*) with the exception of Aceh.[29] Trimedya went on to say that regional regulations based on Islamic law not only contradict the nationalist ideology adopted by the PDI-P, but was also in conflict with the national ideology of Pancasila and the 1945 Constitution. The implementation of *Perda Syariah*, he added, would create social dichotomies that would undermine Indonesia's pluralist model based on the motto 'Unity in Diversity (*Bhineka Tunggal Ika*)'. According to Trimedya, the PDI-P had intensively promoted the four pillars of the national programme initiated by the former chairman of the People's Consultative Assembly, Taufik Kiemas, namely Pancasila, 1945 Constitution, the unitary state (NKRI), and Bhineka Tunggal Ika.

In line with Trimedya's opinion, the chairman of the Indonesian Solidarity Party (PSI), Grace Natalie, also revealed that her party would reject the establishment of regional regulations based on religion.[30] She argued that so far the regional regulations based on religion have led to practices of discrimination and intolerance. Although these statements were not conveyed directly by Joko Widodo, the two parties, namely the PDI-P and PSI, were Jokowi's main supporters. Such views intensified public perceptions and undermined Jokowi's image in the deeply conservative Muslim provinces. A party that also supported Jokowi, namely the United Development Party (PPP, *Partai Persatuan Pembangunan*), took the opposite view nonetheless, stating that they disagreed with the views of the PDI-P and PSI.

In addition to the sharia regulations, a member of the Joko Widodo–Jusuf Kalla campaign team, Siti Musdah Mulia, also noted that Jokowi would abolish the joint ruling made by the Ministry of Religion and the Ministry of Home Affairs related to the requirements for establishing houses of worship, specifically, joint decrees number 8 and number 9 of 2006, concerning the Maintenance of Religious Harmony, Empowerment of Religious Harmony Forums, and Establishment of Houses of Worship.[31] The regulation is considered a violation

Table 7.3 Grievances of West Sumatra-based Islamic activists against Jokowi

No.	Case	Affiliation with Jokowi
	Persecution of Ulama. There have been at least three cases of attacks on ulama. One of them was against KH Umar Basri in Bandung. The leader of the Al Hidayah Islamic Boarding School were victims of a person suspected of having a mental disorder. While the six targets of the case were not Ulama, it was broadcasted that the targets were Ulama. Thirty cases of persecution were fabricated and broadcasted on social media.	The cases of persecution of these Muslim scholars occurred in early 2018, where the perpetrators were alleged people with mental illness. This model of persecution is claimed to mimic the PKI persecution model in 1950s to 1960s where Jokowi and PDI-P have always been accused of having affiliations with the communist movement in Indonesia.
	Criminalization of Habib Rizieq Shihab. The supreme leader of the Islamic Defenders Front (FPI) was by the police to have an improper alleged relationship with Firza Husein. Habib Rizieq Sihab was declared a suspect by the Polda Metro Jaya in May 2017.	Habib Rizieq is the leader of the 212 protest movement which led to Ahok's defeat in the 2017 DKI Jakarta regional election and his incarceration for two years. Ahok (Basuki Tjahaya Purnama) was Jokowi's successor and running mate in the 2012 Jakarta Election.
	Prevention of Ustadz Felix Siaw and Ustadz Abdul Somad to give their sermons in some areas in Indonesia without any legal due process or fair settlement of loss earnings.	Ustadz Felix Siaw is a HTI activist supporting the establishment of the Islamic Khilafah (government based on Islamic law). Cleric Abdul Somad had often criticized the government. The actions against both of them were to curtail the movement carried out by organizations that were considered supporters of Jokowi.
	Issuance of Perppu Number 2 of 2017 concerning CSOs (which was later passed by the DPR into Law No. 5 of 2018) which followed the Dissolution of Hizb ut-Tahrir Indonesia (HTI).	The issuance of the Ormas Perppu was allegedly a form of response to Ahok's defeat in the Jakarta Election and his two year prison sentence due to views on Surat Al Maidah verse 51. In addition, the Public Order Perppu was assumed as an attempt to silence Islamic political power.
	Insult to Al-Quran (Al Maidah verse 51) and Ulama by Basuki Tjahaja Purnama Ahok, former Governor of DKI Jakarta.	Basuki Tjahaya Purnama was the partner of Joko Widodo in the 2012 DKI Jakarta gubernatorial election. They were successfully elected as Governor and Deputy Governor for the period 2012–2017. However, in 2014 Jokowi chose to pair with Jusuf Kalla and was finally elected as president.

Source: Author's summary based on Indonesian media reports.

of human rights and is found to discriminate against members of minority religions in an area where it is not easy to collect 60 signatures to get permission to establish places of worship.

Conclusion

The preceding paragraphs highlight the growing identity politics in Indonesia and the government's response to curb growing Islamism in the country. The action–reaction cycles will continue to play out in conservative Muslim-majority provinces leading to growing antipathies towards winning coalitions helmed by the PDI-P and NU. Identity politics, associated with religion and ethnicity, have strengthened in Indonesia, especially in the province of West Sumatra. While Islamic factors are evident in the identity politics at play in West Sumatra, historical reasons are pivotal as to why presidential candidates supported by the PDI-P and NU will not find significant support in the province. The consequence of a painful historical narrative of oppression during the crackdown of the Revolutionary Government of the Republic of Indonesia (PRRI) from 1958 to 1961 continues to haunt the memories of the Minangkabau people. This memory became a prominent factor in influencing the West Sumatran people's political preferences in the 2014 and 2019 elections. The 2019 election confirms the pattern established in the 2014 election highlighting the importance of historical narrative, ethnicity and religion, which has contributed significantly to the political identity formation of the of Minangkabau people and played its part in shaping voter political preferences in the 2014 and 2019 presidential elections.

Notes

1 See Bland 2019.
2 See Aspinall & Mietzner 2019.
3 See Pepinsky 2019, Warburton 2019, Arifianto 2019.
4 Pepinsky, op. cit.
5 Ibid.
6 See Nasiruddin 2019 and Hamid 2018.
7 See Aspinall 2019.
8 Since the fall of Suharto regime in 1998, certain procedures required to uphold basic democratic standards, like political equality, freedom of speech, and free elections have been introduced in Indonesia. So far it has been largely agreed that electoralism and procedural democracy functions quite well in Indonesia. Elections are held regularly and there has been no backsliding in the form of a military coup. The three constitutionally mandated institutions, the Supreme and the high courts, the president, and the Election Commission are autonomous, demonstrating that a principle separation of powers that has been instituted since the advent of reforms.
9 Team 11, which was chaired by Nurcholish Madjid, verified 48 political parties to run in the 1999 general elections. The selection consisted of administrative and factual verification for the existence of those political parties, starting from the party's structure to the number offices present in the provinces.
10 A declining number of political parties became evident due to the implementation of the electoral threshold in the 1999 general elections and the parliamentary threshold

in both the 2004 and 2009 general elections outlining the minimum requirement of votes necessary to participate in future elections. The parliamentary threshold in 2004 was 2 per cent while in 2009 is was 2.5 per cent and for the 2014 general elections it became 3.5 per cent of total national votes.
11 See Aspinall 2018.
12 Kahin & Kahin 1995.
13 Roadnight 2002.
14 Lijphart 1977, pp. 3–4, Lustick 1979, Reilly 2001, p. 4, Horowitz 1985, pp. 51–55.
15 *Kompas.com* 2014.
16 Iskandar 2018.
17 Detiknews.com 2018b.
18 Detiknews.com 2018a.
19 Kahin 1999, p. 229.
20 Ibid.
21 Syamdani 2009.
22 Ibid, p. 229.
23 Tirto.id 2018.
24 Author's interview with Datuk Majo Kayo, conducted on 22 December 2018.
25 Prokabar.com 2017.
26 Author's interview with Agus Susanto, conducted on 23 July 2017.
27 CNNIndonesia.com 2017.
28 Kamal 2014.
29 Republika.co.id 2014.
30 Tempo.co 2018.
31 *Kompas.com* 2014.

Bibliography

Arifianto, A. 2019, 25 April. 'Is Islam an Increasingly Polarizing Political Cleavage in Indonesia', *Order from Chaos*, Retrieved from www.brookings.edu/blog/order-from-chaos/2019/04/25/is-islam-an-increasingly-polarizing-political-cleavage-in-indonesia/.

Aspinall, E. 2018, 24 May. 'Twenty Years of Indonesian Democracy – How Many More?', *New Mandala*. Retrieved from www.newmandala.org/20-years-reformasi/.

Aspinall, E. 2019, 22 April. 'Indonesia's Election and the Return of Ideological Competition', *New Mandala*. Retrieved from www.newmandala.org/indonesias-election-and-the-return-of-ideological-competition/.

Aspinall, E. & M. Mietzner. 2019. 'Southeast Asia's Troubling Elections: Nondemocratic Pluralism in Indonesia', *Journal of Democracy* Vol. 30 (4): 104–118.

Bland, B. 2019, 3 April. 'The Mind-boggling Challenge of Indonesia's Election Logistics', *The Interpreter*. Retrieved from www.lowyinstitute.org/the-interpreter/mind-boggling-challenge-indonesian-election-logistics.

CNNIndonesia.com. 2017, 18 July. '*Perppu Ormas* Dianggap Dendam Politik Kekalahan Ahok', ['*Perppu Ormas* is Considered as a Political Revenge for Ahok's Defeat']. Retrieved from: www.cnnindonesia.com/nasional/20170718200330-32-228750/perppu-ormas-dianggap-dendam-politik-kekalahan-ahok/.

Detiknews.com. 2018, 9 February. 'Safari Jokowi Merebut Hati di Ranah Minang', ['Jokowi's Roadshow to Attract Minang Voters']. Retrieved from: https://news.detik.com/berita/d-3858647/safari-jokowi-merebut-hati-di-ranah-minang.

Detiknews.com. 2018, 20 September. '10 Kepala Daerah di Sumbar Dukung Jokowi, Ini Alasannya' ['10 Local Chief Executives in West Sumatera Endorses Jokowi. Here Is the Reason']. Retrieved from: https://news.detik.com/berita/4221250/10-kepala-dae-rah-di-sumbar-dukung-jokowi-ini-alasannya.

Hamid, S. 2018, 31 July. 'A Polarised Indonesia? Elections, Intolerance and Religion', *Indonesia at Melbourne*. Retrieved from https://indonesiaatmelbourne.unimelb.edu. au/a-polarised-indonesia-elections-intolerance-and-religion/.

Horowitz, D. 1985. *Ethnic Groups in Conflict*. Berkeley, CA: University of California Press.

Iskandar, I. 2018, 15 February. 'Jokowi and Minang', *Andalas University Blog*. Retrieved from: www.unand.ac.id/id/berita-peristiwa/berita/item/2400-jokowi-dan-minang.html.

Kahin, A.R. 1999. *Rebellion to Integration: West Sumatera and the Indonesian Polity 1926–1988*. Amsterdam: Amsterdam University Press.

Kahin, A.R. & G.M. Kahin. 1995. *Subvertion as Foreign Policy: The Secret Eisenhower and Dulles Debacle in Indonesia*. New York: The New Press.

Kamal, M. 2014, 30 August. 'Lagak Orang Rantau: Tanggapan Atas Tulisan Erwin Natosmal Oemar' ['Nomads Behaviour: A Response to Erwan Natosmal Oemar'], personal blog. Retrieved from: https://mikokamal.wordpress.com/2014/08/30/lagak-orang-rantau-tanggapan-atas-tulisan-erwin-natosmal-oemar/.

Kompas.com. 2014, 15 March. 'Inilah Daftar 109 Anggota DPR dari PDIP Periode 2014–19' ['Here Are the DPR MPs from PDI-P for 2014–19 Term']. Retrieved from: https:// nasional.kompas.com/read/2014/05/15/1039050/Inilah.Daftar.109.Anggota.DPR.dari. PDI-P.Periode.2014-2019.

Kompas.com. 2014, 18 June. 'Jokowi Akan Hapus Peraturan Dua Menteri Soal Pendirian Rumah Ibadah' ['Jokowi Plans to Revoke Dual Ministerial Decree Regarding Houses of Worship']. Retrieved from: https://nasional.kompas.com/read/2014/06/18/1811413/ Jokowi.Akan.Hapus.Peraturan.Dua.Menteri.soal.Pendirian.Rumah.Ibadah.

Lijphart, A. 1977. *Democracy in Plural Societies*. New Haven, CT: Yale University Press.

Lustick, I. 1979. 'Stability in Deeply Divided Societies: Consociationalism versus Control', *World Politics*, Vol. 31 (3): 325–344.

Nasiruddin, D. 2019, 21 April. 'Ending Political Divide in Society – Indonesia Style', *The Star*. Retrieved from www.thestar.com.my/news/regional/2019/04/21/ending-political-divide-in-society-indonesian-style.

Pepinsky, T. 2019, 28 May. 'Religion, Ethnicity, and Indonesia's 2019 Presidential Election', *New Mandala*, Retrieved from www.newmandala.org/religion-ethnicity-and-indonesias-2019-presidential-election/.

Prokabar.com. 2017, 5 October. 'PRRI: Uji Nyali Orang Minang Lawan Soekarno' ['PRRI: A "Critical Test" of the Minangese against Soekarno']. Retrieved from: https://prokabar.com/%E2%80%8Bprri-uji-nyali-orang-minang-lawan-soekarno/.

Reilly, B. 2001. *Democracy in Divided Societies: Electoral Engineering for Conflict Management*. New York: Cambridge University Press.

Republika.co.id. 2014, 4 June. 'Kecuali in Aceh, Jokowi-JK Bakal Larang Perda Syariat Islam' ['Jokowi–Kalla Will Prohibit Islamic Shari'a Regulations, Except in Aceh]'. Retrieved from www.republika.co.id/berita/pemilu/menuju-%20ri-1/14/06/04/n6n15d-kecuali-di-aceh-jokowijk-bakal-larang-syariat-islam.

Roadnight, A. 2002. *United States Policy towards Indonesia in the Truman and Eisenhower Years*. New York: Palgrave Macmillan.

Syamdani. 2009. *PRRI: Pemberontakan atau Bukan?* ['PRRI: Rebellion or Not?']. Padang, Indonesia: Media Pressindo.

Tempo.co. 2018, 17 November. 'Tolak *Perda Syariah*, Grace Natalie: Saya Tak Anti Agama' ['Rejecting Local Shari'a Regulations, Grace Natalie: I Am Not an Anti-Religious Person']. Retrieved from: https://nasional.tempo.co/read/1147272/tolak-perda-syariah-grace-natalie-saya-tak-anti-agama.

Tirto.id. 2018, 10 February. 'Blusukan Jokowi di Lumbung Kemenangan Prabowo, Sumatera Barat' ['Jokowi's Door-to-Door Campaign Visit in West Sumatera, Prabowo's Stronghold']. Retrieved from: https://tirto.id/blusukan-jokowi-di-lumbung-kemenangan-prabowo-sumatera-barat-cEzW.

Warburton, E. 2019, 16 April. 'Polarization in Indonesia: What if Perception is Reality?', *New Mandala*. Retrieved from: www.newmandala.org/how-polarised-is-indonesia/.

8 The 2018 and 2019 elections in South Sulawesi

Jusuf Kalla's decline and the return of Islamists

Dedi Dinarto and Andar Nubowo

Introduction

South Sulawesi is an important province that deserves to be examined in light of the simultaneous regional elections in Indonesia since reforms were instituted in 1998. The province's importance derives from the various power wielders in the province, including prominent political elites from the Party of Functional Groups (*Partai Golongan Karya* or Golkar Party) and influential local Islamic conservative groups. Jusuf Kalla, a prominent Golkar Party cadre who made his way to the national politics, becoming vice president to Susilo Bambang Yudhoyono (2004–2009) and Joko Widodo (2014–2019) hails from this province. Close linkages and interplay between these political elites contribute significantly towards the outcome of regional electoral outcomes in the province. In addition, the relative fluidity of political alliances between candidates and political parties within the province further complicates coalition-building patterns.

In the context of the presidential election, South Sulawesi's importance derives from its position not only as the most populated province in Eastern Indonesia numerically, but it is also a gateway East of the archipelago and a strong barometer of Islamist politics. Based on statistical record from the South Sulawesi Central Bureau of Statistics (*Badan Pusat Statistik Sulawesi Selatan*) (2019), the population in the province reached approximately 9 million in 2018. According to the South Sulawesi General Elections Commission (*Komisi Pemilihan Umum Sulawesi Selatan*) (2018), there were almost 6 million potential voters in the province. Due to the province's high population, clinching a win there by any candidate in the regional election provides considerable leverage for parties thinking of securing a victory in the 2019 presidential election. Understanding the dynamics of electoral politics in South Sulawesi allows one to better comprehend trends and political changes in Indonesian politics at a broader level.

This chapter focuses on the findings of a field trip to South Sulawesi that was carried out in 2018. Trailing significant political events that had taken place in South Sulawesi in the lead up to the regional elections, we seek to understand the workings behind coalition-building between candidates and political parties as well as the role of identity politics aim to mobilise voters. South Sulawesi as a case study provides important insights, including the decline of Jusuf Kalla's influence in the province, an increase in demand from voters for accountability-based leaders, the problem of coordination and logistics from both Jokowi's and Prabowo's campaign team in the province, and the role of Islamic groups in mobilising voters. Indeed, the 2018 Makassar mayoral election and the 2018 South Sulawesi gubernatorial election had demonstrated the diminishing influence of former vice president Jusuf Kalla and his political and business cliques. Further, there had been a significant demand for accountability-based leaders regardless of the political parties that had supported them. Identity politics also played a significant role in the lead up to the 2019 presidential election and was the main reason why Prabowo gained traction among South Sulawesi voters and won most votes in the province. Thus the mayoral election of Makassar and the South Sulawesi gubernatorial election are rightly considered as watershed electoral races in anticipation of the presidential race.

The first part of this chapter provides a brief historical background of how electoral politics in South Sulawesi were organised and studied by Indonesianists. The next section then seeks to analyse the workings behind coalition-building and partnerships between candidates and political parties in the 2018 Makassar mayoral election and the 2018 South Sulawesi gubernatorial election. The third section discusses aspects of the 2019 presidential election from the perspective of the province, focusing specifically on why Jokowi had failed to secure victory despite support from prominent local elites. This section also covers issues of coordination and logistics of both Jokowi's and Prabowo's campaign teams, the role of Islamic groups in South Sulawesi – especially groups that were part of the #2019ChangePresident (*#2019GantiPresiden*) movement – as well as their attempts to influence local electoral politics. The chapter ends with a general conclusion on the political decline of established local elites, the growing demand over accountability-based leaders, the role of identity politics, and the future trajectory of South Sulawesi politics and Indonesian politics at the broader level.

Politics and regional elections in South Sulawesi

Local politics in South Sulawesi had been dominated by two influential groups, the Islamists and the Golkar Party. For the former, its history can be traced to the 1950s when the province was an amphitheatre for the Darul Islam/Indonesian Islamic Army (*Darul Islam/Tentara Islam Indonesia* or DI/TII) rebellion.[1] For the latter, its roots can be traced to the beginning of the New Order (*Orde Baru*) under Suharto as the hegemonic party in the province. In the then Southeast–South Sulawesi Province (*Provinsi Sulawesi Tenggara–Selatan*) – later to be known as South Sulawesi Province after December 1960 – the first ever regional elections of 1955 saw DI/TII elements led by Kahar Muzakkar disrupting the electoral process.[2] Despite the unknown motive, the plan to disrupt the 1955 elections process also occurred in Aceh and West Java. Polling stations were destroyed and at one point in time, members of the polling committee and soldiers were kidnapped followed with thefts of ballot papers and boxes in Makassar, Pare-Pare, and Donggala districts (*kabupaten*) (Feith 1971, Firdausi 2019). The Islamist rebellion itself also had a social-justice dimension which was in opposition to the dominance held by aristocrats in the political and economic sphere. These modernist ideals drew in support from several other Islamic organisations including mainstream organisations like Muhammadiyah (Magenda 1989, Buehler, 2016). Nonetheless, the 1955 election in the province saw the victory of three Islamic parties, including the Council of Indonesian Muslim Associations Party (*Partai Majelis Suryo Muslimin Indonesia* or Masyumi Party), the *Nahdlatul Ulama* (NU) Party, and the Islamic Association Party of Indonesia (*Partai Syarikat Islam Indonesia* or PSII). These three parties had secured more than 700,000 votes in the region, attesting to the strong draw of Islamist politics (Hisyam 2009) as well as close affiliation with local elites (Feith 1971, p. 64).

Under Suharto's New Order, regional and local leaders were directly appointed from Jakarta. While the DI/TII rebellion was exterminated organisationally, remnant networks and its ideology of implementing Islamic law remained (Buehler 2016). Several offshoots were formed from former DI/TII proponents including organisations like *Darul Istiqamah* and *Hidayatullah*, whose activities are focused on Islamic education. On the other hand, the Golkar Party's status as a political vehicle for upward mobility during the New Order allowed for its dominance in the province. The Party's ability to recruit prominent local leaders and elites into its ranks, including the Kalla and Limpo clan, allowed it to dominate party politics even after 1998. There thus appeared to be a divide within the province – that of elite-dominated politics helmed by members of the Golkar Party and Islamic populism propagated by Islamic organisations established by former DI/TII members.

After the fall of the New Order, the Golkar Party remained hegemonic but its dominance and political influence was increasingly dissipated. In the 1999 regional legislative election, the Golkar Party won 16 out of 20 seats in the South Sulawesi House of Representatives (*Dewan Perwakilan Rakyat Daerah Sulawesi Selatan*/DPRD Sulsel). For the 2004 regional legislative elections, the Golkar Party emerged as the party that gained 33 out of 75 seats. In the regional legislative elections of 2009 and 2014, the Golkar Party retained 18 out of 75 and 85 seats respectively. For the 2019 regional legislative elections however, the Golkar Party lost some steam, clinching 13 out of 84 seats (see Table 8.1).

Several studies have sought to explain why the Golkar Party had gradually lost its long time dominance at both the national and local levels in Indonesia (Suryadinata 2007, Tomsa 2007, Syamsuri & Wardani 2018). This was also in line with what was also taking place at the provincial level in South Sulawesi.

Buehler's study (2009) analyses the very first direct regional election that took place in South Sulawesi in 2005 since reforms were instituted. His study focuses on the dynamics of electoral politics in two small regencies (*kecamatan*): Pangkajene and Islands (*kepulauan*) Regency (shortened to Pangkep) and Soppeng. In his study, he noted that support from dominant political parties is not as significant in shaping outcomes towards victory. Rather, cultivating a strong personal network that will aim in (re)election triumphed over all other

Table 8.1 Regional House of Representatives' seats in South Sulawesi (2014 vs. 2019)

Political party	Number of seats (2014)	Number of seats (2019)
Golkar Party	18	13
Democrat Party	11	10
Gerindra	11	11
National Mandate Party (PAN)	9	7
NasDem Party	7	12
United Development Party (PPP)	7	6
Prosperous Justice Party (PKS)	6	8
Indonesian Democratic Party – Struggle (PDI-P)	5	8
Hanura Party	6	1
National Awakening Party (PKB)	3	8

Source: Indonesian General Elections Commission (KPU), compiled by authors.

factors. In another study that focused on party–candidate relationship in the province, Buehler and Tan (2007, p. 65) argued that political parties had minimal influence on whether a particular candidate will win in the province, coming to the same conclusion as the first study mentioned. For the case of the Pangkep election, winning candidate Syafruddin Nur was able to secure 56.9 per cent of votes due to support from the Golkar Party, including the then-governor of South Sulawesi Amin Syam, and the local business community. For the case of the Soppeng election, winning candidate Andi Soetomo spent 25 years serving in various positions at the sub-district level. His career path as a local official allowed him to form a close relationship with the business community. Despite not receiving any formal support from the Golkar Party, Andi still had support of a few individual Golkar Party members, who are also members of his extensive family – to campaign for him.

Although Buehler's analysis covered only two regencies, a general pattern can be concluded. The Golkar Party, despite its decline at the national stage after the New Order fell, had remained an influential political force in the province. Its influence however, had been on the wane even in South Sulawesi. In this chapter, we argue that that reason is because of an increase in resentment towards old established elites, mainly that of Jusuf Kalla and his political and business cliques. While previous studies had demonstrated that patronage played a huge role in electoral wins, in our study we also found that a candidate's track record and the particular career path undertaken is also a distinctively important factor among voters.

Coalition-building and power-brokering in South Sulawesi Province

This section focuses on the coalition-building process in South Sulawesi, demonstrating how candidates and political parties form partnerships at the mayoral, gubernatorial, and national level. In our study, we note that coalition-building and power-brokering were based on the premises of pragmatism and expediency. In addition, the decline of Jusuf Kalla's influence on South Sulawesi politics and an increased demand from the public towards greater accountability from leaders had played a crucial role in the simultaneous elections of 2018 and 2019, quite unlike that of previous elections.

The 2018 Makassar mayoral election

Makassar, the capital city of South Sulawesi, held a mayoral election in 2018 as part of the periodic regional democratic process. Incumbent mayor Mohammad Ramdhan (Danny) Pomanto had served one term and was eager to stay on for another term. He was paired with NasDem Party cadre Indira Mulyasari. His opponent, Munafri Arifuddin, ran together with NasDem Party cadre Andi Rachmatika Dewi. Munafri Arifuddin was then seen as a promising candidate because he had support from ten political parties, namely the NasDem Party, Golkar Party, the Indonesian Democratic Party – Struggle (*Partai Demokrasi Indonesia – Perjuangan* or PDI-P), Great Indonesia Movement Party (*Partai Gerakan Indonesia Raya* or Gerindra Party), People's Conscience Party (*Partai Hati Nurani Rakyat* or Hanura Party), National Awakening Party (*Partai Kebangkitan Bangsa* or PKB), United Development Party (*Partai Persatuan Pembangunan* or PPP), Crescent Star Party (*Partai Bulan Bintang* or PBB), Prosperous and Justice Party (*Partai Keadilan Sejahtera* or PKS), and the Indonesian Justice and Unity Party (*Partai Keadilan dan Persatuan Indonesia* or PKPI). These political parties held 43 out of 50 legislative seats in the parliament (Cipto 2018). Danny Pomanto, incidentally, had no political parties that supported him, forcing him to run independently by collecting a pile of Identity Cards (*Kartu Tanda Penduduk* or KTP) from Makassar populace as an alternative requirement in order to participate in the mayoral election. Despite the absence of political party support, Danny Pomanto successfully collected more than 110,000 KTP, almost two times more than required, and was allowed to contest (Zulfikarnain 2018).

This was a different situation in the 2013 Makassar mayoral election when Danny Pomanto had supported from the Democrat Party (*Partai Demokrat*) and PBB. As a mayor, he enjoyed a reputation as someone who achieved numerous milestones for the city, including improving the environment, boosting the city's finances, and introducing 'smart city' management. In total, he was known to accumulate up to 178 achievements within his 5-year tenure (*Kompas* 2019a). In the economic domain, he succeeded in increasing Makassar's economic growth where the amount of money in circulation in Gross Regional Domestic Product (GRDP) based on current prices in 2018 reached more than 160 trillion Indonesian Rupiah, an increase of 60 trillion Indonesian Rupiah from 2014 (*Kompas* 2019b). Pomanto had also initiated the building of the House of Mamiri Wind (*Baruga Angin Mamiri*) at the mayor's house for discussions, hearings, and meetings, which is considered the first of its kind and was well received (*Kompas* 2019c). Pomanto's contributions were evident to the constituencies he was serving.

Munafri Arifuddin was a Chief Executive Officer (CEO) of a local football club called the *Persatuan Sepakbola Makassar* (Makassar Football United or PSM). He was also close to Jusuf Kalla, a notable entrepreneur and former vice president of the Republic of Indonesia. Munafri married the daughter of Aksa Mahmud who is Jusuf Kalla's brother-in-law. Prior to being involved in the management of his football club, Munafri was working for the Bosowa Corporation, a business conglomerate consisting of automobile, cement, mining, finance, property, and education sectors owned by his father-in-law. As a member of the Golkar Party, a party that is also associated with Jusuf Kalla, it was almost certain that Munafri would capitalise from the advantages he had from his businesses and political connections.

A local pollster called the Celebes Research Centre (CRC) had earlier predicted that Munafri would not stand to win in the mayoral race despite his strong business and political networks, based on surveys of 1,000 participants using multistage random sampling. CRC then went on to predict that Pomanto would gain a significant victory of 72 per cent of votes over Munafri (Indrawan 2018). It is thus curious that, before the publication of the survey, the Makassar Administrative Court of Appeal (*Pengadilan Tinggi Tata Usaha Negara*/PTTUN) ordered the Makassar General Election Commission to disqualify Pomanto from the electoral race. The order from the court was issued in conjunction with Pomanto violating certain regulations and creating conflicts of interest including allegedly using his role as mayor to issue work contracts for temporary employees (Herlina 2018). Pomanto was subsequently disqualified from the Makassar mayoral election, leaving the Munafri–Rachmatika pair as the only human candidates challenging a hypothetical empty ballot box on a technicality. Despite the advantage of being the only candidate, Munafri still lost to the empty ballot box, as he was unable to secure more than 50 per cent of the votes (Hantoro 2018). This event was significant in the sense that it was the first time that a candidate, due to certain circumstances, had lost to a ballot box.

The main reason for such an unprecedented situation to occur in the province was the fact that there had been a growing discontent towards the oligarchy long dominant in South Sulawesi politics, especially that of Jusuf Kalla's business and political cliques. The close relationship between Munafri and Kalla's extended families as well as his business network under the Golkar Party's umbrella became the focal point of criticism among the Makassar populace. While Munafri may have the support of all political parties, this ironically became a liability for his campaign. According to a lecturer from a local university in Makassar, Munafri's defeat symbolised the aggregated resentment of the Makassar constituency towards those who enjoy a close economic and political connection to Jusuf Kalla, seen as a hegemon in the province due to his stature.[3] The problem of economic and social injustice due to the significant wealth gap in the province had become a primary concern among voters in the 2018 mayoral election. Had Pomanto continued to run for the 2018 Makassar mayoral election, he would have won the election primarily due to the excellent track record he had built up.

The 2018 South Sulawesi gubernatorial election

The South Sulawesi gubernatorial election was held similarly on 27 June 2018 in conjuction to other simultaneous elections happening elsewhere in Indonesia. Syahrul Yasin Limpo, who had reached the constitutional term limit of two terms for governor, was slated to be replaced by new office holders. Despite serving as governor of South Sulawesi from 2008 to 2018, Yasin Limpo was known by his prominence as an influential Golkar Party member. He was considered one of among eight party cadres to run for the position of chairman in 2016, although he lost to Setya Novanto (Sarwanto 2016). During the latter half of his tenure as governor, he was publicly condemned by various non-governmental organisations (NGOs) and local fishermen as a result of a controversial project that he spearheaded – that of building artificial islands off the shores of South Sulawesi (Cipto 2016). The project had allegedly circumvented the proper procedures in their haste to issue permits for the developer. In this case, a regional regulation (*peraturan daerah/perda*) on the management of coastline and small islands had not been issued. According to a handful of lecturers from a local university, Yasin Limpo ended his period of service with a poor record despite serving as governor for a decade.[4]

During the 2018 South Sulawesi gubernatorial election, four candidates emerged as potential successors to Syahrul Yasin Limpo's governorship. They included Nurdin Halid, Agus Arifin Nu'mang, Nurdin Abdullah, and Ichsan Yasin Limpo (the incumbent's brother). Nurdin Halid was a prominent figure within the Golkar Party in South Sulawesi and had served as programme coordinator (*Ketua Harian*) for the party at the national level. He was nominated by the Golkar Party, NasDem Party, Hanura, PKB, and PKPI, comprising 35 regional parliamentary seats. His running mate was Aziz Kahar Muzakkar – son of the founder of DI/TII Kahar Muzakkar, who was a member of the Regional Representative Council (*Dewan Perwakilan Daerah*/DPD) of the province.

Agus Arifin Nu'mang was a member of the Gerindra Party and someone who has a strong NU background. His running mate was Tanribali Lamo, a retired army general from South Sulawesi. A handful of political parties, including the Gerindra Party, PBB, and PPP nominated and supported his campaign. Despite having no direct support from the Golkar Party, Nu'mang's close relationship to local elites allowed him to be endorsed by none other than Jusuf Kalla (Kunjana 2018).

Nurdin Abdullah was regent of Bantaeng Regency for two terms (2008–2018). Having a strong academic background in agricultural science, Abdullah used this knowledge to effect in the development of the regency. Building partnerships with Japanese counterparts, Nurdin applied his knowledge of the public health service system and technology on the agricultural sector. As a result of these efforts, Bantaeng Regency saw a significant decrease in the maternal mortality rate and a significant increase in crop yields and diversification. Abdullah's track record then became an asset for him when contesting for a second term. Abdullah was supported by a number of political parties such as the PDI-P, PKS, PAN, and the Indonesian Solidarity Party (*Partai Solidaritas Indonesia* or

PSI) producing a combined total of 20 regional legislative seats. Abdullah's running mate was Andi Sudirman Sulaiman. Sudirman is the brother of Andi Arman Sulaiman, minister of agriculture in the first Joko Widodo (Jokowi) government. They later went on to win in the gubernatorial election.

Ichsan Yasin Limpo who is a brother of Syahrul Yasin Limpo, a prominent business oligarch in the province, was the only candidate who ran independently although he had obtained endorsement from the Democrat Party, United Indonesia Party (*Partai Persatuan Indonesia* or Perindo Party), and the Working Party (*Partai Berkarya*). He was paired with Andi Mudzakar, the former regent of Luwu Regency.

Both local and regional elections in the province demonstrated certain patterns. The excellent track record of certain incumbent candidates is a strong indicator of an eventual re-election. In addition, affiliation with local oligarchs had the effect of being a liability in this case. This is quite evident in the mayoral election when Munafri lost, quite unexpectedly, despite his strong connections to Jusuf Kalla, to an empty ballot box.

Nurdin Abdullah could be elected as governor due primarily to his contributions and track record serving as regent of Bantaeng. On the other hand, candidates like Nurdin Halid, Agus Arifin Nu'mang, and Ichsan Yasin Limpo had failed because of their close ties with Jusuf Kalla's extended cliques and the Golkar Party for Nurdin and Agus, or the larger network of Limpo's own hegemonic presence for Ichsan. Based on an interview with an official from the South Sulawesi gubernatorial office, results of both the mayoral and gubernatorial races in South Sulawesi were indicative of a preference towards candidates who are professional rather than their affiliation or connection.[5]

The 2019 presidential election in South Sulawesi

At the national level, Jokowi and his political opponent Prabowo Subianto were supported by a coalition of political parties. Jokowi's coalition include support by the PDI-P, Golkar Party, PKB, PPP, PBB, NasDem, Hanura Party, PSI, Perindo, and PKPI. Prabowo had the support of Gerindra, PAN, PKS, Democrat Party, and the Berkarya Party.

Apart from formal political party support, each presidential candidate had also cultivated a network of local elites in various regions of Indonesia in order to solicit support. Quite surprisingly, Prabowo did not enjoy any support from the elites in South Sulawesi. Jokowi, on the other hand, had received support and endorsements from various political and business elites in South Sulawesi including Jusuf Kalla, Aksa Mahmud, newly elected governor Nurdin Abdullah, and former governor Syahrul Yasin Limpo. A lecturer from the local national university revealed that Jusuf Kalla's and Aksa Mahmud's political endorsement of Jokowi was a personal one and did not represent an endorsement by the Golkar Party, of which they were members.[6] The Golkar Party, however, did not enjoy a reputation of being loyal to one candidate either. During Prabowo's campaign in Makassar in March 2019, the Golkar Party flag was flown, indicating tacit support. Erwin Aksa, a prominent Golkar member who is also the son of Aksa Mahmud, pledged his support to Prabowo as well.

Nurdin Abdullah, who was supported by Jokowi's closest confidant Haji Isam, publicly declared his support towards the Jokowi–Ma'ruf pair.[7] In a public interview, Nurdin mentioned that he would support a Jokowi presidency but was unable to garner support in South Sulawesi (Wijanarko 2019). This was likely due to strong resistance from Islamists who had pledged their support towards his deputy, Andi Sudirman Sulaiman. Andi apparently had strong ties with the PKS while he himself is a *Rohis* member.[8] Thus, if Nurdin had rallied his supporters to vote for the Jokowi–Maruf pair, he would more likely than not be alienated from his constituency which is mostly anti-Jokowi.

The ineffectiveness of Jusuf Kalla's endorsement for Jokowi in South Sulawesi deserves special attention in this case. Having Jusuf Kalla as running mate and vice-presidential candidate in the presidential election ensured that Jokowi, a new political aspirant then, benefitted from the 'coat-tail effect' which aided in his sweep of South Sulawesi Province in 2014.[9] Kalla's network and his stature – as a successful entrepreneur and pious Muslim – was a tremendous asset. Wielding enormous influence within the ruling Golkar Party then, Kalla's connections and networks allowed the pair to win convincingly in the province, securing 71 per cent of the votes in 2014 (Cipto 2014).

It was different 5 years later however. As then vice president, Jusuf Kalla was quick to publicly declare his support for the Jokowi–Ma'ruf pair for the presidential election in 2019, but this did not amount to much. There had been a growing discontent that is directed towards Jusuf Kalla or elites affiliated with his business and political cliques. Despite having strong ties with Golkar Party's constituencies and Islamist networks particularly when he was active in a local Islamic student group called *Pelajar Islam Indonesia* (Indonesian Islamic Student/PII) as well as originating from a non-aristocrat family, Jusuf Kalla has been perceived to be strongly connected to the established local elites networks who are predominantly controlling the economic resources. A pattern thus emerges: that none of the candidates supported or endorsed by Jusuf Kalla in the 2018 Makassar mayoral election and the South Sulawesi gubernatorial election won. Thus it was no surprise that Jusuf Kalla's support for Jokowi in the 2019 presidential election did not necessarily translate into a victory for Jokowi. Jokowi obtained only 43 per cent of votes while Prabowo went on to win in the province with 57 per cent of votes (Safitri 2019).

In the run-up to the 2019 presidential election, the regional campaign team (*Tim Kampanye Daerah*) of Jokowi–Ma'ruf and that of Prabowo–Sandiaga in South Sulawesi had struggled with funding and logistical issues, lacking coordination among coalitional parties in promoting their respective candidates among constituencies. A local politician from the Perindo Party expressed his concern that the absence of campaign funding constrained political party organisation at the regional level in promoting the Jokowi–Ma'ruf pair.[10] Consequently, there was no meeting among coalition parties 2 months before the election commenced. The PDI-P in particular had a more pragmatic strategy – they campaigned for Jokowi–Ma'ruf based on the incentives that the party would gain from the 'coat-tail effect' in comparison to other coalition political parties.

A similar problem also took place with Prabowo's regional campaign team (*Badan Pemenangan Nasional*/BPN). A legislative candidate from PAN revealed that the campaign team was disorganised and lack financial resources, thus limiting the team from campaigning effectively.[11] How then did Prabowo win in South Sulawesi, despite facing the same disadvantages as his opponent? The following section discusses the role of Islamic organisations in South Sulawesi within the context of the presidential election and how their support was crucial in ensuring a Prabowo–Sandi win in the province.

Islamic organisations and identity politics in South Sulawesi

This section discusses the role of Islamic organisations in South Sulawesi and their influence in shaping electoral outcomes in the province, especially that of the presidential election. While there were no strong evidence that Islamist groups played a pivotal role in the 2018 Makassar mayoral election and the South Sulawesi gubernatorial election, it was a different situation for the 2019 presidential election in the province. These organisations had been influential in shaping public perception through small-scale demonstrations under the hashtag *#2019GantiPresiden*. This political and social movement served as a galvaniser of anti-Jokowi sentiments among various Islamic groups in South Sulawesi that, in turn, had the effect of fostering polarisation of identity. This tipped the scales in favour of a Prabowo–Sandi win in the province.

South Sulawesi and Islamic conservatism

With a majority Muslim population, the South Sulawesi Central Bureau of Statistics in 2018 estimated that Muslims comprise 89.6 per cent of the population at 7 million, followed by Protestants at 7.6 per cent and Catholics at 1.5 per cent. Islam had been the religion of the Sultanates such as that of Gowa, Tallo, Makassar, Luwu, and Bulukumba in the region for centuries and it continues to play an important role under the Indonesian Republic. The Sultan of Gowa and Tallo had converted to Islam in 1605 and made it the religion of their kingdoms (Hisyam 2009). Islam flourished in the region but its narrative was dictated by those in power, especially the aristocrats. This would soon change in the aftermath of Indonesian independence with the emergence of the DI/TII in the province. Although DI/TII originated in West Java by Kartosuwirjo, a former presidential guard Kahar Muzakkar joined the movement and became the leader of the South Sulawesi branch. In addition, Kahar Muzakkar was also a member of the *Hizbul Wathan* (the Muhammadiyah Boy Scouts). This Islamist movement was largely anti-aristocratic and had a populist appeal (Juhannis 2006). The DI/TII movement was initially well received by the rural population. Nonetheless, it became to be seen as a threat to the Unitary Republic as well as among the Pamong Praja (or aristocrats) (Pelras 1981). The DI/TII rebellion was eventually put down in 1962 when Kartosuwirjo was captured. The last DI/TII outpost surrendered in Southeast Sulawesi in 1965.

While the Indonesian military did successfully stem out the movement in the province, DI/TII as an idea did not completely disappear in South Sulawesi. In the aftermath of DI/TII's dissolution in the province, remnant DI/TII leaders started to establish disparate organisations that sought to promote and enforce sharia as inspired by DI/TII primarily through Islamic education and *da'wah* (proselytisation) (Buehler 2016). This was accompanied by the establishment of mainstream *pesantren* or Islamic boarding schools, including Darud Da'wah wal Irsyad (DDI) in Pare-Pare, As'adiyah in Wajo, *Ikatan Masjid dan Mushalla Indonesia Muttahidah* (Indonesian Mosque and Mushalla Muttahidah Association/IMMIM), and Hidayatullah (Hasyim 2009). The influence of DI/TII ideology and conservative values thus found its way back into Muslim society in South Sulawesi. These include the introduction and eventual proliferation of Sharia-inspired regional laws (*Peraturan Daerah/ Perda Syariah*).[12]

Islam thus remains an underlying influence in both the social and political domain of the province. The establishment of the Islamist-inspired Committee for the Preparation of Shariah Enactment (*Komite Persiapan Penegakan Syariah Islam* or KPPSI) in South Sulawesi after 1998 was the next step of the province's underlying inclination towards greater Islamisation. The committee was established for the purposes of implementing Sharia bylaws and was tacitly considered a continuation of DI/TII's ideational struggle within South Sulawesi. Further, Islamic figureheads like Fathul Mu'in Daeng Magading, Ahmad Marzuki Hasan, and Mushin Kahar also set up new Islamic organisations like Wahdah Islamiyyah, Darul Istiqamah Islamic Boarding School (*pesantren*), and a Salafi-inspired Hidayatullah, an extremely influential organisation in the province.[13] The KPPSI had been critical in providing assistance towards Islamic organisations like the Islamic Defenders Front (*Front Pembela Islam* or FPI), Jemaah Islamiyah (JI), and Hizb ut-Tahrir Indonesia (HTI). This is not withstanding the fact that the KPPSI also has connections with mainstream organisations such as NU, Muhammadiyah, and the NU-affiliated Darud Da'wah wal Irsyad (DDI).

In their bid to obtain legitimacy and power in the province, Islamist organisations like Wahdah Islamiyyah, Hidayatullah, and FPI had opted to enact and legislate Sharia bylaws.[14] In addition, these organisations had also shored up their membership base by recruiting and cultivating the young in the hope that they could be future leaders who would promote their brand of Islam. Indeed, these ideologies had been thriving in the province and were the main reason why Prabowo, seen then as their choice of presidential candidate who would propagate their values, won readily in the province.

Identity politics and the 2019 presidential election
in South Sulawesi

A crucial galvaniser of Islamic populism in the context of 2019 presidential election in South Sulawesi was the 212 Movement that had grown out of the protests in Jakarta against Chinese Christian governor Basuki Tjahja Purnama (Ahok) over allegations of blasphemy. The 212 movement in South Sulawesi in particular, had the effect of rallying anti-Jokowi sentiments in the name of Islamic solidarity for their preferred candidate, Prabowo.

Groups like the As'adiyyah (a local traditional Islam group closely associated with NU), Wahdah Islamiyyah, Nahdlatul Ulama, Darul Istiqamah, and Muhammadiyah in Makassar, Wajo, and Pare-Pare also propagated anti-Jokowi sentiments and were of the opinion that the Jokowi–Ma'ruf pair had tried to manipulate pious Muslims for political ends.[15] KH Ma'ruf Amin, though generally seen as a conservative cleric, was viewed as one who had compromised his credentials for the sake of political office under Jokowi. In comparison, the Prabowo–Sandi pair was depicted in an entirely positive light as defenders of Islam by these groups even both of them lack a conservative (*santri*) background.[16]

A handful of influential *kyais* (Muslim clerics) from the As'adiyah *pesantren* in Wajo, South Sulawesi, had also explicitly discouraged their followers and constituencies from voting for the Jokowi–Ma'ruf pair. This was in reference to the fact that the Prabowo–Sandi pair were seen as the lesser evil. Allegorically, the Prabowo–Sandi pair was akin to *kopi pahit* (black coffee) in reference to the fact that, while lacking Islamic credentials, they appeared to be genuine, reflective of the bitter taste of the coffee. On the other hand, the Jokowi–Ma'ruf pair was akin to *kopi susu dengan teh* (coffee with milk combined with tea) in reference to the fact that, while at least one of them had credentials as a pious Muslim (read Ma'ruf Amin), they were smooth-talking and not authentic.[17]

Leaders and members of Muhammadiyah and the local Darul Istiqamah *pesantren* in South Sulawesi were also staunch supporters of the Prabowo–Sandiaga pair. A lot of them were critical of Jokowi's economic policies on welcoming foreign investors including China, seen as benefitting the elites and had no effect on the daily struggles of the average Indonesian. Jokowi was seen as an incompetent leader in the realm of the economy and was especially blamed for the increase in foreign debts. There were also instigations that Jokowi had overwhelmingly depended upon China's economic might, a country still seen as communist and thus antithetical to Islam. In addition, there were rumours of an influx of Chinese workers that threatened to take away jobs reserved for Indonesians through industrial projects. Furthermore, Jokowi was seen to be easily influenced by oligarchs handpicked by him who were hostile to conservative ulamas that were vocal against the administration.[18]

Such anti-Jokowi narratives were successfully propagated and promoted by the #2019GantiPresiden rallies in Makassar in 2018. One of such rallies, its largest scale ever, took place in August 2018. It saw a number of prominent local Islamic groups and politicians in South Sulawesi participating, including politicians from the Prabowo-led Gerindra Party, the National Mandate Party (Gerindra's coalition), and the Prosperous Justice Party (PKS). Prominent individuals include Aziz Kahar Muzakkar (son of the Kahar Muzakkar, founder of DI/TII) (Arfah 2018).[19] Several influential Islamic groups that had pledged their support to the movement included the Heresy Chaser Warriors (*Laskar Pemburu Aliran Sesat* or LPAS), FPI, KPPSI, the Anti Syiah National Alliance (*Aliansi Nasional Anti Syiah Indonesia* or ANNAS) for South Sulawesi, the Muhammadiyah Youth Preparedness Forces Command (*Komando Kesiapsiagaan Angkatan Muda Muhammadiyah* or KOKAM), and *Syabab* (Youth) Hidayatullah (Mulyana 2018). Ustadz Mukhtar Daeng Lau (a member of the Salafi-inspired Islamic group Hidayatullah) took an active interest as chairman of United Islam Forum (*Forum Umat Islam Bersatu* or FUIB) by leading the *#2019GantiPresiden* movement in Makassar. The varied and spontaneous support generated from these events showed that grassroots support for the Prabowo–Sandi pair had indeed superceded that of the political parties. Islamic solidarity was directed against the Jokowi–Ma'ruf pair in the province, tilting the scales in favour of a Prabowo–Sandi win.

Conclusion

When examining South Sulawesi Province in the context of the 2018 Makassar mayoral election, the 2018 South Sulawesi gubernatorial election, and the 2019 presidential election, important patterns about the change and continuity in the way politics was being conducted in the province can be gleaned. First, the dominance and influence of traditional oligarchs in South Sulawesi was seen to be on the decline. This was quite evidently demonstrated by Jusuf Kalla's loss of influence in candidates that he and his associates had supported in the regional elections. Second, accountability by elected leaders towards his constituencies had grown to critical importance in the elections. The defeat of Munafri Arifuddin by a mere empty ballot box during the 2018 Makassar mayoral election and the victory of Nurdin Abdullah in the gubernatorial election was indicative of such a trend.

Identity politics however had remained a fixture in the province. The influence of the Jakarta-inspired *#2019GantiPresiden* movement towards galvanising Muslim solidarity and votes in the province were more effective than campaigns by political parties. This led to an unprecedented Prabowo–Sandi win in the province. While the rise of Islamism across Indonesia has been interpreted in various degrees, the case of South Sulawesi stands as a strong barometer of Islamic politics making a return into Indonesian contemporary politics.

Notes

1 The *Darul Islam/Tentara Islam Indonesia* rebellion movement was officially founded in West Java in August 1949 by Sekarmadji Maridjan Kartosuwiryo after the transfer of sovereignty from the Dutch government to the Indonesian government under the Renville Agreement (*Perjanjian Renville*) in January 1948. The rebellion movement only recognised sharia bylaws as the valid source of law for Indonesia, which is

against the aspiration of nationalists. The movement later began to spread in other areas in Indonesia, including South Sulawesi, Aceh, and Kalimantan. In South Sulawesi, the embryo of the movement began when local guerrilla fighters who previously fought the Dutch were not qualified to serve in the Indonesian Army. Hence, the hatred against the Indonesian government started off. For further details on the origin of Darul Islam, see Dengel 1980.

2 Kahar Muzakkar was a former lieutenant–colonel sent by the Indonesian government to negotiate with the insulted local guerrilla fighters, yet ended up joining the rebellion movement. The peak of the rebellion movement in South Sulawesi was the formation of *Tentara Keamanan Rakyat* (People's Security Army). The army founded by Kahar Muzakkar pledged allegiance to the Darul Islam in West Java in 1953 (Juhannis 2006). For further details, see Buehler, M. 2016.

3 Author's interview with a lecturer from a local Islamic university in Makassar (16 December 2018).

4 Author's focus group discussion with lecturers from national university in Makassar (18 December 2018).

5 Author's interview with an official from the gubernatorial office of South Sulawesi (18 December 2018).

6 Author's interview with a lecturer from national university in Makassar (18 December 2018).

7 Andi Syamsuddin Arsyad, publicly known as Haji Isam, is a coal businessman based in South Kalimantan. He served as the treasurer of Jokowi's national campaign team (*tim kampanye nasional* or TKN) during the 2019 presidential election.

8 *Rohis* or 'Rohani Islam' is an organisation established by the Prosperous Justice Party (PKS) to attract new members. This organisation organises extracurricular activities at the junior and senior high level to attract the young.

9 The 'coattail effect' is widely understood as the tendency for a popular political party leader to attract votes for other candidates of the same party in an election. For further read, see Calvert & Ferejohn, 1983.

10 Author's interview with a local politician from Perindo Party for South Sulawesi Chapter (18 December 2018).

11 Author's interview with a national legislative candidate from National Mandate Party (19 December 2018).

12 For a more detailed overview of the implementation of Sharia bylaws in Bulukumba, South Sulawesi, and its relation with local power brokers, see Buehler (2008). For the case of Gowa, South Sulawesi, women civil servants are obligated to don the *jilbab* and attend Islamic teachings or congregations after office hours, see Khairi, 2012.

13 KH Fathul Mu'in Daeng Maggading was a well-known leader of Muhammadiyah local branch in Makassar and Maros, who also founded a Muhammadiyah activity centre called Ta'mirul Mu'minin. A foundation called *Yayasan Fathul Mu'in* was founded after his demise (currently known as Wahdah Islamiyah). Ahmad Marzuki Hasan established *Yayasan Pembinaan Darul Istiqamah* (The Foundation of Darul Istiqamah Education), which subsequently opened Islamic boarding school in Maros and elsewhere, including Manado, North Sulawesi. Mushin Kahar established the organisation named *Hidayatullah* (Guidance of God).

14 Hidayatullah and Wahdah Islamiyyah were both founded in the 1980s by former ulamas and activists of South Sulawesi's local branch of Muhammadiyah. These organisations were developed extensively through the establishment of the Islamic education system, stemming from early education to university and include the pesantrens, notably in Kalimantan, Sulawesi and Java. These network of Islamic schools, universities, and pesantrens serve as an ideological breeding ground for greater conservatism. Hidayatullah and Wahdah Islamiyyah differ ideologically from Muhammadiyah in terms of leaning towards a more rigorous strand of Islam inspired by the Salafi-Wahabbism of the Middle East.

15 Author's interview with prominent members of local Islamic organisations in Makassar, Wajo, Pare-Pare and Maros (21 December 2018).
16 The term 'santri' was promoted by Clifford Geertz in his book *The Religion of Java*, where the Javanese populace could be categorised into three groups: *abangan* (nominal Muslim), *priyayi* (aristocrats), and *santri* (pious Muslims).
17 Author's interview with a handful of local clerics at As'adiyah Islamic Boarding School (*pesantren*) (20 December 2018).
18 Author's interview with local clerics from Muhammadiyah and Darul Istiqamah in Makassar and Maros (21 December 2018).
19 Gerindra politicians include Agus Arifin Nu'mang, Rusdin Tabi, Sawaluddin Arief, Anwar Wahab, and Bachrianto Bachtiar; PAN politicians include Jamaluddin Jafar, Andi Darwis, and Yusran Paris; and PKS politician was Aryadi Arsal.

Bibliography

Arfah, H. 2018, 12 August. 'Berikut Politisi Sulsel di Deklarasi #2019GantiPresiden Makassar' ['Lists of South Sulawesi Politicians at Makassar #2019ChangePresident']. *Tribun Makassar*. Retrieved from https://makassar.tribunnews.com/2018/08/12/berikut-politisi-sulsel-di-deklarasi-2019gantipresiden-makassar.

Buehler, M. 2009. 'The Rising Importance of Personal Networks in Indonesian Local Politics: An Analysis of District Government Head Elections in South Sulawesi in 2005'. In M. Erb, & P. Sulistiyanto (Eds.). *Deepening Democracy in Indonesia? Direct Elections for Local Leaders (Pilkada)*. Singapore: ISEAS.

Buehler, M. 2016. *The Politics of Shari'a Law: Islamist Activists and the State in Democratizing Indonesia*. Cambridge: Cambridge University Press.

Buehler, M., & P. Tan. 2007. Party-Candidate Relationships in Indonesian Local Politics: A Case Study of the 2005 Regional Elections in Gowa, South Sulawesi Province. *Indonesia*, (84), 41–69.

Calvert, R., & Ferejohn, 1983. J. Coattail Voting in Recent Presidential Elections. *American Political Science Review*, Vol. 77 (2), 407–419.

Cipto, H. 2014, 19 July. 'Hasil Pleno KPUD Sulsel, Jokowi-JK Menang Telak' ['South Sulawesi General Elections Commission Plenary Result, Jokowi-JK Wins Dramatically']. *Kompas.com*. Retrieved from https://regional.kompas.com/read/2014/07/19/23021861/Hasil.Pleno.KPUD.Sulsel.Jokowi-JK.Menang.Telak.

Cipto, H. 2016, 26 April. 'Aktivis Sebut Reklamasi Pantai Losari Rugikan Negara Rp 15 Triliun' ['Activist Claims Losari Beach Reclamation Project Harm Country for 15 Trillion Rupiah']. *Kompas*. Retrieved from https://regional.kompas.com/read/2016/04/26/05093431/Aktivis.Sebut.Reklamasi.Pantai.Losari.Rugikan.Negara.Rp.15.Triliun.

Cipto, H. 2018, 10 January. 'Lawan Petahana, Kerabat Jusuf Kalla Diusung 10 Partai di Pilkada Kota Makassar' ['Ten Political Parties Nominate Jusuf Kalla's Relative in Makassar Mayoral Election Challenging Incumbent']. *Kompas*. Retrieved from https://regional.kompas.com/read/2018/01/10/18463041/lawan-petahana-kerabat-jusuf-kalla-diusung-10-partai-di-pilkada-kota.

Dengel H. 1980. *Darul Islam dan Kartosuwiryo: Angan-angan yang Gagal* (Darul Islam and Kartosuwiryo: Failed Dreams). Jakarta: Pustaka Sinar Harapan.

Feith, H. 1971. *The Indonesian Elections of 1955*. New York: Cornell University Press.

Firdausi, F. 2019, 17 April. 'Sejarah Hari Coblosan Pemilu 1955: Barat Relatif Aman, Timur Rawan' ['Historical Day of 1955 General Elections: West is Relatively Safe,

East is Dangerous']. *Tirto*. Retrieved from https://tirto.id/sejarah-hari-coblosan-pemilu-1955-barat-relatif-aman-timur-rawan-dmq9.

Geertz, C. 1976. *The Religion of Java*. Chicago: The University of Chicago Press.

Hantoro, J. 2018, 27 June. 'Reaksi Calon Tunggal Pilkada Makassar Kalah dari Kolom Kosong' ['Reaction of Single Candidate to Lost against Empty Ballot in Makassar Mayoral Election']. *Tempo.co*. Retrieved from https://pilkada.tempo.co/read/1101473/reaksi-calon-tunggal-pilkada-makassar-kalah-dari-kolom-kosong/full&view=ok.

Herlina, L. 2018, 22 March. 'PTTUN Hadang Danny Pomanto' ['PTTUN Blocks Danny Pomanto']. *Media Indonesia*. Retrieved from https://mediaindonesia.com/read/detail/150627-pt-tun-hadang-danny-pomanto.

Hisyam, M. 2009. The Preparatory Committee for Implementation of Sharia (KPPSI): An Islamic Resurgence in South Sulawesi. In I. Tokoro (Ed.), *Islam in Southeast Asia: Transnational Networks and Local Context Studies*. Tokyo: Tokyo University of Foreign Studies.

Indrawan, A. 2018, 20 March. 'Survei Pilwakot Makassar, Pejawat Unggul' ['Survey on Makassar Mayoral Election, Incumbent Leading']. *Republika*. Retrieved from https://nasional.republika.co.id/berita/nasional/pilkada/18/03/20/p5vvsq365-survei-pilwalkot-makassar-pejawat-unggul.

Juhannis, H. 2006. *The Struggle for Formalist Islam in South Sulawesi: From Darul Islam (DI) to Komite Persiapan Penegakan Syariat Islam (KPPSI)*. Unpublished PhD thesis. Canberra: Australian National University.

Khairi, A. 2012, June. Implications of Shariah by-Law on Moslem Dress Code on Women in Indonesia. *JICSA (Journal of Islamic Civilization in Southeast Asia)*, Vol. 1(1), 36–54.

Kompas 2019a, 23 April. 'Dalam 5 Tahun, Danny Pomanto Ubah Makassar Jadi Kota Dunia yang Nyaman' ['Danny Pomanto Changes Makassar into Comfortable World City in Five Years']. *Kompas*. Retrieved from https://regional.kompas.com/read/2019/04/23/07185821/dalam-5-tahun-danny-pomanto-ubah-makassar-jadi-kota-dunia-yang-nyaman?page=all.

Kompas. 2019b, 10 April. '5 Tahun Jadi Walikota, Danny Pomanto Tingkatkan Ekonomi Makassar' ['Danny Pomanto Revitalizes Makassar's Economy Five Years as Mayor']. *Kompas*. Retrieved from https://regional.kompas.com/read/2019/04/10/23122481/5-tahun-jadi-walikota-danny-pomanto-tingkatkan-ekonomi-makassar.

Kompas. 2019c, 10 April. 'Danny Pomanto Mengubah Makassar Bukan Lagi Kota Demonstrasi' '[Danny Pomanto Changes Makassar Not to Become a "Protest City"']. *Kompas*. Retrieved from https://regional.kompas.com/read/2019/04/10/23122481/5-tahun-jadi-walikota-danny-pomanto-tingkatkan-ekonomi-makassar.

Kunjana, G. 2018, 21 June. 'Elektabilitas Agus Numang-Tanribali Naik karena Didukung JK' ['Agus Numang-Tanribali's Electability Increased due to JK Support']. *Berita Satu*. Retrieved from www.beritasatu.com/investor/497631/elektabilitas-agus-numang-tanribali-naik-karena-didukung-jk.

Magenda, B.D. 1989. *The Surviving Aristocracy in Indonesia: Politics in Three Provinces of the Outer Islands*. Unpublished PhD thesis. Ithaca: Cornell University.

Mulyana, K. 2018, 8 August. 'LPAS Kawal Neno Warisman di Makassar' ['LPAS Guards Neno Warisman in Makassar']. *Sindo Makassar*. Retrieved from https://makassar.sindonews.com/read/12224/1/laskar-pemburu-aliran-sesat-akan-kawal-neno-warisman-di-makassar-1533690524.

Pelras, C. 1981. 'Patron-Client Ties Among the Bugis and Makassarese of South Sulawesi'. In R. Tol, K. Dijk, & G. Acciaioli (Eds.). *Authority and Enterprise Among the Peoples of South Sulawesi*. Leiden: KITLV Press.

Safitri, E. 2019, 19 May. 'Rekapitulasi KPU: Selisih Prabowo-Jokowi di Sulsel 700 Ribu Suara' ['KPU Recapitulation: Prabowo-Jokowi Vote Differences in South Sulawesi Reaches Seven Hundred Thousand Votes']. *Detik*. Retrieved from https://news.detik.com/berita/d-4555738/rekapitulasi-kpu-selisih-prabowo-jokowi-di-sulsel-700-ribu-suara.

Sarwanto, A. 2016, 17 May. 'Setya Novanto Resmi Ditetapkan Jadi Ketum Golkar 2016–2019' ['Setya Novanto Officially Elected 2016–2019 Golkar Chairman']. *CNN Indonesia*. Retrieved from www.cnnindonesia.com/nasional/20160517075856-32-131209/setya-novanto-resmi-ditetapkan-jadi-ketum-golkar-2016-2019.

South Sulawesi Central Bureau of Statistics. 2018. *South Sulawesi Province in Figures 2018*. Makassar: BPS Sulawesi Selatan. Retrieved from https://sulsel.bps.go.id/publication/2018/08/16/73a6daeb04543fd9751dfc34/provinsi-sulawesi-selatan-dalam-angka-2018.html.

South Sulawesi Central Bureau of Statistics. 2019. Jumlah Penduduk Sulawesi Selatan (Number of South Sulawesi Population). *BPS Sulawesi Selatan*. Retrieved from https://sulsel.bps.go.id/quickMap.html.

South Sulawesi General Elections Commission. 2018, 30 August. KPU Sulsel Tetapkan DPT Pemilu 2019 Sebanyak 5.972.161 (South Sulawesi General Elections Commission Set 5,972,161 Final Voters List for 2019 Election). *KPU Sulawesi Selatan*. Retrieved from https://sulsel.kpu.go.id/2018/08/30/kpu-sulsel-tetapkan-dpt-pemilu-2019-ebanyak-5-972-161/.

Suryadinata, L. 2007. 'The Decline of the Hegemonic Party System in Indonesia: Golkar after the Fall of Soeharto'. *Contemporary Southeast Asia*, Vol. 29 (2): 333–358.

Syamsuri, M., & S. Wardani. 2018. 'The Decline of Golkar Party's Hegemony: Golkar's Performance in Facing the Simultaneous Regional Elections in South Sulawesi'. *Literasi Hukum*, Vol. 2 (2): 68–82.

Tomsa, D. 2007, 22 July. 'Bloodied but Unbowed'. *Inside Indonesia*. Retrieved from www.insideindonesia.org/bloodied-but-unbowed.

Wijanarko, T. 2019, 19 April. 'Jokowi Kalah di Sulsel, Nurdin Abdullah Susah Menjelaskan' ['Jokowi Lost in South Sulawesi, Nurdin Abdullah Can Barely Explain']. *Tempo.co*. Retrieved from https://pilpres.tempo.co/read/1197139/jokowi-kalah-di-sulsel-nurdin-abdullah-susah-menjelaskan.

Zulfikarnain. 2018, 8 January. 'Resmi, Danny Pomanto-Indira Mendaftar Sebagai Calon Wali Kota Makassar di KPU' ['Danny Pomanto-Indira Officially Registered Makassar Mayoral Candidate']. *Okezone News*. Retrieved from https://news.okezone.com/read/2018/01/08/340/1841735/resmi-danny-pomanto-indira-mendaftar-sebagai-calon-wali-kota-makassar-di-kpu.

9 The 2018/2019 simultaneous elections in West Kalimantan province and its aftermath

Historical legacies, identity politics, and the politics of partition

Jonathan Chen

Introduction

The province of West Kalimantan tends to be overlooked in studies of Indonesian politics due to the disproportionate amount of attention paid to Java, Indonesia's most populous island and the seat of the nation's capital, Jakarta. The island of Indonesian Kalimantan, particularly the province of West Kalimantan, deserves attention because it has been deemed 'vulnerable (*rawan*)' to money politics and the politicisation of ethnicity, religion, race, and other social divisions (also known collectively in Indonesia as SARA or *Suku, Agama, Ras dan Antargolongan*) by the Election Supervisory Board (*Bawaslu*) and the Indonesian police even before elections began (*Tribun Pontianak* 2019a, Hamdan, *Tribun Pontianak* 2018b). West Kalimantan was ranked third behind Papua (score 3.41) and Maluku (score 3.25) in the Election Vulnerability Index with a score of 3.04 for the 2018 Regional Head Elections (Bawaslu Republik Indonesia 2017), indicating a high level of vulnerability. This assessment ties in with the unique ethnic configuration of the province and its historic links with violence and repression under Suharto's New Order, in light of contemporary political developments in Jakarta in which the province is particularly susceptible as will be shown in the sections below. West Kalimantan is also Indonesia's third-largest province by area (146,807 km²) after Papua (421,891 km²) and Central Kalimantan (152,600 km²) or 1.13 times the size of Java. The abundance of land and the utilisation land for lucrative plantations (usually oil palm), including the politics surrounding partition (*pemekaran*), adds an interesting dimension to the political complexities of the province. Compared to Java, West Kalimantan is sparsely populated (approximately 5.4 million people) and far from the levers of power such that many had considered the province as 'peripheral' in the grand scale of nationwide politics. However, this chapter argues that its vastness and the ethnic heterogeneity and fault lines that have come to define identity politics and how it is conducted in the province, warrants attention, especially with respect to ethnic and political polarisation. In order to understand the complexity of the 2018 West Kalimantan election, a brief introduction to the province's troubled history is required (Heidhues 2003, Davidson 2009, Tanasaldy 2012).

Historical legacies and path dependencies

West Kalimantan province resembles a classic Furnivallesque 'plural society' segregated by ethnic enclaves. For instance, Singakwang is a majority Chinese Hakka town while a large Teochew community reside within Pontianak city and the more urbanised regions. Landak regency has a majority Dayak population while the coastal (*pesisir*) regions of Pontianak, Ketapang, and Mempawah used to be ruled by the Pontianak Sultanate where the majority ethnic Malay population resides. The province's Westerly location in the island of Borneo facing the South China Sea had historically attracted many newcomers (*pendatang*) due to its vast land mass and rich natural resources. Indeed, the Chinese had traded and thrived in West Kalimantan even before the region was colonised. In 1777, Hakka gold and tin miners established the Lanfang Republic – a Chinese state and a *kongsi* federation in West Borneo – that was defeated by the Dutch in 1884 in a series of *kongsi* wars. The Republic had friendly contacts with the Pontianak Sultanate but was considered a thorn over Dutch imperialist designs. The Pontianak Sultanate, on the other hand, was set up in 1771 by explorers hailing from Hadhramaut (present day Yemen) led by an Arab–Malay Sultan (Al Sayyid) with close links to the Riau Sultanate. They were also closely allied with the Sultans of Banjar in the East. A few other Malay principalities were established along the coastal regions in West Borneo such as Sambas and Mempawah, but were subsequently eliminated in a joint Dutch–Pontianak attack.

The Dutch ruled Kalimantan via the Sultanates as their proxies and did not exercise direct control, unlike Java. Even before the Dutch arrived on the scene, the Malay–Muslim Sultanate had imposed its hegemony over the inland non-Muslim Dayaks by forcing them to pay taxes or provide Dayak slaves (Heidhues 1998). The Dayaks, by then, were divided into several clans and had over 400 different languages. Many of the Dayaks in West Kalimantan had converted to Catholicism when Dutch missionaries arrived, although a sizable number still retained their traditional beliefs. In 1946, the autonomous region of West Kalimantan was established and led by Syarif Hamid II, the eighth Sultan of Pontianak and the only president of the State of West Kalimantan until its disestablishment in 1950. During the decolonisation process between 1945 and 1950, proponents of federalism and a Federated Republic of Indonesia (RIS) lost while Syarif Hamid II was discredited and the Sultanate abolished. West Kalimantan lost its autonomous status and was subsequently integrated into the province of Kalimantan (Kahin 1952). In the mid-1960s, West Kalimantan was embroiled in transnational and intra-national conflicts that sharpened ethnic tensions in the province. The province was at the frontline of substantial fighting during the Indonesia–Malaysia confrontation first under the Sukarno government, and subsequently endured acts of mass killings by the military during the New Order, directed at remnant fighters of the Indonesian Communist Party. Due to the province's proximity to Malaysia and its association with the Communist Party, the province endured decades of martial law, governed by de facto military rule from Jakarta by a succession of governors, many of whom were retired Javanese military commanders. This state of affairs lasted until the collapse of the Suharto regime. During this period, the military engaged in forced evictions of the Chinese from inland to coastal regions, as well as large-scale migrations of Javanese and Madurese from Java.

Such policies led to the gradual and unofficial disenfranchisement of the local Dayaks, manifesting in the Dayaks' acute frustration. In 1967, tensions and a conflict between the Dayaks and ethnic Chinese led to the deaths of about 3,000 people and the resettlement of 117,000 Chinese from rural villages to larger cities like Pontianak and Singkawang (Davidson & Kammen 2002). Violence also erupted in 1996 and 1997 between the Dayaks and the Madurese, killing approximately 500 people while turning 75,000 Madurese into refugees. In the wake of the uncertainly surrounding Indonesia's early reform era, ethnic violence broke out in various parts of the vast province (Hawkins 2009, pp. 153–172). In 1999, violence broke out between the Malays and the Madurese in the regency of Sambas resulting in 118 deaths and up to 30,000 Madurese refugees (*The Guardian* 1999). The origins of the riots had its roots in large-scale migrations (also known as transmigration) of Madurese and Javanese during the 1970s and 1980s, which changed the demographic make-up of the province quite significantly. The Dayaks, in particular, felt short-changed as they had only one representative for the office of governor in West Kalimantan during the 32 years of New Order under Suharto (*Kompas* 2012).[1]

West Kalimantan's ethnic diversity can be seen in its distribution and make-up of its various ethnicities, shown in Table 9.1 (total population 4,385,704) (BPS Indonesia 2010).[2] While the locals (Dayak and Malay) made up more than half of the total population, there are significant Javanese, Chinese, and Madurese migrants that are distinct from and do not inter-mix with the locals. This has often led to candidates from the respective ethnic groups contest for elections on an ethnic platform to advance ethnic interests. Such a dynamic, unfortunately, can potentially generate a 'winner-takes-all' conundrum, exacerbating the ethnic divide. This is reflected in the campaigns leading up to the 2018 regional elections, where major candidates had tactically resorted to identity politics in their campaigns in order to secure the most votes from their own ethnic groups.

Table 9.1 Ethnic groups in West Kalimantan

Ethnic group	Population	Percentage (%)
Dayak	1,531,989	34.93
Malay	1,484,085	33.84
Javanese	427,238	9.74
Chinese	358,451	8.17
Madurese	274,869	6.27

Source: Indonesian Statistical Agency (BPS).

Candidates and political parties

It is with this historical background and ethnic composition in mind that one has to consider when looking at the political situation in the province of West Kalimantan. The 2018 gubernatorial election for West Kalimantan featured three candidate pairs (Figure 9.1). The first pair (No. 1) was Milton Crosby and Boyman Harun. Milton was born in Sekadau and was the former regent of Sintang for two terms from 2005–2010 and 2010–2015. He was affiliated with the Democrat Party. Milton's deputy is Boyman Harun, an ethnic Malay born in Ketapang. Boyman was also an ex-regent of Ketapang and served as the local chairman of the National Mandate Party (PAN).

The second candidate pair (No. 2) featured Karolin Margret Natasa and Suryadman Gidot. Karolin was the regent (*bupati*) of Landak and also the daughter of Cornelis, the outgoing governor. She is also a member of the Indonesian House of Representatives (DPR) representing the Indonesian Democratic Party of Struggle (PDI-P) serving two terms from 2009–2017. Her running mate was Suryadman Gidot, an ethnic Dayak born in Bengkayang, who was also regent of Bengkayang from 2010–2015. The Karolin–Gidot candidate pair had been campaigning on an exclusively pan-Dayak platform with strongholds in Landak regency even though the pair received some support from Malay groups such as the Laskar Pemuda Melayu (LPM) (*Tribun Pontianak* 2018c).

The third pairing (No. 3) consisted of Sutarmidji and Ria Norsan. Sutarmidji was the ex-deputy mayor of Pontianak city from 2003–2008 and ex-mayor of Pontianak city from 2013–2018. He was closely affiliated with the Islamic United Development Party (PPP). Sutarmidji's deputy was Ria Norsan, an ethnic Malay and regent of Mempawah for two terms from 2009–2013 and 2013–2018. The Sutarmidji–Norsan candidate pair campaigned on a nationalist platform and were careful to avoid pandering to specific ethnic groups. While Karolin and Milton are ethnic Dayaks, Sutarmidji is an ethnic Javanese, who is closely aligned with the ethnic Malays within the province. The diverse background of these aspiring gubernatorial candidates and their deputies speaks of a new post-1998 generation of local elites (Choi 2014). What is particularly unique is that a series of events and occurrences that took place in Jakarta prior to the elections in West Kalimantan, namely the 2016–2017 Defending Islam Protests (*Aksi Bela Islam*) would emanate beyond Jakarta and entangle itself in the web of ethnic and religious constellations in West Kalimantan, rousing chauvinistic religious and ethnic sentiments that were already lying under the surface. It did not help that the candidates, whether intentional or not, chose deputies along ethnic lines, making overtures to sensitivities regarding ethnicity and religion in their campaigns (Lim 2017).

In earlier days, gubernatorial candidates often paired their candidacy through an informal power-sharing agreement with a different ethnic group in order to minimise conflict in a multi-ethnic environment. Cornelis, the Dayak ex-governor, had a Chinese, Christiandy Sanjaya, as his vice governor for two terms. This strategy however was abandoned, and the reason had partly to do with Cornelis'

Figure 9.1 The three candidate pairs in a local newspaper.

governorship and his reputation of bypassing the appointment of Malays to important political positions from 2008–2018. As a result, tensions between ethnic Dayaks and Malays deteriorated and became much more tenuous (Fubertus Ipur, personal communication, 7 June 2018). Furthermore, it is alleged that during Cornelis' decade-long tenure as provincial governor, most of the appointments for department head (*kepala dinas*) were given to a person of Dayak stock and more often than not a member of his own tribe, the Kanayatan (Fubertus Ipur, personal communication, 7 June 2018). Outright favouritism and nepotism had created unhappiness and jealously not just from the Malays but other non-Kanayatan Dayak tribes as well, exacerbating the 'zero-sum' nature of a political victory. In the process, Cornelis' actions led to a split within the Dayak political constellation, notwithstanding the fact that Milton Crosby, the former regent of Sintang, running against Karolin, came from a different Dayak tribe, and is a Protestant, unlike Cornelis and Karolin, who are Roman Catholics. Such a development demonstrated that the Dayaks are certainly far from being a monolithic group.

The Karolin–Gidot team (No. 2) garnered the most number of seats (27 seats) when competing in the gubernatorial elections and was supported by the Indonesian Democratic Party of Struggle (PDI-P) (15 seats), the Democratic Party (PD) (9 seats) and the locally dominant Indonesian Justice and Unity Party (PKPI) (3 seats). The Sutarmidji–Norsan pair (No. 3) had the next largest number of seats at 25 and was supported by Golkar (9 seats), the NasDem Party (5 seats), the United Development Party (PPP) (4 seats), Hanura (3 seats), the Prosperous Justice Party (PKS) (2 seats) and the National Awakening Party (PKB) (2 seats). Finally, the Milton–Boyman pair (No. 1), which had just managed to reach the threshold of 13 seats, had the Great Indonesia Movement Party (Gerindra) (7 seats) and the National Mandate Party (PAN) (6 seats) for support.

The frontrunners of the 2018 gubernatorial election, were team Karolin–Gidot (No. 2) and Sutarmidji–Norsan (No. 3). Their campaign had been the most aggressive and had roused the greatest interest in the constituencies. According to Maskendari, manager of Karolin's Success Team (*Tim Sukses*), he had been on the ground campaigning in the rural areas focusing on the Dayak vote, going to inland areas like Sintang in a speedboat and on a motorcycle (Maskendari, personal communication, 9 June 2018). The Milton–Boyman team had its supporters but enjoyed a much smaller electoral impact, although it offered an alternative to the two competing pairs. While the Malays make up the majority of the coastal regions, the inland regions dominated by the Dayaks also played a strong factor in the galvanising and mobilising of voter bases.

The Golkar Party supported Sutarmidji because Ria Norsan – its provincial chair – was his vice gubernatorial nominee. The United Development Party (PPP) however was allegedly in a dispute with Sutarmidji then as he was closer to the Djan Faridz faction (*Antara News* 2016) within the party, while much of the PPP leadership in West Kalimantan had been aligned with Romahurmuzy's faction.[3] In essence, the PPP of West Kalimantan only half-heartedly support Sutarmidji's candidacy. The support among the Chinese community is more difficult to ascertain and they tend to back both sides (Anonymous interview, personal communication, 8 June 2018). Even though they form a significant minority within the province, they tend to be politically reticent during election time and are usually pragmatic in their support towards candidates – often not declaring their support until the last minute. The next section seeks to examine in greater detail specific aspects of ethnicity and religion that had defined the contemporary political landscape of West Kalimantan.

Identity politics: the confluence of religion and ethnicity

The growing consciousness of a unified pan-Dayak identity can be traced to the Dayak's exclusion from politics during the New Order period and the need to eradicate the unflattering image of the Dayak as 'primitive' and 'backward'. In the late 1980s, a Dayak-based non-governmental organisation (NGO) named the Pancur Kasih Foundation was established to help build up the Dayak community via a credit union. The Foundation proved to be very well received and its credit union became a huge success (Thung et al. 2004). It later went on to establish the Institute of Dayakology Research and Development (IDRD) in 1991, which focuses on the revitalisation of Dayak customs and heritage. At this point in time, a monthly news magazine was also set up, known as the *Kalimantan Review*. The *Review* focuses on reporting the social, political, economic, and cultural views of the Dayaks, giving a crucial voice and outlet for the Dayak community amid their economic and political marginalisation. After the fall of the Suharto government, these Dayak organisations and bodies had the effect of rousing in the Dayaks a keen sense of ethnic identity and political awakening (Davidson 2003). Even before the New Order had fallen, the appointment of Jacobus Layang, a Dayak career bureaucrat, as regent of Kapuas Hulu in 1994, was politically symbolic and formative. Early into the *Reformasi* period, the Dayaks had begun to assert themselves politically in local elections and came to be dominant and successful in assuming several regencies in West Kalimantan. Cornelis finally broke the mould of Dayak regents by becoming the second Dayak governor of West Kalimantan in 2008 after a lapse of more than four decades. While there are numerous Dayak sub-ethnicities in which Dayak groups differed greatly in many respects, in that particular context 'Dayak' identity became interpreted in a unified, homogenous way (König 2016).

While the ethnic factor had always been emphasised, what had gained tremendous traction was the religious element that tends to be neglected, especially among the Malays who are generally seen as targets of the new Islamic conservatism. Within the last few years, new groups from Jakarta have established their presence in West Kalimantan, further politicising the ethno-religious tension within the province. One of them was the Islamic Defenders Front (FPI), which had gained notoriety in their direct involvement with the 2016–2017 Jakarta protests, also known as the *Aksi Bela Islam* (Action for Defending Islam). The *Aksi* are a series of Islamist protests led by the Islamic Defenders Front group against then-governor of Jakarta Basuki Tjahaja Purnama (popularly known as Ahok), who was accused of committing blasphemy of the Quran from October 2016 to March 2017. Locally, the FPI also had strong connections with certain members of the Alkadrie family of the revived Pontianak Sultanate (Van Klinken 26 July 2007)[4] including the current reigning Sultan, Mahmud Melvin Alkadrie, as well as part of the Alkadrie family who share close ties with controversial preacher Habib Rizieq (Max Yusuf Alkadrie, personal communication, 23 November 2018, *Pontianak Post*, 13 July 2017).[5] In fact, the Sultan was seen hosting an Islamic event alongside the ex-head of the FPI branch of Pontianak, Habib Ishak Ali Al Muthahar. In addition, FPI and other similar Islamic vigilante groups had seemed to gain greater legitimacy especially among conservative Malay communities as a formidable force against vice in the city, in relation to the police who are seen as lackadaisical and subject to corruption (Prof. Syarif Ibrahim Alkadrie, personal communication, 11 June 2018, Habib Ishak Ali Al Muthahar, personal communication, 11 June 2018). In recent years, FPI branches in West Kalimantan had also made inroads as charitable or philanthropic bodies with the initiative of winning the hearts and minds of its Muslim support base. In Mempawah for example, the FPI branch had taken to distributing food and other necessities during the month of Ramadan to the poor and under-privilege (*Pontianak Post* 2018a).

Rather than being a disruptive force, the FPI in West Kalimantan had preached for all Islamic organisations to come together prior to the elections in 2016. The FPI also held rallies with POM (shorthand for *Persatuan Orang Muda Melayu*) or the Malay Youth Association[6] in Pontianak that openly threatened the Dayak community in 2017. These groups infiltrated into the primarily Malay–Muslim organisations, spreading their teaching via proselytisation (*dakwah*) and prayer events. In addition, these groups have also sought to challenge the existing cultural norms and festivities in West Kalimantan. For example, a *Surat Keputusan* (SK) – a regent or mayor's decree that does not require formal approval by the local legislative council (DPRD) and yet considered to be legally enforceable – was seen to be the reason that temporarily halted all forms of Chinese religious processions (also known as *pawai*) on the streets of Pontianak during Imlek (Chinese New Year, CNY) and particularly during *Capgomeh* (15th day of CNY), pressured nonetheless by the local FPI against the Pontianak mayor. There is also a strong Saudi influence in the form of financial aid to Islamic centres to spread their ideology, promoting greater exclusiveness by virtue of religion in the province. In university campuses, the influence of Hizb ut-Tahrir Indonesia (HTI)[7] had been prevalent (Fubertus Ipur, personal communication, 7 June 2018). HTI-affiliated organisations are also influential in terms of building infrastructure like schools and hospitals.

The presence of FPI has caused increased tensions between Dayak and Malay communities, as the Dayak criticised FPI's actions to stage anti-Cornelis' protests as 'Dayak vs FPI', while the Malays see Dayak hostility to FPI and such protests as 'Dayak vs Islam'. The FPI branch in Pontianak had, in the past, invited Habib Rizieq Shihab as special guest for Qur'anic recitation events as well as mass religious meetings in Pontianak (*Antara News* 2012). The most recent invitation however met with a backlash. In April 2017, Cornelis made a strongly worded statement in response to an alleged challenge from FPI Pontianak to invite Habib Rizieq to West Kalimantan. In his speech, Cornelis said that Rizieq's views are not representative of Islam and would be evicted without fail if he set foot in the province (*Pinter Politik* 2017, *Rappler* 2017). At that point in time, Habib Rizieq Shihab was still in Medina although banners could be seen welcoming Rizieq to Pontianak. In response to Cornelis' speech, masses in Aceh also rejected the presence of Cornelis in Aceh when he had to attend a function for the national farmers' and fishermen association officiated by president Joko Widodo on 6 May 2017.

The conflict was worsened and aggravated with statements made by hardline preachers such as Tengku Zulkarnain and local FPI chief Ishak Ali Al-Mutakhar that encouraged the organisation of mass rallies and demonstrations with the tagline of 'Defending the Ulama in Pontianak!' (Aksi Bela Ulama Pontianak 205) (*Detik News* 2017b).[8] This eventually escalated into a planned demonstration march by largely ethnic Malay demonstrators under the banner of 'Defending the Ulama' which occurred on the same day as the start of a Dayak street celebration (Gawai Dayak) (BBC Indonesia 2017). Here, religion is refracted through an ethnic lens that exacerbated the latent tensions between the Dayak and Malay communities.

Tensions were high in the province as the week-long Gawai Dayak Harvest Festival – an annual festival with many Dayak men and women clad in their traditional costumes, carrying their spears and machetes – was interrupted by FPI and POM members who had organised a rally, in lieu of the anti-Ahok rallies that took place in Jakarta, demanding that the police charge West Kalimantan governor Cornelis for insulting the *ulama* (*The Star Online* 2017). In a few social media outlets that were in circulation, young Malay men were seen with their sticks running towards a Dayak group from Flamboyan market along Gajah Mada Street in central Pontianak. At the opposite end, young Dayak men were rushing with their own implements (*Detik News* 2017a). While a full-blown riot was averted and the riot police managed to contain the tensions, it left a bitter taste of things to come.

The use of ethnocentric and religious sloganeering, especially with an eye on the coming regional elections, became the underlying cause for the escalation of tensions between Malays and Dayaks. West Kalimantan, under Cornelis' leadership as governor, was seen as the 'latest lighting rod' for the FPI after the demonstrations in Jakarta which brought down Christian Chinese governor Basuki Tjahaja Purnama (*The Economist* 2017). The FPI and Islamists, spurred on by their victories in the nation's capital, wanted to replace the next governor of West Kalimantan with a Malay–Muslim candidate by weaponising identity politics. In the meantime, Habib Rizieq had denounced Cornelis as a *kafir* (or infidel) while Cornelis had responded back that he would 'butcher' the Islamist if Rizieq were to set foot in West Kalimantan. FPI's Habib Rizieq and his lieutenants appealed to the Malays' discontent incited by Cornelis' discriminatory policies that favoured the Chinese and particularly the Dayaks (A.R. Muzammil, personal communication, 12 June 2018).[9] Haunted by the electoral upset in Jakarta, Cornelis wanted to safeguard his daughter Karolin who was going to run as his replacement in the upcoming gubernatorial election. He thus took a hardline stance against the group, issuing a decree banning FPI and threatened its members with violence if they dared organise another protest in the province (Antonius Situmorang, personal communication, 10 June 2018).

Thus religion and ethnicity, particularly the split between Dayak–Christians and the Malay–Muslims, became amplified and polarised (John Bamba, personal communication, 14 June 2018).[10] Both groups resorted to a revival of historical anachronisms, essentialisms and age-old grievances (Ramadhan 2018)[11] that denigrated the other. Things came to a head when a YouTube video in circulation showed Cornelis as head of the Dayak Adat Council (*Dewan Adat Dayak*, DAD) giving a speech accusing the Malay community as 'colonisers of the Dayak people' (Arifianto and Chen 2018).[12] The video was supposed to be that of a private event among Dayak supporters of Cornelis but somehow got leaked. It was circulated and viewed by individuals and groups including POM. On 7 June 2018, POM reported Cornelis to the police amid allegations that he had given a speech that insulted the province's Malay community. A number of Facebook accounts owned by self-proclaimed Sutarmidji supporters have declared a 'war' against the Dayaks, which was responded in kind by a number of hardline Dayak associations supporting Cornelis and his daughter.

As a result of the recent conflagrations and a potential for election-related violence, both the military and police were mobilised and stationed in various regions parts of West Kalimantan. Two weeks prior to the elections, the police restrained a 1,000-strong Dayak militant group from mobilising in Landak regency with the aim of marching to Pontianak to help friends and relatives thought to be 'persecuted' by the Malays (Fubertus Ipur, personal communication, 19 November 2018).

Decentralised electoral competition, fixed party loyalties, and the politics of partition

Local political elites in West Kalimantan had benefitted from the increased horizontal accountability provided by direct regional elections, allowing for greater participation by marginalised ethnicities such as the Dayaks and the Chinese at the regency and district levels. As a significant minority, political participation by the Chinese had grown and there has been Chinese representation at the mayoral, regency and deputy gubernatorial level despite the trauma of the past under the New Order (Tanasaldy 2012; Hui 2017).[13] Nonetheless, what had transpired in Jakarta by the 212 Movement had casted a pall on greater Chinese participation in politics in West Kalimantan. The predominantly urbanised Teochew (based mainly in Pontianak city) and rural Hakka (based mainly in Singkawang district) safeguarded their interests and influence during the course of the elections through established cultural organisations that control the levers of economy in Pontianak and Singkawang, particularly over the planning and organisation of the annual *Capgomeh* festivities – the major tourist event that brings in much revenue for the province. The Chinese, being predominantly business owners, preferred political stability, and were careful to ensure that all parties of the political spectrum were sufficiently appeased (Lim Keng Sia, personal communication, 22 November 2018).

For Dayaks and Malays, party affiliation is divided along ethnic lines – Dayaks tend to flock to the PDI-P and the minor Indonesian Justice and Unity Party (PKPI) (Teguh et al. 2019),[14] while the Malays prefer the Golkar and Gerindra parties (Yulia Sasti Dwi Putri, personal communication, 9 June 2018).[15] There were some exceptions but it came with its intended risks. Adrianus Asia Sidot, an ex-*bupati* of Landak and a close confidant of Cornelis, was part of the Golkar Party's campaign team that supported Sutarmidji. An extremely influential presence in Dayak circles, his 'defection' had caused a stir and even condemnation among more hardline Dayaks (Adrianus Asia Sidot, personal communication, 12 June 2018).[16] Quite unlike party politics at the national level in which promiscuous power-sharing had led to a situation whereby an opposition had largely failed to emerge (Slater 2018), ethnic fault lines reinforced by religion between the Dayak and the Malays in West Kalimantan are so strong that patronage and power-sharing cannot get both communities to work together. Thus while the anticipated split in Dayak votes due to the presence of Milton Crosby and Boyman Harun as the third candidate pair for governorship may represent an aberration, the results speak more for themselves – Milton and Boyman would only go on to garner an inconsequential 6.65 per cent of the votes (*Kompas* 2018a).[17]

Political pressure to partition West Kalimantan into plausible provinces, districts (*kecamatan*) and cities (kabupaten/kota) is mounting – a reflection of the centrifugal forces arising from ethnic-religious tensions and disagreements (Kimura 2010). While the Jokowi administration had placed a moratorium on further partitions (known as *pemekaran*) (*Kompas* 2018b),[18] politicians like Sutarmidji had continued to campaign for it with the intent of securing votes in particular areas that stand to benefit, even after the gubernatorial elections had ended (*Kompas* 2018c; *Tribun Pontianak* 2019). This had created a situation of a politics of partition in which votes are galvanised based on the alleged financial benefits a certain district or cluster of district would get if partitioned. For instance, 'Kapuas Raya', the name of a new province supported and prioritised by the current governor Sutarmidji, will include Sintang district, Kapuas Hulu, Melawi, Sekadau dan Sanggau. There are also other contenders (*Tribun Sintang* 2019). One of them is the 'Borneo Raya' province. This new province apparently overlaps with the grand design of 'Kapuas Raya' province that will include Sanggau district, Landak, Sekayang, and Bengkayang. These areas have a higher concentration of Kanayatn Dayaks, which is the sub-ethnic Dayak group that are strong supporters of Cornelis. A third new province – 'Tanjung Pura' – will be carved out of the existing Ketapang district and will include Hulu Aik, Kendawangan, Sandai, Jelai, and Ketapang city as its capital. The last plausible new province is known as 'Sambas Raya/Darussalam'. Historically the Sambas area had its own sultanate. This new province will include Sambas Persisir district,

Sambas Darul Makmur, Sanggau Ledo, and Monterado with Sambas city as the capital (Deman Huri, personal communication, 21 November 2018).[19] Territorial partitioning will continue to be an abiding political agenda for the provincial government of West Kalimantan, drawing strong support from its constituents, given the perceived benefits that will be derived from greater autonomy and management – although the question remains whether specific territorial partitions will appease all parties.

Aftermath and implications

With tensions at a peak, the announcement of a Sutarmidji victory did not quell widespread dissatisfaction among hardline Dayak groups. As soon as the results of the *quick count* were out, a media blackout was implemented due to violence breaking out in Landak, a Dayak-majority regency. Several Dayak men took to burning tyres in the streets and publicly slaughtering pigs in imitation of Dayak war traditions as a form of protest against the election results. About 119 inhabitants, mostly Javanese, had to be evacuated from the regency (*Sindonews* 2018). They were targeted because of their prominence in Landak as a community and the fact that Sutarmidji has Javanese roots. Indonesian police had also allegedly laid siege to Cornelis' residence with the expressed purpose of pressuring him to call off all protests originating from the Landak regency, his stronghold (Dian Lestari, personal communication, 22 November 2018). A strong police presence dampened and contained the communal riots and demonstrations, but identity politics did not abate although it did die down eventually (Chen 2019, Setijadi 2018). The division along ethnicity and religion that are regency-based can be seen clearly in the voting patterns of various regencies in West Kalimantan in Tables 9.2 and 9.3.

Table 9.2 Regencies that voted for Sutarmidji–Norsan

Regency (Kabupaten)	No. of votes	Percentage of votes
Kapuas Hulu	62,936	49.6
North Kayong	40,454	**72.7**
Ketapang	124,695	55.1
Pontianak	229,152	**74.8**
Singkawang	51,743	57.0
Kubu Raya	186,833	**71.2**
Melawi	64,123	49.8
Mempawah	87,646	**68.3**
Sambas	224,203	**78.7**

Source: Indonesian Election Commission (KPU).

Note
Bold signifies Sutarmidji–Norsan pair won the particular regency with more than 60 percent of votes being cast.

Table 9.3 Regencies that voted for Karolin–Gidot

Regency (Kabupaten)	No. of votes	Percentage of votes
Bengkayang	85,435	**69.6**
Landak	218,797	**89.1**
Sanggau	124,677	**63.4**
Sekadau	52,134	47.8
Sintang	86,782	44.1

Source: Indonesian Election Commission (KPU).

Note
Bold signifies Karolin–Gidot pair won the particular regency with more than 60 percent of the votes being cast.

From Tables 9.2 and 9.3 (KPU Indonesia 2018), regencies that voted overwhelmingly in favour of Sutarmidji fell into urbanised, coastal areas with a Malay-majority electorate (North Kayong, Pontianak, Kubu Raya, Mempawah, and Sambas). Singkawang, a Hakka-Chinese-dominated city also went to Sutarmidji (Fubertus Ipur, personal communication, 19 November 2018). This could be due to the fact that Sutarmidji is seen as the candidate less likely to create instability for Chinese businesses. On the other hand, inland regencies (Bengkayang and Sanggau) with a majority Dayak electorate had voted for Karolin, with the highest number of votes at 89.1 per cent in Landak. Incidentally, Karolin and Gidot were also ex-regents of Landak and Bengkayang respectively. Sintang's vote was split between Karolin and Crosby.

Ethnic and political divisions persisted throughout the campaign period for the legislative and presidential elections in 2019. Although Sutarmidji had pledged his support for Joko Widodo as presidential candidate,[20] the Malay-dominant electorate in Pontianak and the coastal, urbanised regions thought otherwise. In particular, the #2019ChangePresident movement (or *#2019GantiPresiden*) with close affiliation with the candidature of Prabowo Subianto (Dinarto 2018) made inroads in Pontianak. Prabowo's campaign visit to Pontianak in March 2019 (*Jawapos* 2019) not only demonstrated a strong level of support for Prabowo among the Malay–Muslim electorate but also further reinforced the divisions between the Dayaks and the Malays in their political affiliations, now projected at the national level.

This was evident when the presidential election results at the regional level were concluded in West Kalimantan. Similar to the divisions seen in the gubernatorial elections just months' prior, a clear divide can be seen in the more urbanised, coastal Malay–Muslim-dominated districts that tend to gravitate towards the Prabowo ticket and the inland rural Dayak-majority districts that had overwhelming voted for Jokowi (see Table 9.4). This development followed nationwide patterns of conservative Muslims translating their support into votes for Prabowo.

Table 9.4 2019 presidential election in West Kalimantan

District/city	Prabowo-Sandi (% and no. of votes)	Jokowi-Ma'ruf (% and no. of votes)
Pontianak	**63.49 (214,665)**	36.51 (123,417)
Kubu Raya	**64.87 (191,063)**	35.13 (103,454)
Singkawang City	43.83 (50,212)	**56.17 (64,356)**
Bengkayang	22.04 (30,169)	**77.96 (106,739)**
Sambas	44.65 (135,383)	**55.35 (167,849)**
Landak	13.86 (33,177)	**86.14 (206,240)**
Sanggau	24.34 (60,143)	**75.66 (186,917)**
Sekadau	28.58 (36,596)	**71.42 (91,433)**
Sintang	27.21 (66,952)	**72.79 (179,111)**
Melawi	44.08 (61,750)	**55.92 (78,326)**
Kapuas Hulu	40.01 (59,380)	**59.99 (89,002)**
Ketapang	43.05 (116,086)	**56.95 (153,552)**
North Kayong	**60.11 (38,467)**	39.89 (25,527)
Mempawah	**63.88 (93,414)**	36.12 (52,816)

Source: Indonesian Election Commission (KPU).

Note
Bold signifies the presidential candidate who was declared the winner in the particular district or city.

As seen from Table 9.4 (KPU Indonesia 2019), districts that voted in favour of Prabowo and his running mate (with 60 per cent and above votes) tended to come from the main cities such as Pontianak, Kubu Raya, North Kayong, and Mempawah (coastal, urbanised with a Malay–Muslim majority). These regencies are also where support for the #2019ChangePresident movement was the greatest. On the other hand, while there had been a close fight between the presidential candidates in quite a few districts, certain districts registered an overwhelming support in favour of Jokowi and his running mates, especially in the districts of Landak, Bengkayang, and Sanggau (inland and rural with a Dayak–Christian majority). These are regions where hostilities against the #2019ChangePresident movement and groups like FPI are the greatest. These results correspond to very similar patterns of particular regencies and their strong support of certain kinds of candidates with regencies that had voted in favour of Sutarmidji or Karolin in the 2018 gubernatorial elections in West Kalimantan.

Changes in political party constellation for the simultaneous legislative elections that took place in conjunction with the presidential elections are also interesting to note. While the regional elections had led to a loss in a number of seats previously dominated by prominent Dayaks, many had opted to run for seats in Jakarta for the House of Representatives at the national legislative level in the 2019 elections instead. This includes Cornelis, the former Dayak governor who ran for a seat at the Indonesian House of Representatives (DPR), Adrianus Asia Sidot, who was the former regent of Landak and Lazarus, a DPR Member of Parliament with a strong following in the Dayak heartland.

From Table 9.5 (KPU Indonesia 2019), a few changes in the political party constellation within West Kalimantan can be observed between 2014 and 2019. PKPI, a minor party that used to be a fixture in West Kalimantan politics since 2014 had lost two seats. Perindo, a new political outfit founded in 2015 by media tycoon Hary Tanoesoedibjo, owner of MNC Group (Dian Lestari, personal communication, 21 May 2019) gained a seat.[21] Political parties that had increased their number of seats include the Islamist party PKS (+1), NasDem (+3) and the NU-affiliated PKB (+3). Incidentally, despite its Islamist roots, PKS had pursued populist strategies that appealed to the masses including a campaign to eradicate motorcycle tax and other welfare schemes. The Demokrat Party had declined by three seats. This leaves the Dayak-populated PDI-P as the most dominant political party in West Kalimantan once again with 15 seats, unchanged as in 2014. Thus while Dayak politicians did not manage to perform well overall in the regional elections in 2018 (particularly the gubernatorial election), their prominence in the legislative elections in 2019 for the Regional People's Representative Council (DPRD) and the dominance of PDI-P, a Dayak-majority party in West Kalimantan, more than make up for the earlier losses (Palupi, *Tribunnewswiki.com* 2019). Generally, political party constellation within the province for the year 2019–2024 did not deviate much from national-level trends, with major parties like PDI-P, Golkar, and Gerindra clinching top spots.

Conclusion

On 22 May 2019, when protests and riots broke out in Jakarta in response to the announcement of the presidential election results that showed a Jokowi victory,

Table 9.5 2014 and 2019 legislative election results in West Kalimantan

Political party	2014–2019 (no. of seats)	Political party	2019–2024 (simultaneous elections) (no. of seats)	Change (no. of seats)
PDI-P	15	**PDIP**	15	No change
Golkar	9	**Golkar**	8	−1
Demokrat	9	**Demokrat**	7	−2
Gerindra	7	**Gerindra**	7	No change
PAN	6	**PAN**	5	−1
Hanura	3	**Hanura**	2	−1
PKB	2	**PKB**	5	+3
NasDem	5	**NasDem**	8	+3
PKS	2	**PKS**	3	+1
PKPI	3	**PKPI**	1	−2
PPP	4	**PPP**	3	−1
		Perindo	1	+1
Total	65		65	No change

Source: Author's calculation.

Pontianak met with the same fate. The actions of the protestors were uncannily similar. In Jakarta, a group of unidentified individuals burned down cars parked in front of a special operations tactical unit of the Indonesian national police (abbreviated Brimob) dormitory in KS Tubun road of Petamburan, Tanah Abang (*Detik News* 2019). In Pontianak, a group of protestors carrying firecrackers gathered at the intersection of Jalan Tanjung Raya near a traffic police post and set fire to it on the same day (*Jakarta Post* 2019). While no human casualties had resulted, the police post in Pontianak was razed to the ground and street lamps and CCTV cameras were destroyed (CNN Indonesia 2019). These attacks, which were directed at the Indonesian police in both Jakarta and Pontianak, were apparently due to the circulation of unaccounted news and hoaxes on social media that suggested electoral fraud (Temby 2019). While it demonstrated the increasing reach of Jakarta politics at the periphery of the Indonesian archipelago accentuated by the effect of back-to-back simultaneous elections, it was also a reflection of how polarised ethnic and religious tensions in West Kalimantan has become and how local elections exacerbated pre-existing divisions since democratisation took place in 1999 (Subianto 2009, pp. 327–352).

The simultaneous regional elections of 2018–2019 in West Kalimantan followed a familiar trajectory of ethnic polarisations that had amalgamated with religious cleavages in recent years. The processes and results of the simultaneous regional elections confirms that ethnicity and religious groups matter tremendously in the campaigns as well as in determining the victorious candidates in West Kalimantan. This phenomenon extends into voting patterns for the presidential candidates and their running mates in regencies and districts, whereby specific groups defined by ethnicity congregate or dominate, and tend to vote for a particular political candidate. Fortunately, violence and its spread to other regions in the province had been contained by increased securitisation and vigilance and to a large extent, informed by West Kalimantan's status as a 'vulnerable (*rawan*)' province. However, some academics in the province have predicted that violent conflicts carry the potential of escalating every 30 years (the latest being the widespread ethnic riots during the last years of the New Order in the late 1990s) (Prof. Syarif Ibrahim Alkadrie, personal communication, 11 June 2018, Alkadrie 2010). If this is true, West Kalimantan province certainly warrants greater attention and concern from Indonesian watchers.

Notes

1 There is an exception during the Sukarno years. Oevaang Oeray was governor of West Kalimantan from 1960–1966 and the first ethnic Dayak to hold the position.

2 By 1980, about 1.4 per cent of the province's population consisted of transmigrants. By 1985 the proportion was up to 6 per cent, unevenly distributed. In Sanggau Ledo, where the violence broke out, a full 15 per cent of the population were settlers by 1980, and the proportion is likely to have risen since. By 1984, the percentage of transmigrants going to West Kalimantan as opposed to other provinces had risen from 14.6 to over 25 per cent.

3 The PPP suffered a leadership struggle and was divided into two factions under Djan Faridz and Romahurmuziy after competing national congresses (Muktamar) were held in Jakarta and Surabaya in 2014.

4 The throne of the Pontianak Sultanate was left empty since 1978 when the last Sultan of Pontianak, Syarif Hamid II Alkadrie passed on. In 2004, a nephew of Sultan Hamid II was reinstated as the new sultan. The revived Pontianak Sultanate is one among many other Sultanates who saw the post-1998 democratisation as a window of opportunity to revive old traditions and spheres of influence.

5 The current Sultan started his reign after the death of his father, Sultan Syarif Abubakar Alkadrie, in 2017. He apparently sought FPI endorsement to bolster his credentials because his rule was being challenged by at least two other claimants from rival branches of the Alkadrie family.

6 Each ethnicity in West Kalimantan have their own informal organisation or empowerment groups that can be locality-specific and oftentimes emphasise a very narrow ethnocentric interpretation of tradition and culture. For the case of the Dayak, the most notorious of all is the Dayak Customary Council also known as *Dewan Adat Dayak* (DAD). Others include the *Majelis Adat Budaya Tionghua* (MABT) for the Chinese and the *Ikatan Keluarga Besar Madura* (IKBM) for the Madurese.

7 Hizb ut-Tahrir is a pan-Islamist political organisation which describes its ideology as Islam and its aim as the re-establishment of the Islamic Caliphate.

8 The 'Defend the Ulema' movement was sporadic at first and before June 2017 was a movement specific to West Kalimantan. However, prodded by Habib Rizieq's trial over sexually explicit messages he exchanged with Firza Hussein and charged under the Anti-Pornography law, the alumni of the Jakarta Protest (also known as the Alumni 212) started to officially organise the 'Defend the Ulema' movement on 9 June 2017 with the belief that their leader, as well as other Muslim clerics in their fold, was being wrongfully accused and persecuted by state authorities.

9 According to Muzammil, Cornelis did not accommodate the Malays under his administration. Rather he placed Chinese in influential positions. Cornelis also sought to consolidate Dayak support and fostered a united Dayak voice, citing the Council of Indonesian Ulema (MUI) fatwa for Malay unity in 2007.

10 Historically, the conversion of Dayaks to the Islamic faith had resulted in them disavowing their ethnic identity (he/she will be classified as 'Senganam' or becoming Malays, also known as 'Masuk Melayu'), oftentimes leading to displeasure from the Dayaks themselves (although it must be qualified that in recent years, many have identified themselves as 'Dayak Muslim'). This is quite unique to the province of West Kalimantan and has, in a certain number of ways, contributed to the growing distrust between the two ethnic groups.

11 The main grievances for the Dayak were historical. Apart from repression under the Malay Sultanates, they suffered discrimination under the New Order when Malay governors and civil servants were favoured over the Dayak.

12 Cornelis had also blamed what was a legacy of an exploitative economic model of the Dutch–Malay alliance solely on the Malays. Various Dayak ethnicities however did suffer injustices under the 'Kamit' system (slavery by the Malay Sultan).

13 These figures include Tjhai Chui Mie who was Singkawang first Chinese female mayor, Yansen Akun Effendy who was elected *bupati* (regent) of Sanggau and Christiandy Sanjaya who was deputy governor of West Kalimantan province. These speak of the increasingly diverse political combinations that had benefitted from the decentralisation of politics which had deviated from the Malay–Dayak or Malay–Malay configuration.

14 Interestingly, while PKPI did not manage to surmount the national threshold to secure seats at the national parliament, its political influence in particular regions, such as West Kalimantan, had been significant especially among the Dayaks. PKPI had, in recent years, suffered a schism, and during the time of the gubernatorial elections in

2018, was split between Haris Sudarno and AM Hendropriyono after the 2016 party congress.

15 While Yulia had 'defected' to the Golkar Party as a Christian Dayak, she cites the fact the Golkar sought to present itself as a nationalist rather than an ethnic-based party – at least at the national level. Nonetheless, as a minority ethnic group in the Golkar branch of West Kalimantan, Yulia also expressed disappointment over the party's pragmatic shift towards conservative Islamic candidates. On the other hand, PDI-P is seen as '*Partai Dayak* (Dayak Party)' – externally nationalist, but internally Dayak within the province.

16 In fact, Adrianus revealed that his support for Golkar and in turn the Javanese-Malay candidate of Sutarmidji represented a form of betrayal among Dayaks groups. Reasons for his defection from PDI-P and Cornelis had largely to do with disagreements and rivalry.

17 Sutarmidji would emerge as the winner of the gubernatorial elections, galvanising 51.56 per cent of votes while Karolin came in at 41.4 per cent.

18 North Kalimantan province is the youngest province in Indonesia and Indonesia Borneo, separated from the province of East Kalimantan in October 2012.

19 For more information on the grand design of a possible partitioning of West Kalimantan, see http://bangunindoku.blogspot.com/2013/09/grand-design-pemekaran-provinsi-di.html.

20 Other candidates have also pledged their support for Jokowi including Paolus Hadi (regent of Sanggau), Tjhai Chui Mie (mayor of Singkawang), Citra Duani (regent of Kayong Utara), Antonius L Ain Pamero (deputy regent of Kapuas Hulu), and Hairiah (deputy regent of Sambas).

21 The schism within PKPI affected its ability to garner votes while the Perindo Party had strong roots in West Kalimantan. Perindo's chairman in the province is also Chinese and that helped drew votes from the Chinese.

Bibliography

Alkadrie, S.I. 2010. 'Kasus Kontroversi: Makalah Melayu Dan Patung Naga di Singkawang' ['The Controversial Case: Malay Papers and the Dragon Statue in Singkawang']. Pontianak: Al-Qadrie Centre Press.

Antara News. 2012, 12 December. 'FPI Pontianak Tablig Akbar Hadirkan Habib Rizieq' [Habib Rizieq Welcomed at FPI Pontianak's Tablig Akbar Event]'. Retrieved from https://kalbar.antaranews.com/berita/308721/fpi-pontianak-tablig-akbar-hadirkan-habib-rizieq.

Antara News. 2016, 6 September. 'Sutarmidji: PPP Yang Sah Hasil Muktamar Jakarta' [Sutarmidji: National Congress in Jakarta should be the Legitimate One]'. Retrieved from https://kalbar.antaranews.com/berita/343079/sutarmidji-ppp-yang-sah-hasil-muktamar-jakarta.

Arifianto, A., & J. Chen 2018, 22 May. 'Indonesia's 2018 Regional Elections – West Kalimantan: Identity Politics at the Forefront', *RSIS Commentary*. Retrieved from www.rsis.edu.sg/wp-content/uploads/2018/06/CO18107.pdf.

Bawaslu Republik Indonesia 2017. *Indeks Kerawanan Pemilu Pemilihan Kepala Dearah 2018*. Jakarta.

BBC Indonesia 2017, 22 May. 'Aksi bela ulama di Kalbar "tiru" politik SARA Pilkada J Jakarta' ['Protect-the-Ulama Group in West Kalimantan "Imitates" the Ethno-religious Politics of Jakarta']. Retrieved from www.bbc.com/indonesia/indonesia-39992156.

BPS Indonesia 2010). Propinsi Kalimantan Barat: Jumlah dan Distribusi Penduduk [West Kalimantan Province: Population Size and Distribution]. Retrieved from: https://sp2010.bps.go.id/index.php/site?id=61&wilayah=Kalimantan-Barat

Chen, J. 2019, 1 February. 'Indonesian Presidential Election 2019 – Politics at the Periphery: The "Outer Island" Phenomenon', *RSIS Commentary*. Retrieved from: www.rsis.edu. sg/wp-content/uploads/2019/02/CO19018.pdf.

Choi, N. 2014. 'Local Political Elites in Indonesia: "Risers" and "Holdovers"', *SOJOURN: Journal of Social Issues in Southeast Asia*, Vol. 29 (2): 364–407.

CNN Indonesia. 2019, 29 May. 'Polda Kalbar Bekuk 38 Orang Perusuh Aksi 22 Mei di Pontianak' ['West Kalimantan Regional Police Arrested 38 rioters on 22 May in Pontianak']. Retrieved from www.cnnindonesia.com/nasional/20190522200511-12-397555/polda-kalbar-bekuk-38-orang-perusuh-aksi-22-mei-di-pontianak.

Davidson, J.S. 2003. 'The Politics of Violence on an Indonesian Periphery', *Southeast Asia Research*, Vol. 11 (1): 80–85.

Davidson, J.S., & D. Kammen, 2002. 'Indonesia's Unknown War and the Lineages of Violence in West Kalimantan', *Indonesia*, Vol. 73: 53–87.

Davidson, J.S. 2009. *From Rebellion to Riots: Collective Violence on Indonesian Borneo*. Singapore: National University of Singapore Press.

Detik News. 2017a, 20 May. 'Sempat Ada Insiden, Gawai Dayak di Pontianak Berlangsung Damai' ['Despite Incidences of Riots, Gawai Dayak Festival Proceeds Peacefully in Pontianak']. Retrieved from https://news.detik.com/berita/d-3506946/sempat-ada-insiden-gawai-dayak-di-pontianak-berlangsung-damai.

Detik News. 2017b, 8 June. 'Polisi Melarang, Alumni 212 Tetap akan Gelar Aksi Bela Ulama' ['The Alumni 212 Group will still Hold Demonstrations to Protect the Ulama Despite Prohibition by Police']. Retrieved from https://news.detik.com/berita/d-3524433/polisi-melarang-alumni-212-tetap-akan-gelar-aksi-bela-ulama?_ga=2.2466480.10045 61418.1562309557-725693751.1411612571.

Detik News. 2019, 22 May. 'Polisi: 9 Mobil di Depan Asrama Brimob Petamburan Dibakar OTK' ['Police: 9 Cars in Front of Mobile Brigade Corps Barracks Burned']. Retrieved from https://news.detik.com/berita/d-4559631/polisi-9-mobil-di-depan-asrama-brimob-petamburan-dibakar-otk.

Dinarto, D. 2018, 3 September. '#2019ChangePresident Movement a Game-changer in Next Year's Indonesian Election?', *The Conversation*. Retrieved from https://theconversation. com/2019changepresident-movement-a-game-changer-in-next-years-indonesian-election-101587.

Hawkins, M. 2009. 'Violence and the Construction of Identity: Conflict between the Dayak and Madurese in Kalimantan, Indonesia' in M. Sakai, G. Banks, & J.H. Walker (Eds.). *The Politics of the Periphery in Indonesia: Social and Geographical Perspectives*. Singapore: NUS Press.

Heidhues, M.S. 1998. 'The First Two Sultans of Pontianak', *Archipel*, Vol. 56: 273–294.

Heidhues, M.S. 2003. *Golddiggers, Farmers, and Traders in the 'Chinese Districts' of West Kalimantan, Indonesia*. Ithaca, NY: Cornell University, Southeast Asia Program Publications.

Hui, Y.F. 2017, 27 March. 'Decentralization and Chinese Indonesian Politics: The Case of Singkawang, West Kalimantan', *ISEAS Perspective*, (19). Retrieved from www. iseas.edu.sg/images/pdf/ISEAS_Perspective_2017_19.pdf.

Jakarta Post. 2019, 22 May. 'Post-election Protests Escalate in Pontianak'. Retrieved from www.thejakartapost.com/news/2019/05/22/post-election-protests-escalate-in-pontianak. html.

Jawapos. 2019, 17 March. 'Prabowo Datang, Teriakan '2019 Ganti Presiden' Menggema di Pontianak' ['Shouts of "Change the President in 2019" Reverberates as Prabowo

Arrives in Pontianak']. Retrieved from www.jawapos.com/jpg-today/17/03/2019/prabowo-datang-teriakan-2019-ganti-presiden-menggema-di-pontianak/.

Kahin, G.M. 1952. *Nationalism and Revolution in Indonesia*. Ithaca, NY: Cornell University Press.

Kimura, E. 2010. 'Proliferating Provinces: Territorial Politics in Post-Suharto Indonesia', *Southeast Asia Research*, Vol. 18 (3): 415–449.

Kompas. 2012, 3 July. 'Oeray dan Djerandeng Layak Jadi Pahlawan Nasional' ['Oeray and Djerandeng Deserve to Become National Heroes']. Retrieved from https://nasional.kompas.com/read/2012/07/13/08272480/Oeray.dan.Djerandeng.Layak.Jadi.Pahlawan.Nasional.

Kompas. 2018a, 8 July. 'Rekapitulasi KPU, Sutarmidji-Ria Norsan Unggul di Pilkada Kalbar' ['Recapitulation of KPU: Sutarmidji-Ria Norsan Dominant in the West Kalimantan Regional Elections']. Retrieved from https://regional.kompas.com/read/2018/07/08/22505561/rekapitulasi-kpu-sutarmidji-ria-norsan-unggul-di-pilkada-kalbar.

Kompas. 2018b, 23 July. 'Kepada Wali Kota, Jokowi Isyaratkan Lanjutkan Moratorium Pemekaran Wilayah' ['To All Mayors: Jokowi Hints at the Continuation of the Moratorium on Partitions']. Retrieved from https://nasional.kompas.com/read/2018/07/23/20034651/kepada-wali-kota-jokowi-isyaratkan-lanjutkan-moratorium-pemekaran-wilayah.

Kompas. 2018c, 26 July. 'Gubernur Kalbar Terpilih Prioritaskan Pemekaran Provinsi Kapuas Raya' ['Newly Elected West Kalimantan Governor to Prioritise Expansion of the Kapuas Raya Province']. Retrieved from https://regional.kompas.com/read/2018/07/26/18433851/gubernur-kalbar-terpilih-prioritaskan-pemekaran-provinsi-kapuas-raya.

König, A. 2016. 'Identity Construction and Dayak Ethnic Strife in West Kalimantan, Indonesia', *The Asia Pacific Journal of Anthropology*, Vol. 17 (2): 121–137.

KPU Indonesia. 2018. 'Portal Publikasi Pilkada dan Pemilu Indonesia' [Publication Portal for Simultaneous Local Executive Elections and Indonesian General Elections]. Retrieved from https://infopemilu.kpu.go.id/.

Lim, M. 2017. 'Freedom to Hate: Social media, Algorithmic Enclaves, and the Rise of Tribal Nationalism in Indonesia', *Critical Asian Studies*, Vol. 49 (3): 411–427.

Pinter Politik. 2017, 22 May. 'FPI Tuntut Gubernur Kalbar' ['FPI Presses Demands on West Kalimantan Governor']. Retrieved from https://pinterpolitik.com/fpi-tuntut-gubernur-kalbar/.

Pontianak Post. 2017, 13 July. 'Mengenal Sosok Sultan ke-IX Pontianak, Syarif Machmud Alkadrie' [Get to Know the 9th Sultan of Pontianak, Syarif Machmud Alkadrie]. Retrieved from www.pontianakpost.co.id/mengenal-sosok-sultan-ke-ix-pontianak-syarif-machmud-alkadrie.

Pontianak Post. 2018a, 13 June. 'Pilkada, Kalbar Rawan' ['Regional Elections: West Kalimantan Vulnerable']. Retrieved from www.pontianakpost.co.id/pilkada-kalbar-rawan.

Pontianak Post. 2018b, 13 July. 'Jelang Lebaran, FPI Mempawah Bagikan Ini' ['Prior to Lebaran Holiday, FPI Mempawah Distributes This']. Retrieved from www.pontianakpost.co.id/jelang-lebaran-fpi-mempawah-bagikan-ini.

Ramadhan, D. 2018, 14 November. 'Upaya Dominasi Orang Dayak: Politik Identitas dalam Dinamika Politik Lokal di Kalimantan Barat' ['Efforts to Dominate the Dayaks: Identity Politics in the Dynamics of Local Politics in West Kalimantan'], *Populi Center*. Retrieved from http://populicenter.org/upaya-dominasi-orang-dayak-politik-identitas-dalam-dinamika-politik-lokal-di-kalimantan-barat/.

Rappler. 2017, 8 May. 'Gara-gara tolak kehadiran anggota FPI, Gubernur Kalbar diusir di Aceh' ['West Kalimantan Governor Expelled from Aceh due to his Rejection of FPI Members in Province']. Retrieved from www.rappler.com/indonesia/berita/169206-gubernur-diusir-aceh-karena-usir-anggota-fpi.

Setijadi, C. 2018, 24 September. 'West Kalimantan Gubernatorial Election 2018: Identity Politics Proves Decisive', *ISEAS Perspective*, Vol. 58. Retrieved from www.iseas.edu. sg/images/pdf/ISEAS_Perspective_2018_58@50.pdf.

Sindonews. 2018, 30 June. 'Ricuh Hasil Pilgub Kalbar di Landak, 119 Warga Mengungsi' ['Riots after Declared Election Results in Landak led to the Evacuation 119']. Retrieved from https://daerah.sindonews.com/read/1317697/174/ricuh-hasil-pilgub-kalbar-di-landak-119-warga-mengungsi-1530338222.

Slater, D. 2018. 'Party Cartelization, Indonesian-style: Presidential Power-sharing and the Contingency of Democratic Opposition', *Journal of East Asian Studies*, Vol. 18 (1): 23–46.

Subianto, B. 2009. 'Ethnic Politics and the Rise of the Dayak Bureaucrats in Local Elections: Pilkada in Six Kabupaten in West Kalimantan' in M. Erb & P. Sulistiyanto (Eds.), *Deepening Democracy in Indonesia? Direct Elections for Local Leaders (Pilkada)*. Singapore: ISEAS Publishing.

Tanasaldy, T. 2012. *Regime Change and Ethnic Politics in Indonesia: Dayak Politics of West Kalimantan*. Leiden: KITLV Press.

Temby, Q. 2019, 2 September. 'Disinformation, Violence, and Anti-Chinese Sentiment in Indonesia's 2019 Elections', *ISEAS Perspective* (67). Retrieved from www.iseas.edu. sg/images/pdf/ISEAS_Perspective_2019_67.pdf.

The Economist. 2017, 21 July. 'Indonesia Islamists Open a New Front in Their War on Tolerance'. Retrieved from www.economist.com/asia/2017/07/21/indonesian-islamists-open-a-new-front-in-their-war-on-tolerance.

The Guardian. 1999, 20 March. 'Renewed Ethnic Violence Hits Indonesia as 62 Die in Borneo'. Retrieved from www.theguardian.com/world/1999/mar/20/johnaglionby.

The Star Online. 2017, 27 May. 'A Clash That Wasn't, a Peace That Isn't'. Retrieved from www.thestar.com.my/opinion/columnists/one-mans-meat/2017/05/27/a-clash-that-wasnt-a-peace-that-isnt-tension-was-high-in-indonesias-west-kalimantan-last-weekend-and/.

Thung, J.L., Y. Maunati, & P.M. Kedit. 2004. *The (Re) Construction of the 'Pan Dayak' Identity in Kalimantan and Sarawak: A Study on Minority's Identity, Ethnicity, and Nationality*. Jakarta, Indonesia: LIPI Puslit Kemasyarakatan dan Kebudayaan.

Tribun Pontianak. 2018a, 14 February. 'Kalbar Rawan Praktik Politik Uang Nomor Tujuh se Indonesia' ['Prone to Money Politics, West Kalimantan Ranks Seventh in Indonesia']. Retrieved from http://pontianak.tribunnews.com/2018/02/14/kalbar-rawan-praktik-politik-uangnomor-tujuh-se-indonesia.

Tribun Pontianak. 2018b, 5 April. 'Kalbar Masuk 3 Besar Indeks Kerawanan Pilkada' ['West Kalimantan is Top Three in Regional Election Vulnerability Index']. Retrieved from https://pontianak.tribunnews.com/2018/04/05/kalbar-masuk-3-besar-indeks-kerawanan-pilkada.

Tribun Pontianak. 2018c, 25 April. 'Nyatakan Sikap Politik! Laskar Pemuda Melayu Kalbar Siap Menangkan Karolin–Gidot' ['Expressing their Political Preference! West Kalimantan Malay Youth Warriors Ready for Karolin–Gidot Win']. Retrieved from https://pontianak.tribunnews.com/2018/04/25/nyatakan-sikap-politik-laskar-pemuda-melayu-kalbar-siap-menangkan-karolin-gidot.

Tribun Pontianak. 2019, 3 September. 'Gubernur Kalimantan Barat Sutarmidji Perjuangkan Pemekaran Provinsi Kapuas Raya' ['West Kalimantan Governor Sutarmidji Lobbying for the Expansion of the Kapuas Raya Province']. Retrieved from https://pontianak.tribunnews.com/2019/09/03/sutarmidji-terus-perjuangkan-pemekaran-provinsi-kapuas-raya.

Tribun Sintang. 2019, 5 December. 'Terkait Pemekaran Provinsi Kapuas Raya, Begini Jawaban Bupati Jarot' ['This is Regent Jarot's Answer on the Expansion of Kapuas Raya Province']. Retrieved from https://pontianak.tribunnews.com/2019/12/05/terkait-pemekaran-provinsi-kapuas-raya-begini-jawaban-bupati-jarot.

Tribunnewswiki.com. 2019, 9 September. 'Daftar Anggota DPR RI & DPD RI Daerah Pemilihan Provinsi Kalimantan Barat Periode 2019–2024' ['List of Members for the DPR RI & DPD RI Electoral District of West Kalimantan Province 2019–2024 Period']. Retrieved from www.tribunnewswiki.com/2019/09/09/daftar-anggota-dpr-ri-dpd-ri-daerah-pemilihan-provinsi-kalimantan-barat-periode-2019-2024.

Van Klinken, G. 2007, 26 July. 'Return of the Sultans', *Inside Indonesia*. Retrieved from www.insideindonesia.org/return-of-the-sultans.

List of interviews in Pontianak

Alkadrie, M.Y. [Personal assistant of Sultan Hamid II, Senior advisor, GMNI (youth wing of PDI-P Party)] (23 November 2018).

Alkadrie, S.I. [Former Dean of Faculty of Social Sciences, Tanjungpura University] (11 June 2018).

Al Muthahar, I.A. [West Kalimantan DPRD Members (Gerindra), FPI Leader] (11 June 2018).

Bamba, J. [Former Director, Institute Dayakologi] (14 June 2018).

Dwiputri, Y.S. [Deputy Treasurer, Golkar Party] (9 June 2018).

Huri, D. [Independent Journalist] (21 November 2018).

Ipur, F. [Executive Director, Elpagar] (7 June 2018, 19 November 2018).

Lestari, D. [Senior Reporter, *Tribunnews Pontianak*] (22 November 2018, 21 May 2019).

Lim, K.S. [NGO activist (FITRA Kalbar), Former board member of *Partai Karya Perjuangan* (PAKARPANGAN)] (22 November 2018).

Maskendari [West Kalimantan DPRD Member (PDI-P), Manager of Karolin Campaign Team] (9 June 2018).

Muzammil, A.R. [Board Member, DPW Muhammadiyah West Kalimantan Province and the Malay Traditional and Cultural Assembly of West Kalimantan (MABM Kalbar)] (12 June 2018).

Sidot, A.A. [Former Bupati of Landak, Member of Sutarmidji's success team, Golkar Party] (12 June 2018).

Situmorang, A. [West Kalimantan DPRD Member (Gerindra), Chairman of Milton Crosby Campaign Team] (10 June 2018).

10 Electoral politics in Sumba

The persistence of tradition

Chris Lundry

Introduction

On Friday 12 April 2019 in the capital of East Sumba, Waingapu, supporters of Prabowo Subianto, Jokowi's rival for presidential office, held a rally through the small town's main street. Friday 12 April 2019 was the last day of campaigning before the 'cooling off' period and his supporters made their presence known with boisterously honking horns, revving motorcycles, blaring music, dancing in the back of trucks, and shouting slogans. About 2,000 to 3,000 supporters also descended on a nearby playing field to show their support. This gave the impression of a strong turnout for Prabowo – even though in Sumba and elsewhere in Indonesia, 'professional ralliers' can be paid to organise rallies. Rally-goers are frequently rewarded with food, but are said to be gathering for free food (*Rombangan Makan Gratis*) (interview, Umbu Makambombu, 17 April 2019).

Half an hour later on the same day, another parade took place, and people remained to watch. The parade was a representation of the Passion of the Christ. A young Sumbanese man dressed as Jesus and carrying a heavy cross was enthusiastically kicked, punched, and whipped by several other young men dressed as Roman soldiers. They were followed by perhaps 100 others marching quietly, with some on the periphery passing out fliers reminding people of the importance of the coming week: Good Friday and Easter Sunday, just 2 and 4 days after the election.[1] Reminding voters of Christianity's history of prosecution in the context of Prabowo's association with Islamist groups made perfect political sense.

Despite the show of support for Prabowo, he was trounced in Sumba and East Nusa Tenggara Province (NTT). Repeating a phenomenon that can also be seen in other non-Muslim-majority provinces, 95 per cent of Sumbanese voted for Jokowi. Both Prabowo and Jokowi were Javanese Muslims and had little in common with most Sumbanese. Yet Christian Sumbanese's support for president Jokowi was enormous. As this chapter shows, Sumbanese have little hope for much significant representation on the national or provincial scale, but the history and the role of party politics influences their voting behaviour. For district-level elections, a mixture of tradition, caste, religion, and party creates a unique dynamic.

Brief history of Sumbanese politics

This chapter focuses on Sumba, specifically East Sumba, where the author has done the most field research, but it will also refer to the province of NTT, as data is available at the provincial level and the province allows for a certain degree of generalisation, especially fears concerning the growing Islamisation of national politics. Sumba is predominantly Christian and occupies a peripheral space in Indonesia. It is a province with one of the lowest levels of development in Indonesia, ranking third after the Papua and West Papua provinces, and it continues to lag behind despite recent attempts to bring development and health care (Tanya 2016). Most research on Sumba is anthropological and ethnographic. Historical and political work exists, and Jacqueline Vel's recent work has turned towards politics, albeit from an anthropological perspective (Vel 2008). This author has also conducted research in Sumba, in 2006, 2007, and 2019, including electoral politics (Lundry 2009).

Dutch colonialism arrived late in Sumba, it came under effective Dutch control only at the beginning of the twentieth century, long after the rest of Indonesia was colonised. The Dutch appointed a Council of Rajas as intermediaries just as it did in other regions, but in Sumba the selections were somewhat arbitrary although they did select members from the high caste. Centuries of slave trading by Javanese, Makassarese, Balinese, and others had resulted in three castes: royalty (*maramba*), free men (*kabihu*), and slaves (*ata*), based on who could protect others, who could avoid slavery, and who was enslaved. Until the Dutch 'pacified' Sumba in the early twentieth century, freedom or even one's own life was not guaranteed (Needham 1983, p. 15).

The Council of Rajas was unable to challenge the Dutch, and Sumba remained peripheral. The Second World War brought Japanese occupation and forced labour to build an airfield in Eastern Sumba for an aborted attack on Australia. After the war, the Sumbanese had minimal involvement with the Indonesian Revolution, although the Dutch Calvinist Church renamed itself *Gereja Kristen Sumba* (GKS) to reflect the emerging new political reality (it remained conservative and Dutch-oriented and did not see a great rise in membership until the New Order – see below).

After independence, the Council of Rajas was disbanded in favour of *Dewan Perwakilan Rakyat Daerah* (People's Regional Representative Council), yet the membership remained caste-based, i.e. those from the *maramba* caste. As Keane notes, these elites were able to reinforce their power through the reinstitution of and emphasis on traditional *marapu* rituals.[2] These rituals, as well as the patronage that they represent, still matter in Sumbanese elections (see below). As political consolidation occurred in independent Indonesia, Sumba followed suit, but local patterns of power remained. This relationship was reinforced through their access to education opportunities and control over the process of conversion to Christianity, establishing generational linkages that nominally shifted their justification for ruling from customary power to rationalised power.[3] As independent Indonesia pushed towards modernisation, its politicians and governors needed to reflect this through education and an explicit rules-based system.[4] Their economic dominance was reinforced through their ability to make demands on the lower castes based on cultural privilege, such as livestock. Furthermore, their economic status was retained through their ownership of tools and vehicles and through their ability to give work to those below them (Draing 2009, pp. 174, 204). Access to political and bureaucratic offices meant controlling the distribution of patronage in the form of government funds, including the nepotistic hiring of relatives or clan members.

In West Sumba, 25 per cent of people engaged in the cash economy work for the government, with many more relying on these salaries as employees of government staff, such as cooks, drivers, security guards, etc. (Vel 2008, p. 49). Competition over access to spoils and patronage in the newly democratising context was the main factor in the interregional/clan violence in West Sumba known as *Kamis Berdarah* (Bloody Thursday), which killed 19 people in November 1998.[5] Finally, local electoral rules have been implemented that make it difficult for new candidates, including *maramba*, to run for office. Independent candidates, for example, are required to submit copies of their supporters' identification cards to prove that they have support of 10 per cent of the local population, recently increased from 6.5 per cent, an onerous burden (Vel 2015).

Statistical data from the elections of 1955 is only available at the provincial level – which means Sumba's data is combined with Flores, West Timor, Rote, Savu, and other smaller islands. Flores is predominantly Catholic, which explains the *Partai Katholik*'s 46 per cent in the election. Parkindo, a Christian party, received 18 per cent in the province. These parties received 2.6 and 2 per cent, respectively, in the national election (Feith 1957, pp. 58–59, 71). Although the data is not broken down to the *kabupaten* or lower levels, the two parties receiving 64 per cent of the vote is significant and reflects, for example, GKS lobbying during the election. In 1955, only 5 per cent of Sumbanese identified as Christian.

Yet as the rate of Christianity in Sumba increased, the importance of Christian-oriented parties waned. In the period between the 1955 and the 1978, Christianity quadrupled. By 1986, it had increased almost tenfold. This increase is explained by the New Order's forced implementation of identifying as one of five officially recognised religions following Suharto's ascension in 1965, and the GKS' willingness to exploit this by falsely linking *marapu* with communism, for example.[6] And yet one could make the counterargument that in Sumba many people resisted this classification and retained their identities as followers of *marapu*. During fieldwork in 2007, I was shown a civil servant's ID card that listed *marapu* as his religion (see also: Keane 1997, pp. 44–45). A Constitutional Court ruling in November 2017 (No. 97/PUU-XIV/2016) ruled as unconstitutional the non-recognition of the aforementioned five official religions (plus Confucianism, which was added in 1999), and *marapu* became officially recognised.

Electorally, however, following the consolidation of the New Order and the establishment of Golkar as Suharto's political vehicle, Sumba (and NTT) followed the national pattern.[7] In 1971, Parkindo and *Partai Katolik* support declined, and Golkar received 61.5 per cent of the provincial vote (Biro Humas Komisi Pemilihan Umum 2000, p. 70). Following the consolidation of political parties in 1975–1976, support for Golkar shot up to 90.3 per cent in the 1977 elections. *Partai Demokrasi Indonesia* (Indonesian Democratic Party, PDI), the party that nominally appealed to the Indonesian Christian minority, received just under 8 per cent. Golkar pursued a strategy of coopting *maramba*, understanding that those below them would follow them politically (Draing 2009, pp. 203–204). This pattern was maintained throughout the New Order in Sumba.

The New Order period was also linked to a significant rise in prosperity for Sumbanese, and many Sumbanese made the connection that voting for Golkar was linked to prosperity and development:

> The great strength of the new order establishment in West Sumba was not its capacity for repression, but its record of successful development and maintenance of civil peace over a 30-year period. Its monopolization of power had meant that any civilian who wanted to contribute to the developmentalist project at the political level had to do so through the Golkar organization.
>
> (Mitchell & Gunawan, as cited in Vel 2008, p. 117)

This explained why the Golkar Party remained popular after the abdication of Suharto in 1998, the start of Indonesia's democratisation phase, and the creation of new political parties (48) to contest the 1999 elections – including Catholic- and Christian-oriented parties. During field research in 2006 and 2007, Sumbanese repeatedly told the author that Suharto and Golkar were associated with development, and that it was democratisation that brought poverty. Some civil servants' offices, for example, had larger portraits of Suharto than of president Susilo Bambang Yudhoyono (Lundry 2010).

In the 1999 elections, Golkar received just 22.4 per cent nationally, bested by reform party PDI-P. Yet in NTT, Golkar received a plurality of over 40 per cent of the vote. Christian and Catholic parties again fared poorly, including the *Partai Demokrasi Kasih Bangsa*, formed and led by Manasse Malo, a Sumbanese. Subsequent elections have continued this pattern for local representation, although some of the factors discussed below, such as caste and local support, affect results as well.

Executive politics: province, *kabupaten*, and *kecamatan*

Few Sumbanese have succeeded in politics at the national level in Indonesia. There have been, however a few exceptions, such as Umbu Mehang Kunda and Manasse Malo, who both served in the national *Dewan Perwakilan Rakyat* (Indonesian House of Representatives, DPR). Golkar cadre and former *bupati* of West Sumba, Julianus Pote Leba, took the NTT DPR seat of Charles J. Mesang when he was removed from office for corruption.

Opportunities for Sumbanese to pursue executive politics are more evident at the sub-district (*kecamatan*) and district (*kabupaten*) levels. At the provincial executive level, Sumbanese are simply outvoted. Both Flores and West Timor have populations almost three times that of Sumba (1.83 million, 1.85 million, and 685,186, respectively, based on the 2010 census). There has never been a Sumbanese provincial governor.[8] This also shows the loyalty that the other ethnic groups hold towards their candidates when electing a governor. Each region within the province elects representatives for the provincial DPR, which means that Sumbanese are represented at the provincial legislative level even if they are not at the executive level.

Although some hold aspirations for the national or provincial stage, it is at the *kabupaten* and *kecamatan* level that much of the interesting political theatre takes place, including the relationship between candidates and national parties. Although many Sumbanese voters and politicians are loyal to Golkar and associate it with development during the New Order period, the relationship between local candidates and their parties cannot be taken for granted. Parties are always on the lookout for potentially successful candidates, generally *maramba*, or for figures who may otherwise increase the party vote share in election.[9] Part of this game includes a fair amount of party switching from election to election, and perhaps less party loyalty than might be felt in other areas of Indonesia.

Identification of viable candidates and the two-way dance between them and parties includes consideration of their caste, as *maramba* or, rarely, influential *kabihu* with *maramba* backing. Beyond caste, important considerations include candidates' governing style, connections with other Sumbanese or national elites, education, and ability to bring money to their constituencies. Parties are expected to support and reinforce the high caste status of their candidates (Draing 2009, pp. 203–204). Another consideration is past electoral success. Candidates who have lost previous elections are known to criticise the party that has sponsored them and switch parties in search of a winning formula. In 2019, Palulu P. Ndima, a long-serving Golkar politician who was retiring after the 2019 election, openly supported NasDem candidates (interview, Palulu P. Ndima, 16 April 2019). Parties are also known to withdraw support from candidates who fail to win an election and look for someone else for the subsequent election. Parties and candidates for district chiefs (*bupati*) and sub-district chiefs (*camat*) hire success teams (*Tim Sukses*) in order to campaign on their behalf. Leaders of *Tim Sukses* tend to be recruited from the *maramba* caste because of their influence.

The cementing of the political role of members of the *maramba* caste has persisted. Their roles were formerly important in ceremonies and cultural/spiritual expressions, but the creation of the Council of Rajas by the Dutch set in motion the elite's political domination of Sumba through the period of rationalisation after independence. Through their access to higher education outside Sumba, and their ability then to fill roles in the civil service (a relatively lucrative career), the *marimba* have cemented their dominance. Outside of the main cities of Waingapu (East Sumba) and Waikabubak (West Sumba), caste remains key.

The *maramba*'s cultural and spiritual importance was evident in the East Sumbanese village of Praiyawang. On the night before the election, candidates and supporters came to the traditional *maramba* grounds of the village, where huge monolithic ancestral graves are surrounded by the traditional homes of *maramba*. There, they left offerings for their ancestors in the hopes of interventions on their behalf in the election. As *maramba* Umbu Makambombu explained, 'People of all faiths, Muslim, Christian, came to Kampong Praiyawang to offer betel (*siri penang*) as sacrifices to ancestors, regardless of religion. For the Sumbanese, ancestors are perceived as more concrete spiritual beings than any god or deity' (interview, 17 April 2019). This was confirmed by the Secretary of the Waingapu Elections Commission (*Komisi Pemilihan Umum* or KPU), Christian Umbua Tamu Hawu (interview, 22 April 2019).

In the executive elections for governor of NTT in 2018, there were no candidates from Sumba in the race. This is not surprising as both Flores and West Timor have populations almost three times that of Sumba. Since there were no Sumbanese in the governor's election, party became an important factor. The winner of the election, and the person who garnered the most votes in Sumba, was Viktor Laiskodat, a Protestant from Kupang. His running mate was Josef Nai Soe, from Flores. Laiskodat ran under the NasDem banner, but also in coalition with Golkar. NasDem, a relatively new party founded in 2011, is frequently portrayed as a vehicle for young Indonesians who favour clean government and support diversity, but it also has roots in New Order and *Reformasi*-era Golkar. Its General Secretary, Surya Paloh, was a Golkar cadre for decades prior to forming NasDem and led the Golkar advisory board from 2004–2009. In this case, without a Sumbanese in the race it was the continuing perception of Golkar as the party of development and NasDem as a rising party that pushed Sumbanese support for the Laiskodat-Soe ticket, as well as the increasing popularity of NasDem.

At the executive level, the position of *bupati* is the most fiercely fought over, and viewed as having the most prestige among Sumbanese. There are four *kabupaten* in Sumba – East, Central, West, and Southwest – and here is where the most meaningful politics take place, although the relationship between the central government, parties, and the local *bupati* is important.

One example of the interplay between politician and party can be discerned from the process of redistricting (*pemekaran*) that began in the first decade of the *Reformasi* era. Proposals to subdivide Sumba were filed by people who would gain from the process (although *pemekaran* was initially justified as a cost-saving move as well as to provide more responsive government service, its cost-saving elements have proven dubious). Originally two *kabupaten*, East and West Sumba, *pemekaran* divided the island into four *kabupaten* in 2007: East, West, Southwest, and Central Sumba. Although East Sumba remained intact, the proposal included a plan to divide East Sumba into two *kabupaten*, Northeast and Southeast Sumba. Vel notes the importance of Sumbanese who lived in Jakarta and elsewhere in Indonesia, who were able to use their connections to lobby successfully for *pemekaran* in West Sumba (Vel 2008, pp. 15, 171–200).

The *bupati* of East Sumba, Umbu Mehang Kunda, opposed the division of his *kabupaten*, however, despite it being more than twice the size of the former West Sumba *kabupaten* that was divided into three. There was some opposition from the West Sumba administration prior to *pemekaran*, but it was ineffective. In the East, however, *pemekaran* was staved off.

Credit for the political preservation of East Sumba goes to Kunda. There were various reasons given for the preservation of the *kabupaten*, such as the fear of losing the major rice-producing *kecamatan* Lewa to either Central Sumba or to one or the other proposed subdivisions of East Sumba. Areas where wet rice grow in Sumba are controlled by wealthy elites. In such an arid place where rice does not grow abundantly the loss of this influential constituency would cause significant concern. But the decision also reflects Kunda's personal political capital. He served as the head of Komisi III (charged with law, human rights, and security) in the DPR. He was also a lifetime Golkar loyalist, from the New Order period through the *Reformasi* era. Just prior to Suharto's downfall, Kunda spoke in the DPR against a move by the Islamic-oriented *Partai Pembanguna Persatuan* (United Development Party, PPP) party to remove the need for two parties to support a bill or to sponsor investigations of the government. At the time, there were only three parties – Golkar, PPP, and PDI – and Golkar was firmly entrenched as the party of power in Indonesia. Kunda stated that the proposed change could lead to a 'dictatorship by the majority, or autarchy by the minority' – somewhat disingenuous during the dictatorship of Suharto, but in an Indonesia full of Golkar doublespeak it was sure to please the Golkar leadership (Masuhara 2010, p. 185).

Much of the credit for Kunda's ability to avoid *pemekaran* in East Sumba was due to his loyalty to Golkar, and his ability to deliver Golkar votes in Sumba. Kunda left the DPR in 2000 to serve as the *bupati* of East Sumba from 2000 until his death in office during his second term, in 2008. Sumbanese admired him for being able to represent the island on the national stage, and the airport in Waingapu was renamed after him in 2009.

Kunda's predecessor was Lukas Kaborang. Kaborang's political career started with the Christian-oriented Parkindo, but he soon switched to Golkar with Suharto's consolidation of parties in the early 1970s. He retired in 2000 after serving as *bupati* of East Sumba, but was convinced to return to politics in 2004, running under *Partai Persatuan Demokrasi Kebangsaan* (PPDK, United Democratic Nationhood Party, later *Partai Demokrasi Kebangsaan*, PDK). PPDK made overtures to Kaborang because they knew he already had a constituency in East Sumba, and he frequently spoke of his status as *maramba* and his ability to engage with others of the nobility. In this case, Kaborang had the political capital to insist that he be placed first on the party's list.[10] During the campaign, Kaborang made appeals to his Christian faith and held rallies that served rice with meat, establishing his role as an elite with *maramba* status, as well as a feeling of reciprocity among his constituents. The PPDK won six seats in East Sumba, and Kaborang became the vice chairman of the DPR-D (Vel 2008, p. 206). As Vel notes, 'the victory in East Sumba seemed more a personal success for Lukas Kaborang than a victory for the political party that put him at the top of its list' (Vel 2008, p. 2).

In 2010, Kaborang ran for *bupati* of East Sumba again under the PDK banner, but lost to Gidion Mbiliyora, from Golkar. Because of this failure, Kaborang abandoned PDK and joined NasDem, and won a seat in the subsequent legislative election. Kaborang's departure from PDK and alignment with NasDem is one of the elements credited to NasDem's increasing support – as an influential *maramba*, he brought with him his constituency.

Kaborang's story of an elite using a political party to gain office can be contrasted with the story of Wiyati. She was the director of a women's NGO named Wahana and was approached by *Partai Keadilan dan Persatuan Indonesia* (the Indonesian Justice and Unity Party, PKPI). Unlike the leaders of the party in West Sumba, she did not have elite status. The party, whose platform had emphasised women's issues, thought that she could bring votes because of her role. They put her at the bottom of the candidate list, however, so that those who may have voted for her as a candidate were, in reality, voting for the party and the party's other leading candidates. Wiyati had no chance of winning a seat (Vel 2008, p. 295).

Gidion Mbiliyora was re-elected in 2016 as *bupati* of East Sumba, representing Golkar. His running mate from the previous election, Matius Kitu, fled Golkar and joined NasDem to run against him, but lost. Yet in the run up to the 2019 election, Mbiliyora was removed from his post as the chairman of the East Sumba Golkar Party. He was viewed as being insufficiently supportive of Golkar candidates during the election (Tajukflores.com 2019). After his dismissal, he privately began supporting NasDem candidates, along with retiring Golkar legislator Palulu P. Ndima (interview, Palulu P. Ndima, 2019).

The results of these defections are most visible at the *kabupaten* and national legislative level. At the *kabupaten* level, where votes are more swayed by the backgrounds and status of individual candidates than parties, the defections of Mbiliyora and Ndima to support NasDem translated into a triple boost in the amount of support for the party (see Table 10.1). Yet with other local candidates staying in Golkar, coupled with its robust party machine, Golkar was able to slightly increase its vote total, as did PDI-P. The defections convinced voters who supported other parties such as Gerindra, Hanura, PD, and PKPI to switch; Gerindra was unpopular because it was Prabowo's party, and the others simply did not have much institutional or personal support in the region.

Where the defections had the most effect, however, was at the DPR-RI level. Here, where individual candidates' status and connections to the region matter less, NasDem again nearly tripled its number of votes, PDI-P more than doubled its votes, and Golkar's votes were more than halved (see Table 10.2). Other marginal parties lost significantly as well (Gerindra, PD, Hanura, and PKPI). Given the recent migration of influential Golkar cadres to NasDem it is likely that NasDem will continue to gain steam and perhaps overtake Golkar in subsequent elections.

Table 10.1 Votes for major parties in East Sumba, DPRD–*Kabupaten*, 2014 and 2019

Party	2014	2019
Nasdem	11,881	31,026
PDI-P	14,155	16,764
Golkar	26,905	29,286
Gerindra	15,521	7,281
PD	10,856	7,246
Hanura	8,235	0
PKPI	5,410	3,562

Source: Indonesian Election Commission (KPU).

Table 10.2 Votes for major parties in East Sumba, DPR–RI, 2014 and 2019

Party	2014	2019
Nasdem	13,455	39,424
PDI-P	10,514	26,083
Golkar	33,310	15,855
Gerindra	12,135	4,968
PD	24,752	7,195
Hanura	5,839	3,913
PKPI	4,485	709

Source: Indonesian Election Commission (KPU).

Identity and presidential politics in Sumba and NTT

Identity politics in Sumba play out on an entirely different stage than those of most of the rest of Indonesia. As a predominantly Christian province, political arguments over the nature of the relationship between Islam and politics are of a very different nature. Candidates, for example, are not pressured to exhibit their religious bona fides under pressure of withdrawn support from various groups. Rather, Islam, as a religious practiced by a minority in the province and in Sumba itself, plays an entirely different role in elections.

Although the province and Sumba are both predominantly Christian, Sumbanese – and other residents of NTT – are acutely aware that they remain a small minority in Indonesia. Despite the fact that Islam plays a lesser role in the immediate electoral politics in Sumba, it is still on people's minds when they are thinking about national politics.

Although sectarian violence in Sumba is rare, in November and December of 1998 violence erupted between Christians and Muslims in Kupang, West Timor. Rumours had spread that jihadists from the religious conflict in Ambon were coming to West Timor and that Muslims were destroying Christian churches, and there had been very real violence in Jakarta targeting Christians. Two days of violence followed, with (West Timorese) Christians attacking (Buginese and Javanese) Muslims and burning down homes, kiosks, and mosques. In the aftermath, members of the Christian majority began to agitate and mobilise, opening martial arts training programmes in church basements, for example. Muslims began removing outward signs of piety from their places of business, it was also rumoured that some Muslim stalls began to serve pork. The 'threat' of Islamisation and jihad, however, failed to materialise.

The events in Kupang – and elsewhere in Indonesia at this time – took place in the context of uncertainty and change following the abdication of Suharto and the beginning of the transition to the *Reformasi* era. Although Indonesia's messy transition period to democracy is already two decades old, Islamisation remains a potent topic of conversation. Rhetoric about the Jakarta Charter and the ambitions of Islamists to make Sharia part of national law has made Sumbanese and other predominantly Christian areas of Indonesia wary. When the author was conducting field research in Sumba in 2006 and 2007, Sumbanese and West Timorese (including a former wakil *bupati* from Kupang, Fritz Djubida) very explicitly and openly stated that should Indonesia impose sharia law nationally, a separatist movement would emerge and there would certainly be violence.[11] These sentiments in Sumba and NTT have been echoed in other regions of Indonesia where there are large proportions of Christians as well as predominantly Hindu Bali. For their part, secular Muslim Indonesian nationalists dating back to the founding of the nation have known that imposing sharia would alienate religious minorities. In the 1940s, the founding fathers removed the obligation for Muslims to abide by sharia law from the Constitution (also known as the Jakarta Charter), as they needed to create a unified nation among disparate peoples from different ethnic groups and religions. Residents of Sumba, NTT, and other non-Muslim-majority provinces are acutely aware of this history.

The 2019 presidential campaign reignited much of this wariness about political Islam. Prabowo's campaign had portrayed Jokowi as an impious Muslim. To stave off criticism, Jokowi chose Ma'ruf Amin, a respected Muslim cleric and head of the *Majelis Ulama Indonesia* (Council of Indonesian Ulama), as his running mate. Although Prabowo was not a staunch Muslim, he campaigned on defending Islam from arbitrary state action. Prabowo exploited Jokowi's decision in 2017 to ban Islamist group Hizb ut-Tahrir (HTI) in Indonesia, which fostered the perception among Islamists that Jokowi was 'anti-Islamic'. Other Islamist groups in Indonesia, including those responsible for the persecution of former Jakarta governor Basuki Tjahaja Purnama, openly supported Prabowo. Christians in Sumba were wary of Prabowo and the implications of a Prabowo presidency. In comparison, Jokowi was portrayed as the candidate most supportive of pluralism (interview, Stephanus Makambombu, 15 April 2019). Jokowi's party, PDI-P, also entered a coalition with Golkar. Stepanus Makambombu, a candidate for the DPRD II in 2019, and Palulu P. Ndima, a former legislator in the DPRD I, suggested that this coalition would increase support for Jokowi in the 2019 elections (interview, Stephanus Makambombu, 15 April 2019; interview, Palulu P. Ndima, 16 April 2019).

As the anecdote from the beginning of this chapter shows, actual support for Prabowo's candidacy was minimal despite appearances. Table 10.3 shows the 2019 presidential election results for NTT and the other non-Muslim-majority provinces, with results from 2014 – also between Jokowi and Prabowo – in parentheses. The data show not only an overwhelming victory for Jokowi in all five provinces for both elections, but also a precipitous decline in support for Prabowo between 2014 and 2019. The perception of Prabowo's ticket as supporting Islamisation alienated the Christian and Hindu populations of these provinces, and their voting pattern reflected this.

Viewing Sumba by *kabupaten*, support for Jokowi was extremely high island-wide, between 91 per cent and 96 per cent (see Table 10.4). What little support Prabowo garnered came mainly from cities such as Waingapu in East Sumba and Waikabubak in West Sumba, *kabupaten* capitals where larger Muslim populations were present. Viewing the results of the East Sumba capital Waingapu by *kelurahan* verifies this. Significant support for Prabowo (but never majority support) came from the two *kelurahan* with large Muslim populations: Hambala, the downtown area of Waingapu that is home to three mosques, and Kamalaputi, near the Waingapu port that his home to Kampung Bugis, where ethnically Buginese and religiously Muslim residents live (see Table 10.5). That Jokowi had promised to visit Sumba later in the year also helped his campaign. Soekarno remains, however, the only Indonesian president to have visited the

Table 10.3 Presidential election results from non-Muslim majority provinces

Candidate	Jokowi 2019 (2014)	Prabowo 2019 (2014)
NTT	2,362,041 (1,488,076)	305,615 (769,391)
Bali	2,342,628 (1,535,110)	212,586 (614,241)
West Papua	437,630 (360,379)	108,924 (172,528)
Papua	2,363,009 (2,026,735)	211,032 (769,132)
North Sulawesi	1,218,303 (724,553)	359,131 (620,095)

Source: Indonesian Election Commission (KPU).

Table 10.4 2019 presidential election results from *kabupaten* in Sumba

Candidate	Jokowi	Prabowo
Sumba Timur	119,364 (92%)	10,727 (7%)
Sumba Barat	54,172 (91%)	5,051 (9%)
Sumba Barat Daya	163,936 (96%)	7,371 (4%)
Sumba Tengah	34,895 (92%)	3,115 (8%)

Source: Indonesian Election Commission (KPU).

Table 10.5 2019 presidential election results from Waingapu City

Sub-district (Kecamatan)	Jokowi	Prabowo
Hambala	2,615	1,353
Kamalaputi	2,338	2,057
Kabajawa	4,444	644
Lukukmaru	364	4
Matawai	1,712	292
Mbatakapidu	931	38
Pambotandjara	1,034	21
Total, Waingapu City	13,438	4,409

Source: Indonesian Election Commission (KPU).

island as Jokowi did not make the trip; he sent the minister of Communication and Information, Johnny G. Plate, a Catholic from Flores, instead.

Despite Sumba's Christian majority, there is no outright hostility to Islam, either socially or politically. Sumbanese have welcomed outsiders into their larger cities of Waingapu and Waikabubak with the belief that outsiders bring capital and knowledge, and that a 'rising tide lifts all boats' – everyone will benefit from newcomers' presence, capital, knowledge, and connections. Furthermore, sources attributed the welcoming of outsiders to a Sumbanese culture of hospitality (interview, Arto J. Anapuka, 17 January 2007; interview, David Pajaru Namuwali, 3 February 2007). There have not been widespread acts of interfaith violence as have plagued other regions of Indonesia, nor have there been acts of Islamist terrorism.

Despite its overwhelmingly Protestant and Catholic population, Muslims are also elected to political positions, and there is support for Islamic parties. In 2019, Muslim Ali Oemar Fadaq from Golkar was re-elected and serves as the head of the DPRD–*Kabupaten* Sumba. Although some Sumbanese students at Satya Wacana Christian University in Central Java complained about him being elected when the author was there discussing Sumbanese politics, he represents the Muslim constituency in Waingapu and Golkar's significant political machine and history give him an edge. And, according to Mokambumbu, Muslims in Waingapu tend to discuss openly which candidate they want to support, and rather than splitting their votes among several candidates and (Islamic-leaning) parties, they vote as a bloc (interview, Stephanus Makambombu, 15 April 2019). Hence there will always be enough support for one or two Muslim candidates from Waingapu, but one would be hard pressed to imagine a Muslim *bupati* being elected.

Islamic parties have also supported Muslim and non-Muslim candidates outside the cities. The arrangement between the party and the candidate is mutually beneficial. The party works with a candidate who has social connections and status. Therefore the party can gain access to votes from his *kabihu* (clan) and the nearby region. The party can provide the candidate with infrastructure and support from the party machine that can help to propel the candidate to victory. *Partai Kebangkitan Bangsa* (National Awakening Party, PKB), an Islamic-based party, for example, supported Umar Rosidin, a Muslim, who then rallied his family to support him although they are not all Muslims. PKB also supported candidate Umbu Rihi Paremadjangga, a Christian candidate unable to secure support from another viable party. His family connections and status still allowed him to win. The Islamic nature of these parties is frequently down-played, and as in other places in Indonesia where they are trying to widen their base, Islamic parties will frequently reach out to non-Muslim voters by stressing that their party are corruption-free.

The election system and 2019 controversies

Electoral laws concerning thresholds mean that parties will go in search of can-didates in places such as Sumba. The 2017 electoral law (UU 7/2017) was meant to unify other existing electoral laws and establish new thresholds. In NTT, the law meant that several parties could not field candidates as they did not register a budget or field candidates. This affected *kabupaten*-level elections on Flores, Rote, Sabu, and Sumba. Of the six parties prevented from fielding candidates, three of them are Islamic parties, namely the PKS, the PPP, and PBB. As a result, the three parties could not participate in *kabupaten*-level elections in Sumba, among other places. The PKS and PPP were prevented from contesting East Sumba and the PPP was prevented from contesting West Sumba (Juli 2019). Strategically speaking, this was probably 'no skin off the parties' noses' – being Islamic-oriented parties, they could not have hoped to do well in these predominantly Christian regions outside of the cities and without support from an influential *maramba*-status candidate. With neither an influential candidate nor a constituency of Muslims to vote for the party, running a weak candidate would be a drain on resources better used elsewhere. The other parties that were disqualified include Berkarya, Garuda, and PKPI, from *kabupaten* in Flores.

Nationally, the 2019 election was marked by various 'hoaxes' or false rumours on social media that spread quickly and were meant to undermine various candid-ates. The Jakarta gubernatorial election of 2017 and the fall of Basuki Tjahaja Purnama was due, in part, to rumours and false accusations. This foreshadowed the rumour-mongering campaigns that emerged in the 2019 presidential election. Campaigns for both sides were accused of spreading false rumours.

In Sumba, social media campaigns had minimal impact on the elections as smart phone penetration, especially outside cities, remained low. Even so, rumours were rife – filling the narrative gaps left open by official news sources as well as the general lack of information (Bernardi et al. 2012, pp. 94–95). Rumours that Prabowo wanted to implement sharia nationally reinforced pre-existing positions sceptical of political Islam in Sumba, and may have helped drive voter turnout.

One source of news for East Sumba is the radio station MAXFM. Through daily news programming (along with music and other stories of interest), the radio station provided information on the election, as well as electoral results. Its Facebook page has over 4,750 followers, which is high considering the low Internet penetration in the *kabupaten*. The Facebook page is also a way for Sumbanese outside the region to follow local politics and events.

One story, however, had captured the imagination of Sumbanese – and Indonesians in general. A week prior to the elections, media reported that pre-marked ballots for Jokowi had been found in warehouses in Selangor, Malaysia. The Prabowo campaign cried foul and the KPU investigated, but this called into question, for some people, the legitimacy of the upcoming election.[12]

It was in this context that the Indonesian Election Commission (KPU) in Waingapu reported an insufficient number of ballots for East Sumba. Tensions rose and rumours began to spread that candidates had rigged the election in his or her favour. The author attempted to speak with someone at the KPU office but was accosted and questioned by police and prevented from doing so. The error turned out to be an administrative error – an insufficient number of ballots had been ordered. More ballots arrived in time to prevent a voting day shortage. Following the vote, KPU election officials admitted the problems was a source of stress, but that the problem had been solved (interview, Christian Umbu Tamu Hawu, 22 April 2019).

Implications

Sumba will remain a peripheral region within a peripheral province. Although there are politicians from NTT that have made it to the national stage, they are relatively low in number. And yet the region cannot be discounted in terms of its effects on national politics.

NTT is the only primarily Catholic province in Indonesia but is also home to a large number of Protestants. Along with the other majority Protestant provinces of West Papua, Papua, and North Sulawesi and Hindu-majority Bali, Sumba is influential among secular–nationalist Indonesians of various faiths as they discuss the role of Islam in Indonesia. Should Indonesia attempt to implement sharia a national law, Indonesians' leaders are acutely aware that they are going to face secessionist threats.

Although Golkar remains strong in Sumba, other parties appear to be making headway. NasDem has been gaining in popularity and may be viewed as more supportive of pluralism in the future. Golkar's continued popularity will depend on how the second Jokowi administration, which is in coalition with Golkar, addresses issues that are relevant to residents of Sumba (and NTT). Poverty, education and healthcare, among the worst in Indonesia, demand attention while some national issues may seem abstract for those who are poor. Managing development and outside investment, including the sale of coastal property and rights to traditional land, also remain important issues – and may cause tension between the central and local governments as well as indigenous Sumbanese and newcomers (Vel & Makambombu 2019). Islamic parties will continue to maintain their small constituencies and seats in assemblies, if the pattern of the *Reformasi* era maintains.

And yet the continued popularity of Golkar cannot be taken for granted. One of the reasons Golkar has remained popular in Sumba is its entrenchment during the New Order. During this period, Golkar was able to co-opt *maramba* with political ambitions, and for 32 years was viewed as the only vehicle to electoral success. As such, when politics opened during the *Reformasi* era, many party politics were *maramba*. As the 2019 election showed, however, with the party switching of long-term Golkar politicians such as Mbiliyora and Ndima, future electoral success may hinge on stronger party support for candidates.

The fluid nature of politics in Sumba, including frequent party switching, means that the only reliable predictor of future politics will remain based on caste and status, and the ability to garner support among other influential *maramba*. With a total population of around 5.1 million (based on the 2015 census) and 2.5 million voters, NTT will remain a peripheral region in Indonesia in terms of national politics. In the 2019 presidential election, the margin of loss for Prabowo was around 17 million votes and so the votes from the NTT would not have swung the election either way.

Even when combined with the votes from the other predominantly Christian provinces and predominantly Hindu Bali, which all overwhelmingly voted for Jokowi, it would not be enough to sway the results. In an election in which the question of pluralism was not such a polarising question, and if the result was closer, perhaps other factors would become more important. At the national level, however, 2019 reinforces the peripheral nature of Sumba and NTT. As such, residents will continue to place importance on provincial, *kabupaten*, and *kecamatan*-level politics, where their votes have more impact and where politicians can be expected to be more attentive to their constituents' needs.

Notes

1 The Indonesian government had requested that Christians postpone travel associated with the holidays so that they would be able to vote in the election.

2 Marapu is the indigenous spiritual/cultural system in Sumba. It emphasises social relationships and reverence for ancestors (Kapita 1976a, pp. 37–40, Keane 2007, pp. 156–157).

3 Vel notes that all of the *Bupati*s in West Sumba were *rajas* until 1995 (Vel 2008, p. 9; see also: Kapita 1976b, Forth 1981). A 2007 Master's thesis at Gadjah Mada University argues that opportunities for *hamba* have increased with access to education, including their abilities to eat alongside their masters and may become a civil servant (Sambu 2007, p. 70), and that education would allow the son of a *maramba* and woman from the *hamba* caste could become *maramba* if he was educated. Although an interesting case study, the thesis seems to generalise and the examples within it may be exceptions, not general rules (Sambu 2007).

4 Despite the appearance of rationality, Sumbanese politics are still clearly a mixture of Weber's three types: traditional, charismatic, and rational–legal (Weber 2004).

5 Others have noted the role of access to spoils as a factor in intergroup violence elsewhere in Indonesia, such as Gerry van Klinken's analysis of Christian–Muslim violence in Ambon (van Klinken 2005).

6 Despite Sumba's peripheral nature, the violence of 1965–1967 affected the island as well. In a place as poor as Sumba, Communist appeals to redistribute land resonated

with some, and the party frequently acted as arbiter for landless and powerless poor people. For an account of the post-coup violence in Sumba from the perspective of women, see: Kolimon et al. 2015).

7 Golkar's popularity was, in some senses, mandated. Civil servants and the military, for example, were required to support Golkar. And there was widespread intimidation and corruption during elections.

8 Some Sumbanese have expressed a kind of fatalism to this fact in conversation, although some have stated that perhaps Sumba will become its own province – which is highly unlikely (interview, Palulu P. Ndima, 16 April 2019).

9 Parties also recruit in places such as Sumba in order to increase their national presence and maintain their electoral threshold.

10 In these elections, voters may select a preferred candidate when voting, but their votes are assigned to a party, which is in control of making a ranked list of candidates.

11 Djubida expressed worry over recent political developments, centred in Java and other areas, of creeping Islamisation such as sharia-based bylaws and the increasing strength and perceived impunity in Islamicist groups, concerns that are mirrored in conversations with other Christians throughout the archipelago. NTT, and especially Kupang, was portrayed as the last stronghold of Christian faith, where even Catholics and Protestants forgive former animosity and work together to reject Islamisation. 'If Shari'a is imposed', he stated, 'Flores, Sumba and Timor would declare independence immediately' (interview, Fritz Djubida, 9 November 2006).

12 Following the election, the Prabowo campaign made accusations of systemic fraud and corruption when it was announced that Jokowi had won. The Coordinating Minister for Security and Political Affairs, Wiranto (himself a former general and presidential candidate), announced that there was no widespread or systematic fraud, and that the claims by the Prabowo camp were an attempt to delegitimise the election (Firdaus 2019).

Bibliography

Bernardi, D., P.H. Cheong, C. Lundry, & S. Ruston. 2012. *Narrative Landmines: Rumors, Islamist Extremism, and the Struggle for Strategic Influence.* New Brunswick, NJ: Rutgers University Press.

Biro Humas Komisi Pemilihan Umum. 2000. 'Pemilu Indonesia dalam angka dan fakta tahun 1955–1999' ['Indonesian Elections; Facts and Numbers From 1955–1999']. Jakarta: Biro Human Komisi Pemilihan Umum.

Draing, D. 2009. 'Bertahannya kekuasaan maramba Umalulu' ['The Power Resilience of the Umalulu Maramba']. MA thesis, Salatiga: Universitas Kristen Satya Wacana.

Feith, H. 1957. *The Indonesian Elections of 1955.* Ithaca, NY: Interim Reports Series, Modern Indonesia Project, Cornell University.

Firdaus, A. 2019, 24 April. 'Indonesian Minister: Allegations of Systematic Poll Fraud "Baseless"', *Benar News.* Retrieved from: www.benarnews.org/english/news/indonesian/election-update-04242019151757.html.

Forth, G.L. 1981. *Rindi: An Ethnographic Study of a Traditional Domain in Eastern Sumba.* The Hague: Martinus Nijhoff.

Juli, B.R. 2019, 25 March. 'KPU batalkan kepesertaan 6 partai politik peserta pemilu 2019 pada beberapa kabupaten di NTT' ['KPU Annulled the Participation of 6 Political Parties Contesting the 2019 Election in Several NTT Districts']. *NewsNTT.* Retrieved from: htps://topnewsntt.com/2019/03/25/kpu-batalkan-kepesertaan-6-partai-politik-peserta-pemilu-2019-pada-beberapa-*kabupaten*-di-ntt/.

Kapita, O.H. 1976a. *Masyarakat Sumba dan adat istiadat* ['The Sumbanese Society and Tradition']. Waingapu: Panitia Penerbit Naskah-Naskah Kebudayaan Daerah Sumba, Dewan Penata Layanan Gereja Kristen Sumba.

Kapita, O.H. 1976b. *Sumba di dalam jangkauan jaman* ['Sumba in a New Era']. Waingapu: Panitia Penerbit Naskah-Naskah Kebudayaan Daerah Sumba, Dewan Penata Layanan Gereja Kristen Sumba.

Keane, W. 1997. *Signs of Recognition: Powers and Hazards of Representation in an Indonesian Society*. Berkeley, CA: University of California Press.

Keane, W. 2007. *Christian Moderns: Freedom and Fetish in the Mission Encounter*. Los Angeles, CA: University of California Press.

Kolimon, M., L. Wetangterah, & K. Campbell-Nelson. 2015. *Forbidden Memories: Women's Experiences of 1965 in Eastern Indonesia* (J. Lindsey, Trans.). Clayton, Victoria: Monash University Publishing.

Lundry, C. 2009. *Separatism and State Cohesion in Eastern Indonesia.* PhD thesis. Tempe: Arizona State University.

Lundry, C. 2010. 'Sympathy for the Devil', *Inside Indonesia*, 100. Retrieved from www. insideindonesia.org/sympathy-for-the-devil.

Masuhara, A. 2010. *The End of Personal Rule in Indonesia: Golkar and the Transformation of the Suharto Regime*. Tokyo: Tokyo University Press.

Needham, R. 1983. Sumba and the Slave Trade. Working Paper No. 31. Melbourne: Centre of Southeast Asian Studies, Monash University.

Sambu, K. 2007. 'Feodalisme dalam masyarakat Sumba' ['Feudalism in the Sumba Society']. MA thesis. Jogjakarta: Universitas Gadjah Mada.

Tajukflores.com. 2019, 9 January. 'Melki Laka Lena: Pemberhentian Gidion Mbiliyora sesuai mekanisme' ['Melki Laka Lena: Gideon Mbiliyora's Sacking Follows Existing Mechanisms']. Retrieved from: www.tajukflores.com/artikel/18051/Melki-Laka-Lena-Pemberhentian-Gidion-Mbiliyora-Sesuai-Mekanisme/.

Tanya, D.P. 2016. *Pemanfaatan program janunan kesehetan nasional (JKN) di puskesmas daerah terpencil kabupaten Sumba Timur* [The Utilisation of the National Health Insurance Programme in Remote Public Health Centres in East Sumba Districts]. MA thesis. Jogjakarta: Universitas Gadjah Mada

van Klinken, G. 2005. 'New Actors, New Identities: Post-Suharto Ethnic Violence in Indonesia'. In D.F. Anwar, H. Bouvier, G. Smith, & R. Tol (Eds.), *Violent Internal Conflicts in Asia Pacific: Histories, Political Economies and Policies*. Jakarta: Yayasan Obor Indonesia/LIPI/Lasema-CNRS/KITLV-Jakarta, 2005.

Vel, J.A.C. 2008. *Uma Politics: An Ethnography of Democratization in West Sumba, Indonesia, 1986–2006*. Leiden: KITLV Press.

Vel, J.A.C. 2015, 29 July. 'The Devil is in the Details'. KITLV/Royal Netherlands Institute of Southeast Asian and Caribbean Studies blog. Retrieved from www.kitlv.nl/the-devil-in-the-detail-blog-by-jacqueline-vel/.

Vel, J., & S. Makambombu, 2019. 'Strategic Framing of Adat in Land-Acquisition Politics in East Sumba'. *The Asia Pacific Journal of Anthropology*, Vol. 20 (5): 435–452.

Weber, M. 2004. *The vocation lectures*. D.S. Owen, & T. Strong (Eds.), Livingston, R. (Trans.). Indianapolis, IN: Hackett Publishing Company.

List of interviews

Anapuka, A.J., Kepala Bappeda (Head of the Agency for Regional Development) (Waingapu, 17 January 2007).

Hawu, CUT, secretary of the Waingapu KPU (Waingapu, 22 April 2019).

Makambombu, S., political activist and NasDem candidate for Kota Waingapu DPR (Waingapu, 15 April 2019).

Makambumbu, U., *maramba* and resident of Kampung Adat Praiyawang (Kampung Adat Praiyawang, 17 April 2019).

Naggalanau, D.P.N., Chief of Police for Wulla Waijelu (Wulla Waijelu, 3 February 2007).

Ndima, P.P., former Golkar politician for the NTT DPR (Waingapu, 16 April 2019).

11 Conclusion

What have we learned?

Leonard C. Sebastian
and Alexander R. Arifianto

Concluding observations

Are the 2018 regional elections and 2019 general elections in Indonesia water-shed events in Indonesian politics? Are these elections truly encumbered by divisive identity politics or are they a continuation of political pragmatism and patron–client relationships? Or is it somewhere in between? What have we learned from the eight case studies examining the relationship between religious-based identity politics and how it interacts with the 2018 regional executive elections and the 2019 presidential election in Indonesia?

The chapters presented in this edited volume clearly demonstrated that identity politics were salient during all elections across the board and that it was not limited to the 2016/2017 Defending Islam rallies in Jakarta. This was seen provinces like North Sumatra and West Kalimantan – where there was a history of ethno-religious rivalry and competition between the different ethnic and religious groups who inhabited these provinces, as well as in provinces like West Java and South Sulawesi – where there were strong tilt towards political Islamism within the past two decades. Mobilisation in support of the 2016/2017 Defending Islam Movement in Jakarta conducted by Islamic groups from the two provinces contributed to greater polarisations. Even in provinces where Jokowi managed to score decisive victories against Prabowo – like Central Java, East Java, and East Nusa Tenggara – the use of identity politics to obtain political objectives were prevalent and rampant, albeit in varying degrees and effectiveness.

Religious-based identity politics is not new in Indonesia. It played a predominant role during the 1950s liberal democratic phase and the 1960s Guided Democracy period. Identity politics affiliated with political leanings was also the prelude to the mass killings of alleged members and sympathisers of the Indonesian Communist Party (PKI) by militias. Thirty-two years of Suharto's rule had largely put a lid on free expression. Nonetheless, the post-*Reformasi* landscape saw a rapid surge in various sorts of ideologies propagated, including that of Islamist conservatism and ideas of exclusivity, competing against moderate Islamic interpretations (Feillard & Madinier 2011, van Bruinessen 2013, Sebastian and Nubowo 2019, Arifianto 2020). Gradually, Islamists and their sympathisers in institutions like the Council of Indonesian Ulema (MUI) managed to transform political discourses and state policy through laws such as Law No 21/2008 on Islamic Banking and Law No 33/2014 on Halal Product Assurances, along with hundreds of new local Islamic regulations (*perda syariah*) that were enacted during the past two decades.

Despite slowly gaining followers and socio-political influences, conservative Islamists did not become politically significant nationwide until the 2016/2017 Defending Islam rallies against former governor Basuki Tjahaja Purnama (Ahok) of Jakarta. Given their popularity and influence in numerous regions such as West Kalimantan, West Sumatra, and South Sulawesi, the rallies were able to rouse a following of approximately 1 million supporters within a short timeframe. Bolstered by the momentum from the rallies, the Islamists then turned these rallies into a archipelagic-wide populist movement that swept up anti-Jokowi sentiments and was a primary obstacle for president Jokowi's attempt at winning a second 5-year presidential term. After the objectives of these participants were met – resulting in Ahok's re-election defeat and subsequent conviction for allegedly committing a religious blasphemy – the Islamist activists transformed their group unto a political movement. Commonly called the 'Alumni 212' movement, they transformed into a movement with the goal of electing Muslim officeholders from all levels (from presidency to regents and mayors) who pledged to enact and implement 'pro-Muslim' policies and transform the Indonesian state and society to become more Islamic.

Indonesian politics scholars have struggled to interpret the rise of the Defending Islam movements and the role of its activists in shaping the 2018/2019 Indonesian elections. Scholars affiliated with both oligarchy and liberal pluralist schools in Indonesian Studies have rightly pointed to the flaws of Indonesia's post-*Reformasi* democracy. They noted the predominance of a small group of political and economic elites (e.g. Robison & Hadiz 2004, Winters 2011), the persistent of a clientelistic system (e.g. Aspinall & Berenschot 2019), and the increasing tendencies by the country's political elites to subvert the democratic system in order to suppress their rivals (e.g. Mietzner 2018, Power 2018). However, scholars from both schools have failed to fully take into account the reasons why identity politics had resurfaced in Indonesia, why did it become salient during the 2018/2019 Indonesian elections, and why it will likely play an important role in Indonesian politics in the foreseeable future.

Based on the chapters in this edited volume, we argue scholars should pay attention to the role of ideology as drivers of political motivation for the Islamist groups, instead of treating it as something that can easily be subverted by power and material considerations. Many Alumni 212 activists were motivated by the desire for political change. They were the most vociferous in carrying out their respective campaigns to oust Jokowi – seen as a less pious Muslim in their eyes. These activist groups – committed to their goals – did not mind spending their own financial resources and manpower to campaign for Jokowi's rival, Prabowo Subianto. The high level of loyalty and dedication these volunteers channelled towards their campaigns resulted in a surge of support for Prabowo, although

Jokowi eventually emerged as winner of the presidential election. Case studies in North Sumatra, East Java, and South Sulawesi had demonstrated the strong support and solidarity of Islamist clerics and their followers had pledged and generated towards Prabowo during and after campaign season. We argue that paying more attention to the different historical and socio-political features of different Indonesian regions would greatly help one to understand the reasons why identity politics had become salient in certain Indonesian regions.

Alumni 212 and the 2018/2019 elections

The widespread use of identity-based politics during the presidential election campaign was a consequence of the mobilisation of the former Defending Islam Movement activists, – commonly known as Alumni 212 – in numerous localities throughout Indonesia. In provinces such as East Java and West Kalimantan, the Alumni 212 activists were the primary volunteers for the Prabowo campaign and supplied much of the manpower for its campaign activities within the provinces. Based on observations from these provinces, members and party cadres from pro-Prabowo political parties like Gerindra and PAN were not as effective in their campaign efforts due to the fact that they did not have both financial and manpower resource to support Prabowo's cause in the regions. Rather, it was the Alumni 212 activists and their sponsors that supplied and generated the most traction for the Prabowo campaign and for Prabowo-supporting groups like *#2019GantiPresiden.* They ranged from those originating from hardline groups like *Hizb ut-Tahrir Indonesia* (HTI), Wahdah Islamiyah, and the Indonesian Islamic Propagation Council (DDII) to more mainstream Islamic groups like Muhammadiyah (as seen in the provinces of North Sumatra and West Kalimantan) as well as some *kyais* affiliated with the *Nahdlatul Ulama* (NU) (as observed in Madura and East Java).

The Alumni 212 volunteers provided much needed arsenal for Prabowo campaign's efforts in challenging Jokowi during the 2019 presidential election. Prabowo's landslide victory in West Java and South Sulawesi and his lead in the West Coast of North Sumatra and in Pontianak and its suburbs in West Kalimantan can be attributed to their commitment to campaign on behalf of Prabowo as well as the religiously inspired attacks launched against the Jokowi campaign. Even in provinces where Jokowi eventually won such as East Java, Alumni 212 also had a strong presence initially, until a combination of last-minute efforts by pro-Jokowi volunteers tipped the scales in favour of Jokowi.

The involvement of Alumni 212 supporters in terms of endorsements and financial contributions as well as the use of identity politics to polarise various constituencies certainly helped Prabowo clinch a large voter base, threatening the incumbency of Jokowi.

Identity politics in the regions: a mixed bag

Despite the salience of religious and ethnic identity politics at the national level, the use of identity politics during the outcome of the 2018 regional executive elections (*Pilkada*) did not always yield its intended electoral effects, as demonstrated in the various case studies featured in this edited volume. In regions such as West Kalimantan and North Sumatra, conservative Islamists constituted a significant part of the population in a context where there exists a long history of ethno-religious contestation between different groups living in disparate regions. There is evidence to show that identity politics were salient during the gubernatorial elections within these provinces.

As Jonathan Chen observed in his chapter, local ethno-religious-based competition between Malay and Javanese Muslims versus Dayak Christians became politicised under the conditions of the regional elections as external actors such as FPI and other Islamist groups made their way into West Kalimantan, polarising the already tenuous relations between the various ethnicities. Malay–Muslims supported the gubernatorial candidacy of Pontianak mayor Sutarmidji, while Dayak Christians supported Karolin Margaret Natasa, daughter of outgoing governor Cornelis, who was widely accused of favouring the Dayaks during his decade-long reign as governor of the province. The fact that FPI provincial leaders had strong links with key local elites such as certain members within the revived Sultanate of Pontianak certainly helped to make it an influential player among the Muslim community in the province. On election day, West Kalimantan voters voted largely on ethno-religious lines, with Sutarmidji winning over Natasa in a campaign fraught by identity politics and negative campaigning carried out by both sides.

In North Sumatra, the long-standing rivalry between the mostly Christian Batak and the Islamic ethnic Malays and Javanese were made worse with the entrance of Djarot Saiful Hidayat, former vice governor of Jakarta under Ahok, and Edy Rahmayadi, who was backed by a majority of conservative Islamic clerics and groups within the province. As shown in Chapter 6, written by Tiola and Adhi Primarizki, pre-existing ethno-religious divisions were further polarised given Djarot's nomination as governor of North Sumatra by the Indonesian Democratic Party of Struggle (PDI-P) and the use of identity politics by both candidates and their supporters throughout the campaign. On election day, North Sumatran voters voted largely on ethno-religious lines, with Edy winning over Djarot.

A similar phenomenon was also seen in West Sumatra, where Prabowo managed to win overwhelmingly against Jokowi by a margin of 86 per cent. As elaborated by Adri Wanto and Leonard Sebastian in Chapter 7, the victory was attributed to the historical legacy of the 1950's PRRI/Permesta rebellion, which highly impacted the lives of the province's residences. It motivated them against supporting any PDI-P Party candidates for national and local offices due to the party's affiliation with Indonesia's founding president Sukarno who ordered a repressive crackdown against the rebellion. In all three races, candidates supported by conservative Islamist groups managed to win both elections over their rivals who were perceived to be supported by president Jokowi and the nationalist PDI-P Party.

The victory of Islamist-based candidates in these two provinces does not mean that identity-based strategies are always successful when deployed in other Indonesian regions. As seen in Chapter 3 by Keoni Marzuki and Chaula R. Anindya, Bandung mayor Ridwan Kamil managed to prevail over Islamist-backed opponents Sudrajat and Ahmad Syaikhu. Ridwan Kamil's candidacy was helped by the fact that he recruited Tasikmalaya regent Uu Ruzhanul Ulum as his running mate. The latter has strong Islamic credentials that were derived from his status as a descendant of the Miftahul Huda Islamic boarding school's founder – one of the most influential *pesantren* in West Java. Ridwan Kamil was also helped by the fact that he ran in a four-way race, which might split the votes of the conservative Islamists away from the Sudrajat–Syaikhu pair to other candidates.

While there was evidence of identity politics in the East and Central Java gubernatorial races, the impact were not as significant if compared to the other gubernatorial contests described above. In East Java, the two gubernatorial candidates, Saifullah Yusuf and Khofifah Indar Parawansa, have ties with the Nahdlatul Ulama (NU) – the largest Islamic organisation within the province. Both candidates are known for their moderate approach when it comes to religious-related issues. The predominance of traditionalist Muslims in the province and the presence of nationalist and syncretic Muslims (*abangan*) in the PDI-P ensured that radical religious rhetoric was moderated during the campaigns. Identity politics, however, became significant during the last few days of the campaign. Alexander Arifianto showed how the Alumni 212 activists launched a series of black campaigns against Saifullah's running mate Puti Guntur Soekarno. The Gerindra Party and the PKS opportunistically switched their allegiances to Khofifah, leading to an eventual victory in the East Java gubernatorial election.

Meanwhile, in Central Java, incumbent governor Ganjar Pranowo from the PDI-P competed against Gerindra candidate Sudirman Said during the gubernatorial election. Conservative Islamists from the cities of Yogyakarta and Solo were staunch supporters of Sudirman. This constituency allowed Sudirman to increase his vote share towards the end of the campaign. However, Ganjar appointed Taj Yasin Maimoen, son of influential senior NU *kyai* Maimun Zubair, to become his running mate. Ganjar also aligned himself with NU in the province. Following such a move, Ganjar eventually won by a 59 per cent electoral margin due to strong support from the PDI-P and NU supporters in the province. As highlighted by Syafiq Hasyim, most Central Javanese residents, especially those who were considered to be *abangan* two to three decades ago, now perceive themselves as traditionalist Muslims affiliated with NU. This new phenomenon helped explain the predominance of moderate forms of Islam within the province. Many of these voters had either aligned themselves with the PDI-P or with the NU-affiliated National Awakening Party (PKB), ensuring Jokowi's overwhelming victory in the presidential race and Ganjar's victory in the Central Java gubernatorial race.

The role of traditional elite families and networks

In both South Sulawesi and East Nusa Tenggara, identity politics played a relatively insignificant role in regional elections. In South Sulawesi, local politics were dominated by the increasing discontent directed at influential political dynasties who have dominated local politics for more than two decades since *Reformasi* – namely the Kallas and the Limpos. As shown by Dedi Dinarto and Andar Nubowo in Chapter 8, this discontent was demonstrated clearly in the race for the Makassar mayor. Munafri Arifuddin, the only officially approved mayoral candidate who was related to the Kalla family, lost to an 'empty ballot/ none of the above' box, making him the first ever candidate losing to an 'empty ballot' in an Indonesian election. In the gubernatorial election, Ichsan Yasin Limpo, brother of former governor Syahrul Yasin Limpo, did not win the election. On the other hand, Nurdin Abdullah, a candidate from a non-dynastic background who won praise for his accomplishments during his decade-long tenure as regent of Bentaeng, eventually won the election. Candidates with close linkages to local political dynasties and with the Golkar Party (a party with roots to Suharto and the New Order) ironically failed to win. This showed that voters were rejecting family/dynasty politics in favour of candidates with a track record of improving and developing their respective localities.

Lastly, in Sumba, East Nusa Tenggara province, Chris Lundry (Chapter 10) finds local candidates linked with those of nobility (*maramba*) more likely to win local executive and legislative races when compared to those without connections or endorsement from a *maramba*. Nevertheless, there is also a signal that local Sumbanese politics, long dominated by the Golkar Party, are increasingly fragmented as candidates from new parties such as the National Democratic (*NasDem*) Party are winning local races. However, these candidates were endorsed by the *maramba* as well, indicating that while the Golkar Party may seem to be fragmenting, the nobility's influence in local Sumbanese politics still remained strong.

Final takeaway points

We conclude that identity politics are prevalent at politics at the national level and will remain so for the forseeable future given the strength of conservative Islamist forces. Nonetheless, there are several other mitigating factors found in the various regions and provinces of Indonesia that either promote or forestall its prominence. These includes the following factors:

1   *Historical conditions*: including past ethno-religious conflict and political contestations that may or may not include either ethnic conflicts (e.g. affecting ethnic Chinese and Madurese migrants in West Kalimantan) or past regional rebellions (e.g. the *Darul Islam* movement in West Java and PRRI rebellion in West Sumatra). As shown in the West Sumatra chapter and the West Kalimantan chapter, past history of regional conflicts and identity-based politics are helping to promote the influence of the trajectory of contemporary politics in these regions. This means that the increasing expression of religiosity and conservative Islamism in the two regions (as well as in others) are often related to past history of regional grievances

against the national government that also incorporates religious dimension into it.

2 *Socio-political conditions*: specific socio-political conditions within a specific Indonesian region also helped to either increase the prevalence of identity politics or decrease its prevalence in other contexts. For instance, as Syafiq Hasyim has highlighted in his Central Java chapter, the predominance of *abangan* political culture (which provides support for the prevalence of nationalist parties like the PDI-P) combined with moderate expressions of Islam (which gives opportunity for moderate groups like NU and its affiliated party PKB to grow and dominate in local politics). In the outer islands, such conditions include the existence of non-Muslim-majority regions such as in North Sulawesi, Bali, East Nusa Tenggara, and Papua, with a different set of political aspirations and a concern about their future in an Indonesia dominated by conservative and hardline Islamists. As shown by Chris Lundry in his Sumba chapter, these drove voters living in East Nusa Tenggara to overwhelmingly vote for Jokowi during the 2019 presidential election. However, contemporary politics also helps to shape socio-political conditions, as seen in the 2016/2017 Defending Islam rallies and how it shaped regional politics and helped to motivate deeply conservative regions like West Java, West Sumatra and West Kalimantan to vote both for Prabowo Subianto's presidential candidacy as well as for gubernatorial candidates that were perceived to represent conservative Islamist political aspirations in these regions.

These historical and demographical conditions had helped minimise the impact of identity politics in certain regions that we have discussed earlier. Central and East Java, two provinces with the second and third-largest number of voters in Indonesia respectively, tend to have both features (large number of *abangan* and moderate Islamic voters) stated above. Together with the non-Muslim-majority regions in the outer island, these regions contributed a large number of votes towards Jokowi's landslide victory over Prabowo in the presidential election.

However, despite Prabowo's loss in the presidential election race, the influence of activists of Alumni 212 during the campaign, and the massive grassroots support the movement received from conservative Islamic clerics and organisations throughout Indonesia, demonstrated that the conservative Islamist voter base is a force to be reckoned with. In the context of the simultaneous elections, their voice remained important more than 2 years after the Defending Islam rallies made them an influential constituency that commands a substantial number of votes.

Identity politics has now become part and parcel of Indonesian politics. Even though the Islamists lost their candidate Prabowo Subianto in the presidential election, they are still a sizable voting constituency and would not give up on their goals of further Islamising the Indonesian state and society with their preferred candidates. The widespread support received by the Alumni 212 and conservative Islamist groups and preachers, especially in Prabowo strongholds like West Java and West Sumatra, ensured that they remain relevant and will compete for support in future elections.

This edited volume has shown the impact of identity politics on democratic politics in Indonesia at the regional levels. Its impact and effectiveness however depend on the specific historical and socio-political conditions that had prevailed. Nonetheless, it is a political instrument that is commonly used in religiously diverse and multi-ethnic states like that of Indonesia to shore up support and consolidate votes. Given the tilt towards greater Islamic conservatism in numerous Indonesian regions, we can expect the continuance of such politics, especially those motivated by Islamist goals and ideologies, to dominate the political landscape.

Bibliography

Arifianto, A.R. 2020. 'Rising Islamism and the Struggle for Islamic Authority in Post-*Reformasi* Indonesia', *Trans-National and -Regional Studies of Asia*, Vol. 8 (1): 37–50. Retrieved from https://doi.org/10.1017/trn.2019.10.

Aspinall, E., & W. Berenschot. 2019. *Democracy for Sale: Elections, Clientelism, and the State in Indonesia.* Ithaca, NY: Cornell University Press.

Feillard, A., & R. Madinier. 2011. *The End of Innocence? Indonesian Islam and the Temptations of Radicalism.* Singapore: National University of Singapore Press.

Mietzner, M. 2018. 'Fighting Illiberalism with Illiberalism: Islamist Populism and Democratic Deconsolidation in Indonesia', *Pacific Affairs*, Vol. 91 (2): 261–282.

Power, T.P. 2018. 'Jokowi's Authoritarian Turn and Indonesia's Democratic Decline', *Bulletin of Indonesian Economic Studies*, Vol. 54 (3): 307–338.

Robison, R., & V. Hadiz. 2004. *Reorganising Power in Indonesia: The Politics of Oligarchy in an Age of Markets.* New York: Routledge.

Sebastian, L.C., & A. Nubowo. 2019. *The Conservative Turn in Indonesian Islam: Implications for the 2019 Presidential Elections*, Asie Visions, 106, Paris: Ifri. Retrieved from: www.ifri.org/en/publications/notes-de-lifri/asie-visions/conservative-turn-indonesian-islam-implications-2019.

van Bruinessen, M. 2013. 'Introduction: Contemporary Developments in Indonesian Islam and the "Conservative Turn" of the Early of Twenty-first Century'. In M. van Bruinessen (Ed.), *Contemporary Developments in Indonesian Islam: Explaining the 'Conservative Turn'*. Singapore: ISEAS-Yusof Ishak Institute.

Winters, J.A. 2011. *Oligarchy.* New York: Cambridge University Press.

Index

Page numbers in **bold** denote tables, those in *italics* denote figures.

Printed in the United States
by Baker & Taylor Publisher Services